The
MULTICULTURAL
MYSTIQUE

The
MULTICULTURAL
MYSTIQUE
The Liberal Case against
DIVERSITY

H. E.
BABER

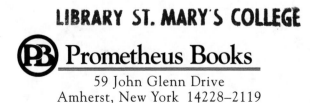
Prometheus Books

59 John Glenn Drive
Amherst, New York 14228–2119

Published 2008 by Prometheus Books

The Multicultural Mystique: The Liberal Case against Diversity. Copyright © 2008 by H. E. Baber. All rights reserved. No part of this publication may be reproduced, stored in a retrieval system, or transmitted in any form or by any means, digital, electronic, mechanical, photocopying, recording, or otherwise, or conveyed via the Internet or a Web site without prior written permission of the publisher, except in the case of brief quotations embodied in critical articles and reviews.

Inquiries should be addressed to
Prometheus Books
59 John Glenn Drive
Amherst, New York 14228–2119
VOICE: 716–691–0133, ext. 210
FAX: 716–691–0137
WWW.PROMETHEUSBOOKS.COM

12 11 10 09 08   5 4 3 2 1

Library of Congress Cataloging-in-Publication Data

Baber, H. E.
    The multicultural mystique : the liberal case against diversity / by H. E. Baber.
        p. cm.
    Includes bibliographical references and index.
    ISBN 978–1–59102–553–5
    1. Multiculturalism. 2. Liberalism. I. Title.

BD175.5.M84B33 2008
305.8001—dc22

2007051690

Printed in the United States of America on acid-free paper

CONTENTS

IS MULTICULTURALISM GOOD FOR ANYONE?

Little Indian, Sioux or Crow,
Little frosty Eskimo,
Little Turk or Japanee,
O! don't you wish that you were me?[1]
—Robert Louis Stevenson, *A Child's Garden of Verses*

"Multiculturalism has always been an embattled idea," Salman Rushdie remarked recently, "but the battle has grown fiercer of late. In this, it is terrorism that is setting the agenda, goading us to respond: terrorism, whose goal it is to turn the differences between us into divisions and then to use those divisions as justifications. No question about it: it's harder to celebrate polyculture when Belgian women are being persuaded by Belgians 'of North African descent' to blow themselves—and others—up."[2]

A decade ago Susan Okin asked whether multiculturalism was bad for women. After 9/11 and the war in Afghanistan, the London bombings, riots in French immigrant ghettos, and gang warfare on Australian beaches, we have begun to wonder whether multiculturalism is good for anyone and, most particularly, whether it is good for immigrants, people of color, and others whom it is supposed to benefit. I shall argue that it is not—and, in particular, that "plural monoculturalism," the doctrine that a good society ought to be a "salad bowl" where diverse groups maintaining their separate identities interact peacefully without coalescing, is especially hard on members of racial and ethnic minorities.

Multiculturalists assume that, all other things being equal, immigrants and members of ethnic minorities want to maintain separate identities and preserve their ancestral cultures. Is that really so? In chapter 1, I pose the question of whether people *like* their cultures. The answer is not obvious. Culture is not something we choose and it is not something of which most of us are aware. Some cultures are highly restrictive and impose burdens on their members; others lock people into unjust, corrupt, inefficient systems that perpetuate poverty and human misery. Perhaps instead of affirming the value of such cultures or adopting policies aimed at preserving them, we should, insofar as we are interested in promoting human welfare and individual rights, be working to dismantle them or at least helping their members to escape. Multiculturalism affirms the value of diverse cultures and seeks to preserve them. It may be that this program harms members of such cultures, whose interests are better served by opportunities to escape from their cultures.

Multiculturalism, however, is a moving target, so my task in chapter 2 will be to fix the target. Multiculturalism is sometimes understood innocuously as genetic diversity, so that a "multicultural" society is one that includes citizens of diverse ethnic origins. Multiculturalism has also been understood as the recognition that the artifacts and practices of diverse cultures may enrich our own. In quite a different sense, multiculturalism is the doctrine that we ought to understand and value diverse cultures on their own terms rather than judging them by our own cultural standards. Finally, multiculturalism may be identified with the plural monoculturalist "salad bowl" doctrine. It is multiculturalism understood in this last sense that I argue is bad for (almost) everyone.

This is not to say that genetic diversity is bad: culture does not track kinship. Indeed, "plural monoculturalism," the salad bowl doctrine, is objectionable precisely because, when taken seriously, it implies that culture *should* track kinship so that within genetically heterogeneous societies, indigenous peoples, members of racial minorities, and immigrants and their descendents ought to maintain some degree of communal cohesion and cultural distinctiveness. Arguably, most immigrants and members of ethnic minorities can, will, should, and, above all, *want* to assimilate to the majority culture. If they cluster in ethnic enclaves it is most often because they are prevented from joining the mainstream by discrimination in education and employment, social isolation, and stereotyping, exacerbated in some cases by the ideology and policies associated with multiculturalism. Plural monoculturalism, as I argue in chapter 3, is bad for (almost) everyone because it restricts choice by burdening members of minority groups with an obligation to maintain ethnic identity and making assimilation more difficult.

In chapter 4, I argue that there is compelling reason to believe that most people do not want to live in a plural monoculturalist "salad bowl." Ethnic and racial identities are *ascribed*, that is, they are assigned at birth rather than chosen and they are *immutable*. Some individuals can "pass"—at the risk of censure if discovered—but none can opt out. Where multiculturalism is taken seriously ethnicity and race are, in addition, *socially salient* and *scripted*: in a multicultural society, we take them to predict, explain, and prescribe behavior. Most people do not want others to predict or explain their behavior by reference to race and ethnicity or to be pressured into acting according to associated scripts. That is why it is a truism that people "want to be treated as individuals" and not "put into boxes." Consequently, most people prefer not to live under the multiculturalist regime. The burden of proof is on multiculturalists to show that things are otherwise—and this they have not done.

Communitarians will disagree with the suggestion that ethnic affiliations are simply constraints on individual choice. They hold that kinship networks, ethnic groups, and other natural communities in which our character, values, and desires are formed are not external constraints but essential components of who we are, and they argue that persistence of such organic communities enriches our lives and contributes to human flourishing. Liberals like me do not deny that our cultures and the communities in which we are embedded form our habits, preferences, and "values." We note, however, that there is no preestablished harmony. We cannot assume that people like their cultures and we certainly cannot assume that people wish to identify with cultures to which they are connected solely by ancestral bloodlines.

The communitarian picture is attractive only so long as we assume that even if individuals do not choose their natural affiliations, most prefer to remain in the communities within which they are embedded. This assumption is false. After the internationally notorious honor killing of Fadime Sahindal in Sweden, it was representatives of immigrant associations who complained that the government's well-meaning attempts to respect the cohesiveness of ethnic communities and accommodate immigrants' cultural practices ghettoized immigrants and deprived them of equal protection under the law. In Canada, largely because of protests by Canadian Muslim women, a proposal to establish civil courts for Muslims operating under sharia law was unexpectedly scotched. When Paris burned, in spite of attempts to spin the riots as the beginnings of a separatist movement or Islamic jihad, residents of immigrant housing projects complained that they were effectively locked out of the mainstream by discrimination and geographic isolation and that even after two or three generations they were not regarded as fully French.

For white Americans, ethnic identification is largely a matter of choice, since whiteness in the United States and Europe is nonsalient and, as it were, transparent. This is, indeed, the fundamental characteristic of "white privilege": to be white is, in an important sense, to lack racial identity, to be "just regular" as regards race. Moreover, white Americans can choose how ethnic they want to be and, within limits, with which ethnic group they identify. White Americans can make a fuss about their Italian, Polish, German, Irish, or Scandinavian identity, attempt to learn ancestral languages, dabble in genealogy, and decorate their homes with ethnic knickknacks or they can just ignore the whole thing without anyone thinking the worse of them for it. As I note in chapter 5, however, this is a luxury that people of color do not have. Members of visible minorities are expected to identify with their ancestral culture, express pride in their ethnic identity, and follow their assigned ethnic "scripts." Those who do not, risk being castigated as "inauthentic" or "self-hating."

In this chapter I also address the important question, rarely discussed, of when, if ever, ethnic diversity ends. Do multiculturalists imagine that the salad bowl is forever and that ethnic minorities will maintain distinct cultural identities in perpetuity without coalescing? It is hard to see how such an arrangement could be maintained without the establishment of a virtual millet system of semiautonomous communities maintaining their own schools, institutions, and, perhaps, systems of personal law with the approval and support of the state. Historically in the United States immigrants assimilate by the second or, at latest, third generation. If multiculturalists' goal is not merely temporary accommodation but the maintenance in perpetuity of distinct ethnic communities, "benign neglect" may not be enough. It may be necessary to establish policies to support cultural preservationists in imposing exit costs from ethnic enclaves, to discourage "miscegenation," and otherwise take proactive measures to preserve ethnic communities.

This poses a hard question for multiculturalists. Is their goal to promote individual liberty, in particular to see to it that individuals who wish to maintain distinct cultural identities are not penalized, or is their aim to support the persistence of separate communities defined by bloodlines? If we assume that all or most people prefer to maintain and identify with ancestral cultures this question does not arise. That, however, is an assumption that we cannot make, so there is a hard choice. Do we want to promote the liberty and rights of all individuals regardless of race or ethnic origin or do we, in the interests of cultural diversity, want to adopt a scheme of special incentives, disincentives, and accommodations to encourage otherwise reluctant individuals, who can be genetically associated with the ethnically defined communities we want to preserve, to remain in ethnic communities or reestablish contact with them?

We cannot, of course, assume that all members of minorities regard their ethnic identity as an unwanted burden. Indeed, some choose to live in ethnic communities and maintain their ancestral customs. In chapter 6, I consider a range of cases in which individuals choose to live in ethnic enclaves. Their sincere avowals and choices when exit is feasible, however, strongly suggest that for most the decision to live within these communities is a response to the difficulty of negotiating the mainstream culture, ongoing discrimination, exclusion from the larger society, and high costs of exit rather than a reflection of what they would prefer. Policies intended to preserve such communities make it more difficult for individuals to get out.

Where communities are bound by religious conviction and practice, the question of policy is especially vexed, since the state's interest in protecting individual rights and promoting individual welfare may be at odds with its commitment to respecting religious freedom. This concern is currently pressing in European countries with significant Muslim populations, but it was posed in its clearest and starkest terms by the US government's quandary in dealing with the Amish. In the 1972 *Yoder* decision, the US Supreme Court ruled that the Amish were exempted from state education requirements and could pull their children out of school after eighth grade.

The Yoder decision highlights an in-house dispute between Rawlsian political liberals, who recognize some special status for so-called values—particularly religious values—and utilitarian liberals like me, for whom the desire to conform to religious or other "values" is no different from any other desire and no more or less worthy of consideration.

Arguably, all other things being equal, most members of ethnic communities want to get out. Arguably, most members of ethnic minorities regard the "scripts" and role obligations their ascribed identities impose as burdens rather than benefits and would prefer to assimilate.

Should people get what they want? Reflecting on the malaise of privileged individuals in affluent countries, social critics worry that getting what we want does not always make us happy and that expanding the range of options individuals enjoy may make them worse off. In chapter 7, I address objections to my fundamental assumption that having the widest possible range of opportunities to satisfy our desires makes us better off. Granting that sometimes our choices are uninformed and do not reflect our true preferences and that sometimes we may be confused by the range of options available to us so that we don't know what we want, I argue that when we satisfy our informed preferences we are better off.

Unfazed, many multiculturalists, particularly in the United States, hold that members of ethnic minorities who prefer to assimilate to the dominant culture should not get what they want. Some suggest that the desire of minorities and immigrants to assimilate is a symptom of low self-esteem, a pathology responsible for all manner of self-destructive and antisocial behavior. Drawing on the literature of postcolonialism and identity politics, they argue that the desire of members of these groups to shed their ethnic identities and assimilate to the dominant culture is a consequence of "internalizing" the values of the oppressor, in particular the oppressor's assumption that they are inferior. In chapter 8, on the cult of cultural self-affirmation, I discuss and criticize this conventional wisdom.

According to the received view, multiculturalism recognizes ethnic diversity and enables individuals to pursue their culturally diverse lifestyles without interference or penalty. I argue in chapter 9, on identity-making, that multiculturalist doctrines and policies enhance, modify, and, in some cases, *create* minority identities. Where national and cultural identity has worn thin, oppositional minority identities became attractive to a minority of youth in particular. Multiculturalists facilitate the formation of oppositional identities by a program of "making offense." In response to the supposed sensitivities of minorities—who are rarely consulted on these matters—they urge that apparently innocuous practices current in the dominant culture are offensive, exclusionary, or demeaning and, often, in so doing *confer* objectionable meanings on these practices. Making offense contributes to the formation of oppositional identities and promotes the perception of ethnic minorities as victim groups that require special accommodation. It also supports the establishment of a variety of programs, facilities, and institutions to cater for the supposed special needs of minorities. Once this multiculturalism industry is established, it functions as a source of jobs and grants for stakeholders and so perpetuates itself.

In chapter 10, I discuss the making of the multicultural mystique and the industry that it supports: how it came into being, why it was incorporated into what was during the latter part of the twentieth century regarded as enlightened common sense, how it was promulgated and promoted, and what interests it was supposed to serve.

What is the solution? My suggestions in chapter 11 are speculative but are, at the very least, educated guesses: enforce antidiscrimination regulations and establish affirmative action policies to reduce the effects of ongoing discrimination; reinstate school busing to integrate schools and adopt proactive policies to integrate neighborhoods; recognize that economic inequality is a problem and address it.

This is all old hat. The consensus is that it was tried and failed. I beg to differ. Within months after the Civil Rights Act of 1964, prohibiting racial discrimination in education, housing, and employment, had been passed, Alex Haley's *Autobiography of Malcolm X* was published and established a new agenda of black power and black separatism. There was a long hot summer of race riots, and, by the spring of 1968 when Martin Luther King Jr. was assassinated, it was a commonplace in the social milieu where I operated that King was little better than an Uncle Tom and that the civil rights movement he had led was an "accommodationist" program. Lyndon Johnson's Great

Society collapsed under his support for the Vietnam War. During the 1970s, when I came of age, Nixon was on trial and everything stank. By the end of the decade, we were ready for Reagan's conservative Morning in America. Americans were convinced that the liberal agenda had been tried and failed.

But that wasn't so. We Americans didn't give the liberal program a fair shot. We rejected social democracy and set about dismantling the welfare state, such as it was. And we rejected integration and assimilation in favor of multiculturalism. Worst of all, liberals who should have known better got onto the bandwagon. Now that we've seen the consequences, however, most of us are not so enthusiastic, contrary to what conservatives imagine.

The alternative to multiculturalism is not exclusion—it is integration and assimilation: inclusion in the most serious sense. The current essay is a defense of the Old Time Religion—as old as Cynics like Diogenes, who proclaimed himself a citizen of the world; as old as the Gnostics, who made the case that we were not our bodies, so that ancestry, kinship, and ancestral culture were constraints on who we were as individuals and did us harm; and as old as Christianity, which absorbed the Hellenistic ideal and, in response to Jewish notions of tribal loyalty, proclaimed that in Christ there was no male or female, Greek or Jew, slave or free.

We are, all of us, citizens of the world—and the cosmos. This is the message of liberation.

NOTES

1. http://www.bartleby.com/188/129.html.

2. S. Rushdie, "What This Cultural Debate Needs Is More Dirt, Less Pure Stupidity," TimesOnline, December 10, 2005, http://www.timesonline .co.uk/article/0,,1072-1918306,00.html.

Chapter 1

DO PEOPLE LIKE THEIR CULTURES?

Par ma foi, il y a plus de quarante ans que je dis de la prose, sans que
j'en susse rien.

—Molière, *Le Bourgeois Gentilhomme*

Does multiculturalism make us more free or less free? The answer seems obvious at first: multiculturalism, which supports the coexistence and equal dignity of diverse cultures, expands the range of cultural options and therefore enhances human freedom.

But there's a logical trick here, a fallacy. Even if there is a wide range of cultural options available within a multicultural society, it does not follow that there is a wide range of cultural options open to any given individual within that society. Indeed, multiculturalism restricts freedom by locking individuals into unchosen identities, affiliations, and social arrangements, some of which are themselves highly restrictive.

Liberals value individual freedom. Multiculturalism restricts individual freedom. That is the liberal case against multiculturalism.

CHOICES

Like M. Jourdain—Molière's bourgeois gentleman who didn't realize he'd been speaking prose all his life—most people don't know that they live in "cultures." They view local social arrangements as unalterable facts of life, like death and taxes, rush hour traffic or the irritating minutiae of office politics chronicled in *Dilbert*.

Do people like their cultures? That is like asking whether people like their phone numbers. I don't know how my phone number was assigned and I do not think that there is any way I could get it changed. I had no choice about it, in any case. I might idly wish that my phone number were more memorable or that I could get an arrangement of alphanumeric characters that expressed something about my personal history or preoccupations—like a vanity license place. But that is not the way things work: you take what you get. This is the way most people understand their cultures, which are for them no more a matter of choice than phone numbers or, for that matter, the laws of nature, and certainly not something that they think about. People are stuck with their cultures, and, on the face of it at least, there is no reason to think that they like them.

Nevertheless, on the world stage, people strive for ethnic "self-determination." Michael Lind, speculating on "the world after Bush" in the *Prospect* notes:

> The fact is that most of the people engaged in political violence today—from the Basque country to the Philippines—are not fighting for individual rights, nor for that matter are they fighting to establish an Islamist caliphate. Most are fighting for a national homeland for the ethnic nation to which they belong. For most human beings other than deracinated north Atlantic elites, the question of the unit of government is more important than the form of government, which can be settled later, after a stateless nation has obtained its own state.

Political revolutionaries do indeed fight to establish ethnically defined national homelands. We should ask, however, *why*. Arguably, it is because in most circumstances capturing tribal turf is the only way to secure individual rights. Multiethnic states in which the individual rights of all citizens are equally protected regardless of their ethnic origin or tribal affiliation are anomalous, and, in most cases, even where the official regulations guarantee equal rights to all citizens, these regulations are not taken seriously. Tribes take care of their own, and interethnic peace is always fragile: in most multiethnic nations, if you are a member of a minority tribe you are living on sufferance. "Tribal clashes" and ethnic cleansing are always a real and present danger.

We citizens of the global north, and we Americans in particular, imagine that multiethnic democracies where the rights of all individuals are secure "regardless of race, creed or color" are a norm or default to which all nations naturally will revert—if only they can be liberated from brutal dictators or corrupt regimes. Nationalist revolutionaries know better.

If you are tribal, you do not have the option of affiliating with other tribes or joining deracinated elites. You may not like your culture, but you are locked into it, and the only way to secure individual rights in the tribal system is by achieving ethnic "self-determination" and group rights—turf, power, and, if possible, statehood for your tribe. It is better to be a member of a tribe that has turf, power, and political independence under virtually any conditions than it is to be a member of a powerless, stateless minority on another tribe's turf. Consequently, if you, as a member of an ethnic minority, can choose between an ostensibly democratic multiethnic state and a national homeland—even a national homeland under the thumb of a dictator from your tribe—you will choose the latter in the interest of securing individual rights for you and your tribe mates.

We cannot therefore infer that, apart from we members of the deracinated North Atlantic elite, most people like their cultures and want to preserve them or they value cultural preservation and group rights rather than individual rights. People live tribally because they have no other viable options. They take care of their own because they know that only their own will take care of them. They fight for turf and prefer ethnic "self-determination" to incorporation in multiethnic states because they know that in most such systems, official commitments to liberty, equality, and fraternity are a sham. They follow the rules of their cultures and perpetuate them because they have no choice.

Do people like their cultures? Maybe some do and some don't. We cannot, however, assume that all or most people like their cultures. We cannot assume that most people, particularly members of non-Western societies, prefer to preserve their cultures or that immigrants and members of ethnic minorities in the West prefer not to assimilate, and we cannot assume that the interests of cultural preservationists should trump the interests of assimilationists.

Some individuals may like their cultures. Culture, as we are often reminded, is not merely external: individuals' beliefs, values, and aspirations are formed by their cultures. But culture also constrains, and the rational choices individuals make in response to the constraints imposed by their cultures reinforce these constraints. Even if no one likes the system, any individual who opts out unilaterally will be worse off. Working the system perpetuates it, but refusing to work the system does nothing to undermine it and only leaves refuseniks worse off. So, in developing countries riddled with corruption, paying bribes feeds the beast, but not paying bribes would starve out individuals long before it starved the beast. When I was foolish enough to send a T-shirt to my friend Lila, who was working for a Kenyan publishing firm, she had to pay twice the cost of the shirt in "fees" to extract it from the local post office. You either paid or you couldn't collect your mail. You might not like the system, but you couldn't beat it.

We, the privileged few, have a wider range of options and recognize that our cultures and the social rules that constitute them are local and revisable—that is to say, we know that we live in a culture. We have choices. We are accustomed to getting what we want and imagine that other people are, for the most part, getting what they want too— that their cultural practices and social arrangements are the way they like things. This assumption is unwarranted.

Do most people like their cultures? We can't assume that they don't, but we can't assume that they do, because most have no choice.

KENYA

I didn't understand this myself until I got to Kenya. After two years of collecting frequent flyer miles, I managed to piggyback my journey onto a trip back east to our son's graduation from Johns Hopkins, my grad school alma mater. My first stop, at Heathrow, was nothing exciting. As half of a transatlantic couple, I'd visited family in England often. Apart from that, however, I hadn't traveled much, so when I got back on the plane, I hung on the TV map on the seatback in front of me, watching the plane cross the channel and fly southeastward across continental Europe. When the Mediterranean came into view, I melted. This was the first place I'd seen, even if only from two miles in the air, that seemed truly Other. The plane-icon jerked across the screen of the TV map, which periodically displayed helpful information about the temperature and wind speed in the stratosphere, across the Mediterranean and into Africa, the most foreign of all foreign places.

After negotiating the Nairobi airport, which had the ambience of a provincial Greyhound bus station, I was collected by my friend Lila, and we drove down the airport road and through the industrial district to her house in South B, a middle-class neighborhood near downtown Nairobi. Kenya, as I first saw it, was as foreign as I could have wished. Ragged bands of pedestrians drifted down the road, which cut through a semi-arid plain that sprouted thorny acacia trees. Lila's house was in a gated community, between a burnt-out Catholic church and a bombed-out mosque. The approach was lined with small businesses operating out of "kiosks," booths tacked together out of concrete blocks, rubble, and corrugated iron. Inside the gated community, the house was itself fortified with walls and iron bars. It was maintained by a fifteen-year-old housegirl from up-country who soon after my stay got pregnant and was dismissed. The house stank of sour rags.

There was no microwave or washing machine in Lila's house, nor the usual suite of labor-saving devices. The supply of electricity was sporadic; it was cheaper and more efficient to employ housegirls who were exchanged regularly as they inevitably got pregnant or were caught stealing. Electricity was unreliable, but labor was cheap. The pots in the kitchen had no handles: they had half-inch lips around the top edge that housegirls picked up with their bare fingers. Pots like this, Lila told me, were beaten out of hubcaps by local *fundis*; handles and potholders were luxuries, and there was no point in investing in them, since housegirls were accustomed to picking up pots by their lips with their bare hands. This was middle-class life in Nairobi, the life of teachers, doctors, engineers, lawyers, and businesspeople—the life of privileged Kenyans.

Downtown, there was perhaps a square mile that approximated a normal first-world city. Lila and I sat in posh downtown bars and watched American and European tourists, who would remember Kenya only as a game park with hotel facilities, as they packed into minivans to be ferried to local wildlife preserves. Beyond the square mile, an inaccessible never-never land for most Kenyans, Nairobi was a maze of impassible streets, filth, and squalor. It was the London of Gay's *Beggar's Opera* and Hogarth's *Gin Lane*, a casualty of the Industrial Revolution, replete with runaway and throwaway kids, begging and stealing. Lila warned me to keep the car windows rolled up: street urchins packing human feces extorted money from careless motorists by threatening to smear them if they didn't stand and deliver.

Lila's firm, which published books for the education market, had organized a series of seminars for primary school teachers up-country in Meru, on the east side of Mount Kenya, to promote their books, and I tagged along to help out. We drove up along the side of the mountain to primary schools "on the tarmac"—just off the main road—to conduct seminars for teachers in the area and, we hoped, to sell books. The country was sweet and lovely, with houses, schools, and churches built foursquare in stone, reminding me of the west of England. We drove past donkey carts packed with rice, one- and two-donkey carts, and occasionally donkey troikas. Trucks packed with *miraa*, a mild stimulant also known as khat and grown up-country, whizzed by on their way to market as we pushed northward packed into our company car with boxes of books.

The teachers, who came by foot from remote villages to the seminars, could have been teachers from Topeka or Cleveland—they were teachers like me and behaved like teachers everywhere, chatting and enjoying their day, and trying to pick up free copies of books as I did myself when I went to conferences. In the course of cheap charter flights, I'd very briefly been to Brussels and Amsterdam and later traveled to Iceland and to China. These places felt alien to me in a way that Kenya didn't. Whether it was language, religion, or some shared history, it seemed to me that they were my people, my own, locked into an intolerable situation. It was one thing to imagine exotic, primitive people in remote South Sea islands living strange lives, but it was chilling to see people who spoke English—people like me—living under these conditions. The acacia trees and free-ranging goats in the city streets may have been exotic, as they seemed to me when I landed, but the people I met were not. They were my people, caught in an evil net and unable to extricate themselves.

Lunchtime came and went, but the caterer who had been hired to bring hot meals from the nearest town was nowhere in sight. The teachers chatted and entertained themselves; we apologized and did what we could to kill time. No one was happy about the delay, but no one was surprised. Kenya, Lila explained, operated on "African time." When lunch finally came, almost two hours late, the caterer explained that her van had been stuck behind an overturned truck that blocked the road. Whether or not this was true—and we didn't bother investigating—it was plausible. Roads were quite often impassible for one reason or another and it could be hours before traffic accidents were cleared up.

No one particularly liked African Time (those teachers were hungry), but it was a fact of life and there was no way to avoid it. You couldn't count on the roads being clear or the electricity being turned on or the phones working or any of the other prerequisites for carrying through plans, keeping to schedules, or operating efficiently. Black-outs and other cock-ups that occasionally stopped business in the United States were a daily occurrence in Kenya. That, I discovered, was the most intractable deficit in the "developing" world—not individual poverty, which could have been addressed, but the absence of reliable public goods and services. Resistance was futile. You could no more escape African Time than you could opt out of the patronage system or avoid interminable waits on line to negotiate with innumerable functionaries to pay "fees." If everyone behaved differently, things might have been better, but any individual who tried to beat the system was doomed to failure and frustration. The only rational response was to work the system—and so to perpetuate it.

To say the system was corrupt, however, would be misleading, since corruption assumes a prior uncorrupt state, a time in which there was an efficient, transparent, fair system in place that had decayed. There never was such a time, even if during colonial days the British had tried to impose one for limited purposes. Kenyans operated according to a tribal patronage scheme, which was until recently in human history universal. From top to bottom, people took care of their own—their families and tribe mates, cronies and clients. President Moi, then in his last days in power, extracted tribute and bankrolled his retainers; he promoted the flower industry, operated by his Kalinjin tribe mates at the expense of Kikuyu coffee growers. Jobs in the bureaucracy and police force were concessions: functionaries worked for the state with the understanding that their positions entitled them to extract additional fees to supplement their income, like waiters working salary plus tips or the universally hated tax collectors in the Gospels who took a cut as a matter of course. When Barack Obama visited his father's ancestral village in Kenya, an elderly lady interviewed on the evening news exulted that with Obama as a big man in the United States, the village was now sure to get an airport, which would put it on the map. That was the way the system worked.

After the seminar was over, we drove north to conduct seminars at two more village schools along the road in the rain shadow of Mount Kenya and finally to Timau, in more open, semi-arid country where we approached the school and a great stone church under construction along an avenue of soaring eucalyptus trees. I had heard the presentation to English teachers three times by then, and the Swahili talk was beyond my ken, so I stayed outside chatting with the headmaster. He complimented me on my sunburn, which he said he understood was much sought after by Europeans, and wondered whether it hurt (it did) and expressed puzzlement that at my advanced age I hadn't been to Africa before. He said he'd heard that Americans, when they graduated from college, took a year or two off to travel around the world. I explained that while Americans were rich, most of us weren't that rich, that few of us traveled abroad and that for most who did, it was a once-in-a-lifetime experience.

Travel for Kenyans, he said, simply wasn't feasible. When you were young and working you spent all your money on school fees and uniforms and everything else it took to give your kids a good start and a decent chance in life. Once the kids were on their own, you'd reached the mandatory retirement age and there was no money for travel. He wanted to see the United States but didn't see any way—yet, he mused, he sometimes thought if he could put together just the money for a round trip flight he would go, even if all he could do was sit in the airport for a few hours and then fly back.

Everyone I spoke to in Kenya wanted out, temporarily or, if possible, permanently. Those who could joined the brain drain, but for most, exit wasn't feasible. They especially wanted to get to the United States. At that time, before America's global prestige collapsed, some Kenyans named their children after US presidents, and, I was told, there were quite a few Clinton Mwangis running around. I wondered why they wanted to get to the United States and not the United Kingdom, which was closer both geographically and culturally. Kenyans seemed to me Brits: in taste, décor, and habits, middle-class life in Kenya approximated provincial England. Visiting a family farm in Meru, I could have been in Swindon: the living room suite was exactly like the one my in-laws got from Chalford Chairs, the pattern in the carpet was the same, and the paterfamilias's facetious running commentary on the evening news was exactly like my father-in-law's.

Some Kenyans I spoke to explained that whereas in England, they believed, they could only be immigrants, in the United States, they could become Americans. What mattered, it seemed, wasn't just wealth or luxury but the idea of a better life in some intangible sense, a fairer, more decent social arrangement and the chance to be truly part of it.

GROWING UP TRIBAL

Coming from a tribal territory in northern New Jersey, I understood the Kenyan system quite well. In Paterson, the gritty city where I was born and the shooting site (in more than one sense) for several episodes of *The Sopranos*, everyone was ethnically tagged and everyone knew what everyone else "was"—whether Italian or Jewish, Dutch or Irish, Polish, German, or Greek. Moreover, what one *was*, was of paramount importance because it was a commonplace that you took care of your own—first family, then clan, beyond that tribe mates, but no further, unless political deals were struck or money changed hands. It was taken for granted that jobs and political appointments, when they were not bought and sold outright, were allocated along ethnic lines and that all institutions, particularly government and unions, were corrupt. This was multiculturalism as I knew it.

I learned how the system operated when, after high school, I worked as a clerk-typist for a bus company in Paterson. I sat in a large room full of women at banks of desks, carrels not yet having been popularized, typing charter orders and date-stamping cash register tapes from the busses. Once a week I filed drivers' pay slips, noting that, depending on seniority and overtime, they made twice to four times what I earned. There was nothing to learn at my job, nothing to achieve and no way to show your stuff. There was no way to do the job well rather than poorly—you either did it or you didn't—and efficiency was as pointless as fighting African Time. On the first day, after finishing my tasks, I asked my supervisor for more work. She and the assembled company laughed and cracked jokes. "Hmmm. Why don't you sort your paperclips, Hon. Ha, ha, ha. And when you're done, you can sort your rubber bands." Welcome to adult life—join the club. You're here from 8:30 to 5:00 and your job is to fill time: look busy.

The other women at the office filled time by gabbing—and I listened in. I sat between Lois and Mrs. Kuhn, both of whom were married even though they were not much older than I was. Their chief preoccupation was getting "set up" and getting pregnant. Being set up meant having the down payment for a house and a matched set of good china. Getting pregnant was the ticket out of the office. There was no point in having any other ambitions or goals, because there was nothing more that was, for all practical purposes, possible.

The jobs we did were boring. There was no possibility of achievement or advancement, and, short of getting pregnant, there was no way out. Lois, Mrs. Kuhn, and the rest could only grin and bear it. They joked about the blunders of middle management, the three dispatchers recruited from the all-male ranks of bus drivers who had a wood-paneled office all to themselves and whose inability to write legibly or do simple arithmetic was legendary. We knew that we could do better, but we also knew that there was nothing we could do about it: office girls could never become dispatchers because only bus drivers could, and, of course, women could not be bus drivers. That wasn't a matter of preference or ability; it wasn't that we preferred sitting around date-stamping tapes and gabbing or that we thought we couldn't master bus driving. It was just the way things were.

By the time I got my job, the Civil Rights Act had been passed and the help wanted ads were no longer classified as "Help Wanted—Male" and "Help Wanted—Female." All were "Help Wanted—Male or Female." But everyone knew that this was a mere formality—one of many official regulations that no one took seriously. Everyone knew you had to be a man to get a job as bus driver, just as you had to be Italian to get a job as a pipe fitter: that was the way things worked. Everyone knew that official rules and regulations were never taken seriously: unions were run by the Mob, cops were on the take, politicians were all crooks, and candy stores were fronts for the numbers racket; honesty, fairness, and impartiality were myths for children—

you followed the unofficial rules, the real ones, and you took care of your own. And in the end even that was dicey because, as everyone knew, everyone was out for themselves.

In later years, when I watched *The Sopranos*, I remembered that system and the tribal code, noting Tony Soprano's unshakable conviction that you could only trust blood, that you had no serious obligations to "strangers," and the consequences of his occasional lapses. After beating up Ralphie, a self-made man and good earner, because he had killed a teenage prostitute who reminded Tony of his daughter, Tony is reprimanded by consigliere Silvio Dante, who rehearses the relevant articles of the code. For Silvio, Tony's behavior simply makes no sense. "That girl was a stranger," Silvio reminds Tony. "She wasn't your wife, your daughter, your sister, your niece or your *goomah*. And she was just a whore."

Silvio just didn't get it. The idea of impartial justice, the idea that from the moral point of view everyone counts as one and no one counts for more or less than one, the idea that you should do unto others as you would have them do unto you, or unto your wife, daughter, sister, niece, or *goomah* was beyond Silvio's intellectual horizon. Even Tony, who had an inkling of a different code, finer instincts, and supreme power as a mob boss, couldn't beat the system and had to make amends by giving Ralphie a promotion. No one, not even a tribal chieftain, could buck the system without endangering himself and his mates: that is how the tribal system perpetuated itself.

TRIBAL GAMES AND RATIONAL CHOICE

Among deracinated elites in affluent Western countries, things are very different: tribal affiliation is a sentimental fantasy, so we can take up ethnicity as a hobby or ignore it as we please. Organizing political units to track cultural groups is of no importance for us. It does not matter whether our tribe mates are in power, because we can count on impersonal, formal mechanisms to secure our rights and trust that we will be treated fairly.

As a thought experiment, suppose that you, an American, lived in a town near the Canadian border, and it turned out that, because of a surveying error, your neighborhood was in fact in Canada. Would it matter? And if it did, how much would it matter and in what ways? Would you immediately put your house on the market, pack your bags, and flee? Would there be a train of emigrants clogging the highways, heading south to American refugee camps? Would you worry that Canadians might launch a campaign of ethnic cleansing with the support of the Canadian government?

You might worry about higher taxes, as you would if you had discovered that your house, which you thought was in an unincorporated area, turned out to be within the city limits—but then, of course, you would find out that your taxes bought you into a single-payer health-care scheme. You might wonder what kinds of income tax forms you'd have to fill out, how the school system worked, whether your kids would have to learn French, and how to deal with Canadian money. But it wouldn't be as big a deal as it would be if you were a Greek Cypriot and discovered you were living in Turkish Cyprus, a Sunni in a Baghdad Shiite neighborhood, or a gang member living in a competing gang's territory. You wouldn't worry about physical violence or discrimination in Canada—the worst you could expect would be jokes and teasing: "You're a hoser now, eh?"

It's quite another thing in tribal areas, where competing ethnic groups maintain an uneasy truce. In times of peace there will be negotiation and log rolling. If your tribe is dominant, you and your kin will get political favors, construction contracts, and union jobs; if your tribe is a minority but has enough clout to negotiate, deals will be cut; but if your tribe does not have clout, you will get nothing. You had better take care of your own, because if you break the contract they will not take care of you—and no one else will either because they are committed to taking care of their own: in the tribal system individual rights are mediated through the tribal machinery, and there is no effective higher court of appeal. Anyone who tries to opt out of the system unilaterally will be worse off for it, so no one, much as he might personally dislike the system, can safely opt out. And if the peace breaks, you will be in real trouble. You are best off in any case if your tribe has its own turf, and, as a rational self-interested chooser within the tribal system, that is what you will try to achieve—not because you want to preserve your culture or because you have an interest in group rights but because it is the only way you can secure your own individual rights and well-being. It may be that no one particularly likes the system, but no one dares to stop playing and so the system perpetuates itself. That's the way it was in New Jersey.

There are lots of games like this—games that most people don't particularly want to play but that keep going on because no one dares to be the first to quit. Everyone knows these games. Suppose you live in a high-crime area where the streets are deserted at night because no one wants to risk going outside after dark. You are stuck in your house because you don't dare go out into those deserted streets. As a rational, self-interested chooser, you won't go out because you know that your neighbors are also rational, self-interested choosers who won't go out because they know that neither you nor any of their other neighbors will venture to be the first to go out. So nobody goes out—even though everyone knows that they would all be better off if everyone went out and took back the night from the muggers and rapists. This is one of the classic paradoxes of rational choice—a game in which each player is doing the best that he can for himself *given everyone else's choices* but in which everyone would do better if *everyone* made different choices.

Do people like their cultures and want to keep playing the tribal game? Maybe they do. But we can't assume that they do, because, apart from a few who are very desperate or very lucky, players can't opt out.

SLUMMING

After five months of typing charter orders, stamping tapes, and filing pay slips, I packed away my sorted paper clips and went off to an expensive private college in the Midwest for rich underachievers. I was both very desperate and very lucky. When I got to the Midwest, I thought I'd died and gone to heaven: it wasn't only that I had gotten out of the office and didn't have to spend my days imprisoned from 8:30 to 5:00 coping with excruciating boredom—I had escaped from the tangled web of tribalism and corruption. I had come to a place where there were no tribal territories or no-go areas, where the world operated according to explicit, formal regulations rather than the thousand unwritten rules that governed tribal life, where there was openness and transparency. I saw that it was incomparably better. I was in a place where people at least pretended to care about fairness, honesty, and impartiality and, whatever prejudices they may have harbored, had the decency to feel shame. If they were hypocritical, that seemed to me immeasurably better than what I had known in the tribal world I came from: they at least were *embarrassed* about racism and corruption.

I was appalled that my classmates didn't appreciate this. Instead, they deplored what they saw as the blandness of the Midwest and the hypocrisy of the bourgeoisie. They went slumming to observe urban ethnic subcultures and the subculture of the working class, which, on the received view, were more interesting, more "real," and more conducive to human flourishing than their own.

I went on a weekend field trip organized by the college chaplain for my social ethics class to study Chicago ethnic neighborhoods. After breakfast at a church in Lincoln Park and a lecture by the minister on what he called "urban dynamics," tour guides from the parish, which catered to young families who were gentrifying the area, took us to a select group of neighborhoods where we could observe Ethnics in their natural habitats. We went to the South Side to view blacks and then to a neighborhood populated by hillbillies whom, we were told, should be called "Mountain People." Finally, as the sun set over remote prairies, we went to a bleak factory district on the west side dominated by a monumental Catholic church to see the White Ethnics. The area looked like Paterson. As our tour guide prattled on about Polish immigrants and Upton Sinclair's exposé of conditions in the stockyards, and as my classmates ogled old ladies in babushkas waiting at a bus stop, I wondered whether any college students had toured Paterson, seen me in my native habitat, and speculated as to whether I was a White Ethnic or a Mountain Person.

My classmates didn't get it. They viewed the working-class Ethnics we "studied" on our expedition as specimens of exotic cultures. They admired, or claimed to admire, these specimens whom they breathlessly characterized as "real"—not hypocritical, conventional, and uptight like members of the Anglo middle class—but they could not imagine themselves walking in their moccasins. I had walked in their moccasins and knew that they were caught in an evil net from which they could not extricate themselves. I knew that it wasn't only the external circumstances of their lives that oppressed them but the cultures they perpetuated through their actions and choices, because the cost of exit was beyond their means and because for them, the only alternative to following the cultural rules was failing to follow the rules and suffering the consequences.

I didn't like my culture. My classmates certainly didn't like theirs, but they never even considered the possibility that the Ethnics we'd observed might not like their cultures either. It didn't occur to them that these Ethnics might have wanted out, that they did not get out because they were effectively excluded from the mainstream culture by prejudice, discrimination, and economic disadvantage, or that they might have been deeply, and legitimately, offended by our viewing them. Arguably, whatever pressures there may be or may have been on non-Western people, immigrants, or members of ethnic minorities to adopt Western ways or assimilate to the dominant culture, the chief difficulty they face is exclusion—by members of culturally dominant groups who, for all their talk about integration, man the barricades, by economic disadvantage and discrimination, and by self-perpetuating systems that lock them into tribal games and ghettos from which they cannot escape.

At this point, multiculturalists who have been champing at the bit will object that this is not what multiculturalism is all about. It is not about tribalism, corruption, or patronage systems either in the United States or elsewhere. It is certainly not about female genital mutilation, violence, or crime. It is about the rich mosaic of people of all different colors interacting peacefully while maintaining their traditions within cohesive ethnic communities. It is, above all, voluntary—not a matter of being "locked in" or "locked out" but about celebrating ethnic identity and diversity. It is, in other words, a fantasy.

Therefore, before going any further, it is worth getting clear about what multiculturalism is.

Chapter 2

A PHILOSOPHICAL PRELUDE

*What Is
Multiculturalism?*

I spent last week wearing my linguist hat at a workshop on an obscure language spoken by a small, indigenous people. I promised I would not identify these people in public. Suffice it to say, they are non-Westerners.

One of the researchers showed a video of two women having a conversation in the language. They were confident and witty. One of them was arresting in the precise elegance of her gestures. The other one drew in the viewer with her warm irony. They did not seem "exotic"—they could easily have been two women at a Starbucks. One would imagine they were talking about how cute their kids were or something of the sort.

Except that their conversation was about how their husbands rarely let them leave the house.

This is ordinary in their society: women are expected to stay home to cook and take care of children—of which they are also expected to have as many as 10 or more. To go against the husband's wishes is to risk a beating, sanctioned by the village. To leave the society is to risk being killed.

Thus these women can only grin and bear it. It's all they know.

They talk about it with the same resigned "we're all in it together"
jokes as casually as we talk about rush hour traffic.

—John McWhorter[1]

Those who speak do not know and those who know do not speak.

—Lao Tsu

"Multiculturalism" is, at the very least, ambiguous, and the
current tendency to conflate culture and ethnicity or race
further muddles the discussion. At its most innocuous, multiculturalism means nothing more than genetic diversity, a fact of life in societies that have experienced mass immigration. It is also a fact of life
in such societies that recent immigrants and others maintain distinct
cultures and form cohesive communities within the larger society.
Multiculturalism understood in this way is simply a demographic fact.

Most of the time, however, when people discuss multiculturalism,
they are not talking about the composition of societies, about the
ethnic origin of their members, or about citizens' affiliations, traditions, or practices but about how we should view and respond to the
facts of genetic and cultural diversity. And in much of the discussion,
genetic and cultural diversity are conflated. As a consequence, multiculturalism has been understood as four quite different agendas, which
are distinct and separable.

First, multiculturalists accept genetic diversity and hold that individuals should not be disadvantaged or excluded from full participation in their societies in virtue of race or ethnic origin. Second, they
regard the incorporation of artifacts and customs native to other cultures into their own as normal and desirable. Third, they suggest that
we should be "sensitive" to the value of diverse cultures, even where
their traditions and practices are objectionable by our own standards—
a more controversial commitment. Finally, and most controversially,
multiculturalists reject assimilation as an ideal, holding instead that
multiethnic societies should support the persistence of cohesive ethnic
communities, which coexist peacefully and interact without coa-

lescing. They hold that immigrants and members of ethnic minorities should not be expected to assimilate to the dominant culture and reject the melting pot in favor of a salad bowl model of cultural diversity.

My quarrel is with multiculturalism understood in this last sense, what Amartya Sen characterizes as "plural monoculturalism" and peripherally with cultural "sensitivity." I shall argue that plural monoculturalism is bad not only because it undermines social cohesion and sets back the interests of the culturally dominant majority but because it constrains and harms immigrants and members of ethnic minorities. Multiculturalism harms them, first, because the traditions and practices of some cultural groups set back the interests of their members and, in some cases, violate their rights as citizens and, second, because the persistence of distinct cultural communities defined by bloodlines, and the expectation that "diverse" individuals will identify with them in some manner, harms individuals who are associated with them.

Disputes about multiculturalism generate enormous heat and often little light, because *multiculturalism* is ill-defined and because these commitments are rarely distinguished—that is, because when we argue about multiculturalism we do not know what we are talking about. We shall therefore begin by getting clear about the distinctions between the various commitments and agendas that are popularly understood as "multiculturalism."

MULTICULTURALISM AS THE ACCEPTANCE OF GENETIC DIVERSITY

Sometimes when people talk about multiculturalism they do not have culture in mind at all: their concern is biology. They understand a multicultural society as one that comprises citizens of different races and ethnic backgrounds, where there are no genetic tests for citizenship, and where individuals are not excluded from full participation because of ancestry. Racists who hold that societies should maintain ethnic purity reject multiculturalism understood in this way.

Most Americans rightly repudiate racism. They do not see why it should be a good thing for any nation to be genetically homogeneous. There may not be anything particularly good about a society that is genetically diverse—in which people have a variety of skin tones, hair colors and textures, facial features, and body types—but there is nothing bad about it either. We certainly ought to reject policies and practices that exclude individuals from full social participation or relegate them to second-class status because of ancestry, ethnic identity, or appearance. All people of good will are, in this sense and to this extent, multiculturalists.

MULTICULTURALISM AS HYBRIDITY

Multiculturalism as it is most often understood, however, has nothing to do either with genetics or with the way in which people ought to organize their lives. Rather, it is a thesis about the value of artifacts and practices of diverse cultures in enriching our own. A society is multicultural in this sense if it is one where the customs, cuisines, and artifacts that originate in diverse cultures are available.

Multiculturalism understood in this way is "hybridity"—a good thing, because it provides more variety and so more options for everyone. There is no reason to believe that the superficial aspects of Anglo culture are inherently superior to those of other cultures, and in fact there is compelling reason to believe that some aspects are inherently inferior, for example, cuisine. Indeed, the one component of Anglo culture that is arguably superior to all comparable cultural products is the English language, a monument to hybridity, which, with its complete dual vocabulary, is, according to urban legend, "the only language that has a Thesaurus, or needs one."

Some people do, however, object to hybridity in the interests of maintaining cultural purity. They imagine that the introduction of "foreign elements" will somehow muddle native culture or undermine indigenous practices. This fear of hybridity at its most bizarre, the form it typically takes in the United States, is the strange worry that Spanish will drive out English. So, beating the drum for cultural preservation, English-only advocates have managed to pass resolutions declaring English to be the "official language" in thirty states. On the world stage, English has had its ups and downs, and upon independence a number of former British colonies have tried, without success, to adopt alternative official languages. Such programs inevitably fail, not only because English is the language of world powers or because it is de facto the world's lingua franca, but because by virtue of its hybridity English throws off pidgins and creoles and gobbles up local languages.

Language aside, it is hard to see why anyone should worry about hybridity or, indeed, what it is that they worry about. Cultures are never static, so it is not clear what cultural purity comes to. Cultural purists may take a snapshot at a particular time and declare the culture at that time to be "pure," but the selection of a time is external and arbitrary. "Pure" is what philosophers, in the spirit of lexical inflation, call a "syncategorematic" term: it takes its meaning from the expression it modifies. If we ask, for example, whether an animal is "purebred," we need to be clear about what *kind* of animal we are talking about; a horse/donkey hybrid is a pure mule. When it comes to languages and cultures, which change over time and vary by location, the notion of purity is even more problematic. To establish criteria for purity we have to choose a time and place to set the standard, and such choices are largely arbitrary. I speak what I understand is pure American English, the industry standard that prevails in parts of the Mid-Atlantic states and Midwest, which is to say, I don't "have an accent." But then, nobody thinks that they do. Cultural purity is problematic for the same reason: the industry standard is set by people with various interests, not something inherent in the order of nature. It is a matter of decision rather than discovery. It is a matter of deciding where, and when, to take the snapshot of a culture that is to set the standard.

I used to hang out on a Beliefnet message board for "reconstructionist" pagans who were much concerned about cultural purity. The board's habitués were keen to reconstruct the pure folk religions of their (real or imagined) Celtic, Norse, or Greco-Roman forebears. Those on the Hellenismos and Religio Romana section, which I frequented, worried about which gods belonged to the Greco-Roman pantheon in its "pure" form. The received view was that *real* Hellenismos was defined by Homer, Hesiod, and the Parthenon frieze, and was restricted to the deities of "classical" Greece. Isis, Serapis, and Cybele were out. This would have been news to the Greeks as early as the fourth century BC. The choice of a particular time to take the snapshot of Greek culture at its purest, the definition of "classical" Greek culture and religion, is external to the culture and to a great extent arbitrary. It was *we*, or at least our relatively recent forebears, who decided that the fifth century BC was Greece's floruit, the paradigm and height of ancient civilization to which "archaic" Greece was a mere prelude and Hellenistic Greece was a decadent, mongrelized postlude. The culture of ancient Greece and its religion changed over time, and picking that time to take a snapshot of the culture in its pure form was largely arbitrary and reflected the interests of cultural outsiders.

By the same token, the notion that American and British cultures, or, more broadly, "Western Civilization," have been, in some times and at some places, uniquely "pure" is, at best, deeply problematic. Interaction with other cultures and mass immigration are nothing new. Cultures have always changed, for better or for worse, through the operation of internal forces and through interaction with other cultures so that what were once novelties or "foreign elements" become quintessentially native. Amartya Sen recollects "a definitive description of the unquestionable Englishness of an Englishwoman in a London paper: 'She is as English as daffodils or chicken tikka masala.'" Reflecting further on the hybridity of contemporary English and Indian cuisine he writes:

> Indian and British food can genuinely claim to be multicultural.
> India had no chili until the Portuguese brought it to India from
> America, but it is effectively used in a wide range of Indian food

today and seems to be a dominant element in most types of curries. It is plentifully present in a mouth-burning form in vindaloo, which, as its name indicates, carries the immigrant memory of combining wine with potatoes. Tandoori cooking might have been perfected in India, but it originally came to India from West Asia. Curry powder, on the other hand, is a distinctly English invention, unknown in India before Lord Clive, and evolved, I imagine, in the British army mess. And we are beginning to see the emergence of new styles of preparing Indian food, offered in sophisticated subcontinental restaurants in London.[2]

Nowadays supermarket chains in the United Kingdom stock twenty different kinds of curry sauce and canned mulligatawny soup, which have become native English fare. Most people agree that this is a good thing, since "classical" British cuisine leaves much to be desired. We could, if we chose, *define* proper, pure English food as the stuff that was served up in England a century ago, dominated by boiled beef and overcooked vegetables. Even if we did, however, the choice of 1906 would have been arbitrary. Why not 1806? Or some time prior to 1066, before the decadent French corrupted English culture and the Anglo-Saxon language?

Some Americans, too, imagine that there is a classical period when our culture and cuisine were pure. These days Americans who are keen on cultural preservation and who worry that the latest wave of mass immigration will swamp "pure" American culture latch onto the 1950s at some indeterminate midwestern location, improved by retrospection and filtered through the medium of TV sitcoms. But this is as arbitrary as choosing any other time to take that snapshot. As al Qaeda operatives knew and most Americans only realized after 9/11, New York is an American city—as American as Oshkosh or Kalamazoo. Tautologously, what is in America is American, just as any word in common English usage is English—as I was reminded by a copy editor who chided me for italicizing "ceteris paribus" and "de facto" as "foreign" words. Tikka masala is as English as daffodils, and *loompya*, tortillas, and couscous are as American as hamburgers, bagels, and spaghetti, which, in turn, are as American as turkey, squash, cornbread, succotash, and other native fare we turn out on Thanksgiving when we "do American" in earnest.

Besides being arbitrary in their selection of a standard, cultural purists are disconcertingly selective about which "foreign" elements they tolerate. During a rally for immigration law reform last year, some local residents in my town near the Mexican border were outraged that participants carried both American and Mexican flags and sang "The Star-Spangled Banner" in Spanish—a sure indication, they opined, that Mexican immigrants would not learn English, could not assimilate, and intended to take over. None seemed to mind the Swedish flag at our local IKEA. I doubt, too, that they would have worried if citizens of Lake Wobegon, Minnesota, sang "The Star-Spangled Banner" in Swedish at a civic event celebrating their real or imagined Scandinavian heritage. And I do not think there would be a dry eye in the house if a sentimental docudrama depicted masses of immigrants pushing down the gangplank to Ellis Island singing "The Star-Spangled Banner" in Russian, Yiddish, or Italian.

Mercifully, however, most Americans are not cultural purists. "Pure" American culture is lavishly hybrid, and most of us like it that way; that is why we favor what is commonly called "multiculturalism." Upon Googling the keyword "multiculturalism," there are many hits for advertisements in local papers for "multicultural faires" at which ethnic cuisine from around the world is served, Native American blankets and beadwork are exhibited, and students from local elementary schools dressed in ethnic costumes sewn by their moms rehearse folk dances from Africa, the Balkans, and the British Isles. All this is good fun, and it is hard to see why anyone should object.

This is what most people understand as multiculturalism. It is enjoyable, enriching, and in no way objectionable, *since participation is strictly voluntary.* We can take part in these multicultural festivals and eat in ethnic restaurants as we please and we can, at least temporarily, take on whatever ethnic identity we choose as part of the fantasy. You don't have to be Jewish to love Levi's Real Jewish Rye, as an old TV commercial had it, you don't have to be Italian to enjoy the San Gennaro Festa, and you don't have to be Irish to celebrate St. Patrick's Day. Theologian Karl Barth describes his amazement on coming to America for the first time during Chicago's annual St. Patrick's Day festivities to see the Chicago River dyed bright green and a black woman wearing a button that said, "Kiss me, I'm Irish." As an American reading Barth's memoir, I did a double take—what was the big deal?—until I realized it was a big deal, and a good one.

Critics of multiculturalism get bad press because the common perception is that we object to these harmless customs and practices. That is not what is at issue. When it comes to the harmless, superficial features of culture—food, costume, music and dance, language, entertainment, and crafts—the more the better. As Susan Okin famously argued, however, it is quite another matter when it comes to some of the deep features of culture, including the role of women and practices that enforce that role. Jazz, curry, and salsa dancing enrich culture; female genital mutilation, forced marriage, and wife beating do not.

MULTICULTURALISM AS CULTURAL SENSITIVITY

So long as we restrict ourselves to what Stanley Fish has called "boutique multiculturalism"—the stuff of multicultural faires and holiday celebrations—we can probably agree that absorbing features of diverse cultures is a good thing.[3] Beyond the boutique, however, cultural affirmation is at best a mixed bag, and cultural relativism—understood *substantively* as the doctrine that there are no universal or cross-cultural standards against which the beliefs, practices, and mores of diverse cultures can be assessed—is surely a thesis we ought to reject.

Most of us believe that cultural relativism understood as a substantive thesis about the equality of all cultures is false. If there are no cross-cultural values or standards, then illiteracy is as good as literacy, creation myths are as good as scientific cosmology, and human sacrifice is just another cultural practice on a par with Fourth of July fireworks or Mardi Gras. If literacy, education, scientific achievement, technical sophistication, and political liberty are good things—and autocracy, corruption, militarism, tribalism, and racism are bad things—it follows that not all cultures are equal. Literate, cosmopolitan, technically advanced cultures are better than illiterate tribal cultures where people eke out a bare living through hunting and gathering or primitive agriculture. Cultures that promote education and value liberty, equality, and fraternity, we believe, are better than those whose members wage war with competing clans for land, slaves, beasts, and wives, and keep women as chattel. Cultures that tolerate or support these latter practices are, by any reasonable standards, defective.

Defective cultures are like diseases or injuries. We don't, or shouldn't, pretend that a broken leg or case of the flu is a good thing to make injured or ill people feel better; we recognize that disease and injury make people worse off and aim to cure them. Cultural relativism doesn't do anyone any favors—least of all members of the defective cultures whom it is intended to benefit. It is hard to see why anyone with a serious interest in human rights or well-being would balk at the suggestion that some cultures are bad for the people who live in them or why the characterization of cultures as "defective" should have shock value—as it does.

Cultural relativism gains plausibility in part because we are inclined to identify cultures with habits and practices that are trivial, superficial, or innocuous, such as costume, cuisine, and language rather than the deep features of culture that are constitutive of serious cultural identity: the structure of the family, the roles assigned to men and women, the obligations imposed by kinship and group membership, the way in which outsiders are viewed and treated, religious convictions and ethical commitments, the value placed on various character traits and practices, assumptions about the value of education and the feasibility of social change, and a whole host of practices that manifest and enforce these fundamental features of the culture. Identifying cultures with their innocuous, superficial accoutrements, we rehearse urban legends about missionaries forcing natives to wear pants in order to "civilize" them. Surely, we believe, Western dress is not the mark of civilization, and surely minorities should not be sent the message that white bread is superior to tortillas, kebobs, or curries. And surely that is true. But the serious critique of cultural relativism is not directed at hybridity in costume or cuisine or motivated by naive views about the superiority of white Anglo diet or dress. Rather, critics note, the deep features of some cultures are disadvantageous to individuals who live in them.

Cultural relativism, however, gains further plausibility from the tacit assumption that culture is inextricably linked to the genetic endowment of individual participants. Given this assumption, we read any hint that a culture is primitive, backward, or inferior as tantamount to the claim that native members of that culture are genetically defective. And that is a thesis that we are, with good reason, keen to repudiate.

Cultural relativism *as a methodology* represented the repudiation of that thesis, which enjoyed remarkable popularity among both the educated general public and academics concerned with the study of human culture as little as a century ago. As a *methodology*, cultural relativism does not assert that all cultural practices are equally good. Rather, it represents a commitment to studying cultures on their own terms without making value judgments—in particular, without assuming that any deviation from the model of European culture is a defect. It represents a repudiation of an earlier pseudo-science of race that purported to have established a biological basis for the inferiority of non-European cultures. This is the doctrine against which advocates of cultural sensitivity are reacting, and, in this respect at least, they have the best of intentions even if the popular response to their program has been wrongheaded. To understand the response, it is crucial to understand the history.

During the early years of the twentieth century, eugenics—the program of selective breeding to improve human stock suggested by Sir Francis Galton in *Human Genius* and elsewhere—was in vogue among public intellectuals in the United States. Among those supporting this program were Oliver Wendell Holmes, who wrote the majority opinion in the 1927 Supreme Court decision upholding Virginia's forced sterilization law, and prominent progressives like Margaret Sanger.[4] The eugenics movement, as it figured in American popular culture during a period of mass immigration, also promoted notions about the relative fitness and social desirability of various ethnic groups. Predictably, eugenics attempted to provide scientific backing for the widespread sentiment that the most recent immigrant groups, Southern Europeans and Jews, were the least genetically fit and the most prone to criminality. Indeed, various authors, including Stephen Jay Gould, have suggested that restrictions on immigration passed in the United States during the 1920s were motivated by the goals of eugenics, in particular, a desire to exclude "inferior" races from the national gene pool.[5]

Contemporary anthropologists' sympathetic accounts of traditional societies are the result of a revolution in anthropology, a field of study that was born in sin. Before Franz Boas and his star pupil Margaret Mead transformed their discipline, anthropologists influenced by Social Darwinist notions and racist theories went about collecting bones and measuring the skulls of "primitive" people in hopes of producing what they took to be a properly scientific, biological explanation for the primitive character of their cultures. This research program was the supposed scientific basis for the ideology of colonialism. "Primitive" people, on this account, benefited from incorporation into superior cultures but only as a permanent servant class insofar as their genetic deficits rendered them incapable of full participation.

Anthropologists who repudiated this research program adopted cultural relativism as a methodology not because these racist doctrines were politically incorrect but because they were bad science. Taking the structure and institutions of modern Western societies as a universal paradigm, attempting to understand other cultures in those terms, and judging them defective because they did not fit the model undermined any serious attempt to explain how such cultures actually operated. It was rather like taking Latin grammar as the universal linguistic paradigm and declaring split infinitives in English "ungrammatical" because Latin infinitives could not be split. Latin grammar is a bad fit for languages with Germanic verb systems and an impossible fit for non-Indo-European languages. To understand how a language works is to understand it on its own terms—and so it is with cultures. Moreover, biological accounts were simply not illuminating when it came to understanding and explaining culture. Measuring skulls and thighbones does not go any way toward explaining why people behave as they do.

Anthropology, however, found its way into popular culture, where cultural relativism, which anthropologists adopted as a *methodology*, a way of studying culture, was read as a *substantive* thesis about the equal value of all cultures and practices. Like history, anthropology is an academic discipline that produces literature nonexperts can read for enjoyment—and it was indeed a pleasure to read the sympathetic accounts of participant-observers in exotic cultures. Besides being informative, this literature enlarged our sympathies in the way that all good social history does. Thumbing through *National Geographic* or watching TV documentaries about Polynesians and Eskimos, hunter-gatherers in the Amazon rain forest, and peasant farmers in sub-Saharan Africa, we learned that they weren't all simply "natives" on a rampage, shaking spears and looking for missionaries to cook.

Like most popular social history, however, this literature repre-sented its subjects and their lives in a favorable light and focused on the interesting bits—the music and dance, love affairs and mornings on the lagoon, the rites of passage, potlatches, and ceremonies. That is, after all, why such literature becomes popular. No one with a taste for social history wants to read about poverty, disease, or other human miseries; about the narrowness and constraint of the village world; or about the drudgery and tedium of daily life. If we have a taste for accounts of life in Elizabethan England, we want to watch costume dramas set in the royal court and read about the lives and loves of the aristocracy, not the brutality and squalor of life downstairs, in the urban slums, or in rural villages. And if we have a taste for anthro-pology, we want to read Margaret Mead.

Listen to Mead describe the beginning of a day in Samoa:

THE LIFE of the day begins at dawn, or if the moon has shown until daylight, the shouts of the young men may be heard before dawn from the hillside. Uneasy in the night, populous with ghosts, they shout lustily to one another as they hasten with their work. As the dawn begins to fall among the soft brown roofs and the slender palm trees stand out against a colourless, gleaming sea, lovers slip home from trysts beneath the palm trees or in the shadow of beached canoes, that the light may find each sleeper in his appointed place. Cocks crow, negligently, and a shrill-voiced bird cries from the breadfruit trees. The insistent roar of the reef seems muted to an undertone for the sounds of a waking village. . . . The whole village, sheeted and frowsy, stirs, rubs its eyes, and stumbles towards the beach. "Talofa!" "Talofa!" "Will the journey start to-day?" "Is it bonito fishing your lordship is going?" Girls stop to giggle over some young ne'er-do-well who escaped during the night from an angry father's pursuit and to venture a shrewd guess that the daughter knew more about his presence than she told.

There was, perhaps, a hidden agenda, an implicit critique of modern Western societies "seared with trade, bleared, smeared with toil" and cramped by sexual taboos, as well as an attempt to lay to rest the ghost of racism and undermine the colonialist ideology with which it was associated. The laudable aim of this project was to show that "primitive" cultures were as complex and interesting as those that were supposed to be more advanced and, in many respects, kinder, gentler, and more conducive to human flourishing.

Whatever the agenda, this was the literature that shaped a generation. We read it for pleasure and we read it in undergraduate intro courses in the social sciences where instructors preached incessantly on two themes. First, they stressed that we should not judge the beliefs or practices of non-Western peoples by our local cultural standards or condemn practices that we, because of our own enculturation, found peculiar or distasteful. Second, they warned us that even well-meaning attempts to improve, educate, modernize, Westernize, and most especially to Christianize the natives had disastrous consequences: traditional cultures were coherent and fragile—any interference could bring about social collapse and leave the natives much worse off.

The suggestion that some cultures were better than others or that some cultural practices were simply bad and ought to be stopped was taboo. And given the history of racism, colonialism, and the exploitation of indigenous peoples, there was a good reason for the taboo. This suggestion that some cultural practices were bad was, as Jared Diamond points out, a dangerous idea. Diamond notes, for example, that the idea that tribal peoples often damage their environments and make war is dangerous:

> Why is this idea dangerous? Because too many people today believe that a reason not to mistreat tribal people is that they are too nice or wise or peaceful to do those evil things, which only we evil citizens of state governments do. The idea is dangerous because, if you believe that that's the reason not to mistreat tribal peoples, then proof of the idea's truth would suggest that it's OK to mistreat them. In fact, the evidence seems to me overwhelming that the dangerous idea is true. But we should treat other people well because of ethical reasons, not because of naïve anthropological theories that will almost surely prove false.[6]

Recent events have brought home to us that this is a dangerous idea we have to face. In the global south, tribalism breeds corruption, which impedes development, and tribal warfare is endemic. Women are everywhere subordinate and almost always mistreated. The greater part of the population of most "developing" countries is mired in poverty not only or primarily, as we were carefully taught, because colonial powers appropriated their resources or exploited them but because their cultures, from which they cannot extricate themselves, are defective.

Immigrants from these countries bring their cultures with them. Excluded from the mainstream and confined to ghettos by poverty, ignorance, discrimination, and the muddled multicultural policies of receiving countries, they perpetuate the cultural practices that lock in poverty, promote tribal conflict, and oppress women in their countries of origin. When, inevitably, their exclusion causes trouble—when patriarchs murder girls who "dishonor" their families, when youths riot in the streets of immigrant suburbs, or suicide bombers blow up busses—we notice. Then, politicians who have not made any serious effort to provide the support and resources to integrate them, or to eliminate discrimination in education and employment, blame them for "keeping to themselves" and rejecting mainstream cultural values.

The multiculturalist policies that were adopted in Western European countries experiencing mass immigration harmed immigrants. In the interests of cultural sensitivity, politicians and bureaucrats treated immigrants, their children, and their children's children as members of distinct "communities" and accommodated cultural practices that set back the interests of their members. So, in Sweden, where the age of legal marriage for native Swedes is eighteen, girls from immigrant families were legally allowed to marry as young as fifteen to accommodate cultural practices—hardly a benefit for children subject to forced marriage. In the same spirit, the British government chose to deal with its Muslim minority through the mediation of self-appointed "community leaders"—ignoring the interests of liberal Muslims and all Muslim women.

Apart from "community leaders" and others who make their living in the multiculturalism business, cultural sensitivity does not do anyone any favors and it is especially hard on the immigrants and members of minority groups it is supposed to benefit. That is one reason why we should reject plural monoculturalism—the doctrine of the salad bowl—in favor of the assimilationist melting pot: some cultures are oppressive to their members and embody practices that violate individual rights. There is, however, another reason, which strangely is not often heard: the expectation that individuals will identify with ancestral cultures and affiliate with cohesive ethnic communities is oppressive in and of itself because it constrains individual choice.

MULTICULTURALISM AS PLURAL MONOCULTURALISM

Plural monoculturalism is the doctrine that individuals ought to remain faithful to their ancestral cultures and that a multiethnic society ought to be a "salad bowl" where diverse groups, maintaining their separate identities, interact peacefully without coalescing. It is the doctrine that individuals, in the interests of "authenticity," ought to maintain, reestablish, or invent connections to their ancestral cultures, however remote; that the development and persistence of ethnic communities should be encouraged; and that individuals should identify—and be identified—with their ancestral cultures unto the second, third, and nth generations. This is the version of multiculturalism that I shall argue is bad for (almost) everyone and that hereafter, unless otherwise indicated, will be what I mean by "multiculturalism."

Some of the consequences of multiculturalism thus understood have been disastrous. To see this, consider one especially egregious example—the policies forbidding transracial adoptions, promoted by the National Association of Black Social Workers in the interest of cultural preservation, described by black legal scholar Richard Thompson Ford: "The presumptions underlying race-matching policies are sharply articulated in a 1972 NABSW [National Association of Black Social Workers] resolution, which read in part, 'Black children belong physically, and psychologically and culturally in black families in order that they receive the total sense of themselves and develop a sound projection of their future . . . black children in white homes are cut off from the healthy development of themselves as black people.'"[7] Citing a range of cases in which agencies, operating according to the canons of multiculturalism, sought to block transracial adoptions against the express wishes of birth parents and without any serious consideration for what might reasonably be construed as the welfare of the children involved, Ford notes that the policy assumed "a racial and almost biological conception of cultural difference, something that one carries in the blood" and permanently relegated most black children put up for adoption to the foster care system.[8]

The only rationale for this program is what might be called Serious Cultural Genetics, the assumption that culture is, in some sense, genetically coded so that individuals, regardless of their desires or the cultures in which they are in fact embedded, are biologically bound to ancestral cultures. This doctrine, Ford suggests, has its roots in German Romanticism, in particular in the writings of Herder, and came to fruition in Nazi racist ideology.

Serious Cultural Genetics is immune to empirical falsification. Social workers who, as Ford notes, were insistent on placing black children with black families and keeping Native American children on the reservation did not imagine that black children in white homes would nevertheless exhibit some distinctively black cultural traits or that Indian children adopted as infants would miraculously grow up speaking Hopi to the amazement of their white adoptive parents. They worried that these children would *not*—that they would be detached from the culture of their ancestors and blood kin and so, in some indescribable way, be worse off for failing to receive a "total sense of themselves." It is left as an exercise for the reader to figure out what this means.

Although it seems unlikely that most multiculturalists are serious racists, many seem to believe that the doctrine of inherent cultural differences between members of different races is, at the very least, a good myth that should be cultivated, and that even where appropriate cultural practices do not exist, they ought to be invented. In this spirit, during the 1960s American sociologist Ron Karenga invented Kwanzaa to provide black Americans with an African cultural heritage. Along the same lines, Susan B. Anthony is supposed to have remarked that even if the state of primitive matriarchy postulated by Elizabeth Cady Stanton and other early feminists were not a historical reality, it was good to believe that such a state had existed because it "encouraged women."

This is the version of multiculturalism that, whether based on racist assumptions about the genetic basis of culture or adopted as a good myth to "encourage" members of disadvantaged minorities, I shall argue is not good for anyone. The very idea that black children would be better off being kicked around the foster care system than they would be in white adoptive homes, that immigrant women in Canada would benefit from access to sharia courts—a proposal seriously pursued recently until it was squashed by Canadian Muslim women's protests—or that the preservation of ancestral cultures trumped individual rights and interests is the reductio of plural monoculturalism.

MULTICULTURALISM AS A RESPONSE TO RACISM

The wisest mentor I have had, a theologian, cautioned me that in reading historical theology, it was of the utmost importance to read historically and to ask in particular what views theologians were interested in repudiating. Church history is full of strange disputes and doctrines that seem incomprehensible or, at best, unmotivated, until we recognize the follies their authors aimed to repudiate. So it is with multiculturalism and a number of doctrines with which it is packaged. They are easy to dismiss but in fairness need to be considered within their historical context and criticized within their historical context, with special attention to avoiding the follies to which their authors were responding.

As Americans, we are reacting against a peculiarly disgraceful form of institutionalized racism. Even if very few people seriously believe that cultural traits are genetically coded, a great many believe that the quality of a culture reflects upon the individual character of its native participants, so that if a culture is inferior, that is evidence that its members are, at least on the average, inferior to native members of superior cultures. Where there's smoke there's fire—so they believe. While there might be a few exceptional members of inferior cultures who could cut it by the standards of civilized societies, the majority cannot.

In fact culture is a historical accident, which is not even remotely or indirectly linked to genetics. As Diamond argues compellingly in *Guns, Germs, and Steel*, there are a thousand reasons why some cultures progress while others stagnate, including access to trade routes, the availability of large mammals that can be domesticated, and plain, dumb luck—a hard saying for most of us who want simple answers.

Nevertheless, reacting against assumptions about the tie between culture and race, Americans, intent on repudiating racism, felt that they had to prove that all cultures were equally good and, in particular, that cultures previously deemed primitive, defective, or inferior were better than they were cracked up to be. By the same token, white Anglos in the West read the behavior of others who repudiated their ancestral cultures and sought to assimilate or adopt Western ways as manifestations of "self-hatred"—evidence that, bamboozled by colonialist and racist propaganda, they believed that they, or at least their relatives, were genetically inferior. That is why many of us, in the interest of repudiating racism, promoted cultural self-affirmation and plural monoculturalism, policies that, as we shall see, set back the interests of the very people they were intended to support.

NOTES

1. John McWhorter, "Tribes v. Westerners," *New York Sun*, October 12, 2006.

2. http://www.pierretristam.com/Bobst/library/wf-58.htm.

3. S. Fish, "Boutique Multiculturalism, or, Why Liberals Are Incapable of Thinking about Hate Speech," *Critical Inquiry* 23, no. 2 (1997).

4. H. Bruinius, *Better for All: The Secret History of Forced Sterilization and the Quest for Racial Purity* (New York: Knopf), 2006.

5. "Eugenics," Wikipedia entry, http://en.wikipedia.org/wiki/Eugenics.

6. Jared Diamond, *Edge*, World Question Center, http://www.edge.org/q2006/q06_print.html#diamond.

7. Richard T. Ford, *Racial Culture: A Critique* (Princeton, NJ: Princeton University Press 2006), p. 83.

8. Ibid., p. 86.

Chapter 3

THE COSTS OF MULTICULTURALISM

Today we combine two concepts of liberty: one has its origins in the 18th century, founded on emancipation from tradition and authority. The other, originating in anti-imperialist anthropology, is based on the equal dignity of cultures which could not be evaluated merely on the basis of our criteria. Relativism demands that we see our values simply as the beliefs of the particular tribe we call the West. Multiculturalism is the result of this process. . . . As a result, we can turn a blind eye to how others live and suffer once they've been parked in the ghetto of their particularity. . . .

This is the **paradox of multiculturalism**: it accords the same treatment to all communities, but not to the people who form them, denying them the freedom to liberate themselves from their own traditions. . . . [U]nder the guise of respecting specificity, individuals are imprisoned in an ethnic or racial definition, and plunged back into the restrictive mould from which they were supposedly in the process of being freed. Black people, Arabs, Pakistanis and Muslims are imprisoned in their history and assigned, as in the colonial era, to residence in their epidermis. . . . Multiculturalism is a racism of the anti-racists: it chains people to their roots.[1]

Is multiculturalism a good thing? That depends on whether it makes it easier for people to get what they want or blocks them. This is, at least, how we should address the question if we are *liberals*, that is, if we believe that liberty is of paramount importance and if we believe, as I do, that the Good Life consists of nothing more or less than the freedom to get what we want.

Does multiculturalism restrict individual freedom or enhance it? Does it liberate people, in particular immigrants and members of ethnic minorities, or does it thwart them? Most discussion of multiculturalism evades these questions insofar as it *assumes* that multiculturalism expands individual options and makes it easier for members of traditionally disadvantaged groups to get what they want. That is what I shall dispute. Multiculturalism has its costs, and they are significant ones, particularly for immigrants and members of visible minorities.

MULTICULTURALISM AS LIBERTY: THE CONVENTIONAL DEFENSE

The conventional defense of multiculturalism rests on two closely related assumptions. First, multiculturalists assume that (normal) people—members of cultural minority communities in particular—*like* their cultures. Second, it assumes that exit from minority communities is relatively unproblematic for most members. These assumptions hang together: if we assume that exit from minority communities is unproblematic, then we should take individuals' identification with these communities as strong evidence that they prefer maintaining their distinct cultures. We may then conclude, as multiculturalists do, that attempts to mandate or even encourage assimilation impede them from getting what they want.

London mayor Ken Livingstone, in a recent op-ed essay, articulates with great clarity the conventional defense of multiculturalism, which rests on these assumptions:

Multiculturalism versus its opponents is simply one manifestation of the age-long struggle between liberty and its opponents. It is not about personal differences of opinion but between the values of an open and a closed society.

The principles on which multiculturalism rests are not new. The foundations of liberalism and multiculturalism were outlined in great clarity in what is justifiably the most famous political essay in British history, John Stuart Mill's *On Liberty*. In Mill's original formulation: "The sole end for which mankind are warranted . . . in interfering with the liberty of action of any of their number is self-protection . . . the only purpose for which power can be rightfully exercised over any member of a . . . community, against his will, is to prevent harm to others." This, the classic formulation of liberalism, is, of course, what is frequently paraphrased as "You should be able to do anything you want provided it does not interfere with others."

Its basis is simple. Every individual who exists is unique and wishes to pursue their life in a different way. The individual must be able to choose for themselves. Those who oppose "multiculturalism"—that is, the right to pursue different cultural values subject only to the restriction that they should not interfere with the similar right for others—are merely playing the same roles as those who previously thought Protestants should be prohibited from practicing their religion in Catholic countries, that Jews were not entitled to vote, and atheists should not be allowed to be MPs.[2]

Most people are hesitant to criticize multiculturalism because they do not want to deny immigrants, ethnic minorities, or anyone else the freedom to maintain their religious traditions or to impose alien values and practices upon others. The debate, consequently, is framed as one between progressive advocates of choice and conservatives who would restrict individual choice, between proponents of cultural diversity who support the right of diverse individuals to do as they wish and opponents of diversity who aim to enforce conformity to majority values and practices. On this account, multiculturalism promotes the interests of minorities at the expense of majority interests and so the fundamental question posed is whether accommodating minorities, through the implementation of multicultural policies, sets back the interests of the culturally dominant majority.

Framing the issue in this way is seriously misleading. It *assumes* that multiculturalism expands the scope of individual choice and, in particular, that it benefits immigrants and members of ethnic minorities by freeing them to maintain their diverse cultures. Indeed, it assumes that assimilation is, at best, a *cost* that members of minority groups incur, a Faustian bargain they make in the interests of social acceptance, political participation, and material advantage.

That is something we cannot assume. For immigrants and members of ethnic minorities, multiculturalism opens up some options but closes off others. When multiculturalism is taken seriously it benefits those immigrants and members of ethnic minorities who want to preserve distinct cultural traditions and maintain cohesive ethnic communities at the expense of those who would prefer to assimilate.

Livingstone imagines that multiculturalism protects the *right* of individuals to "pursue different cultural values." He imagines that it is comparable to political guarantees of religious liberty protecting the rights of Protestants in Catholic countries and the right of Jews and atheists to maintain their religious commitments or lack thereof in the face of pressures to affiliate with the dominant religion. The assumption is that many or even most members of ethnic minorities *prefer* to "pursue different cultural values"; we rarely talk about the rights of individuals to do things that they do not want to do. Popular rhetoric on the Right begins with the same assumption, but whereas Livingstone defends what he takes to be the right of immigrants and members of ethnic minorities to get what they want, conservatives fault them for allegedly rejecting mainstream values and practices and for keeping to themselves. Both conventional multiculturalists and their conservative critics assume that assimilation is unproblematic and, indeed, that there is significant pressure on members of ethnic minority groups to join the mainstream.

This assumption is manifestly false. Assimilation is simply out of reach for many new immigrants, who do not speak the language, are unfamiliar with the customs and practices of receiving countries, are visibly marked as members of "immigrant communities," and are in countless ways excluded from the mainstream. You cannot assimilate at will and you cannot unilaterally declare yourself white. Social exclusion and discrimination are still a fact of life, and, even privileged members of traditionally disadvantaged groups who have overcome those barriers, are pressed to identify with their ancestral cultures.

Listen to Keith Richburg, a black American journalist reflecting on his three-year stint in Nairobi as an African bureau chief for the *Washington Post* covering news in Kenya and neighboring African countries. Richburg does not "identify" with Africa or with Africans and he thanks God that his remote ancestors left—conceding the fact that they left for the New World in chains: "[I]f things had been different," he writes, "I might have been one of them—or might have met some similarly anonymous fate in one of the countless ongoing civil wars or tribal clashes on this brutal continent. And so I thank God my ancestor survived that voyage."

> Does that sound shocking? Does it sound almost like a justification for the terrible crime of slavery? Does it sound like this black man has forgotten his African roots? Of course it does, all that and more. . . . It might have been easier for me to just keep all of these emotions bottled up inside. Maybe I should have just written a standard book on Africa that would have talked broadly about the politics, the possibilities, the prospects for change.
>
> But I'm tired of lying. . . . Talk to me about Africa and my black roots and my kinship with my African brothers and I'll throw it back in your face, and then I'll rub your nose in the images of the rotting flesh.

Leaving Africa, and none too soon, Richburg continues:

> I'm beaten down, weary, ready to leave all of these lurid images behind me, ready to go home . . . Africa. Birthplace of civilization. My ancestral homeland. I came here thinking I might find a little bit of that missing piece of myself. But Africa chewed me up and spit

me back out again. . . . It wasn't supposed to turn out this way. I really did come here with an open mind, wanting to love the place, love the people. I would love to end this journey now on a high note, to see hope amid the chaos. . . . But while I know that "Afrocentrism" has become fashionable for many black Americans searching for identity, I know it cannot work for me. . . . I am an American, a black American, and I feel no connection to this strange and violent place. . . .

I'm leaving Africa now, so I don't care anymore about the turmoil. . . . [F]rom now on, I will be seeing it from afar, maybe watching it on television like millions of other Americans. . . . [N]one of it affects me, because I feel no attachment to the place or the people.

And why should I feel anything more? Because my skin is black? Because some ancestor of mine, four centuries ago, was wrenched from this place and sent to America, and because I now look like those others whose ancestors were left behind? . . . I have been here, and I have seen—and frankly, I want no part of it.[3]

If Richburg sounds petulant and defensive, that is not his fault. He is responding to the entrenched dogmas of multiculturalism, according to which our identity is inextricably bound up with our genetic heritage: that we ought to identify with ancestral cultures and feel kinship with remote relatives from our ancestral homelands and that if we fail to do so we are at fault.

We cannot assume that this is so—and there is no reason to believe that it *should* be so. Some immigrants and members of minorities want to preserve distinct cultures and communities; others do not. And there is an irreconcilable conflict of interests between cultural preservationists and assimilationists. Multiculturalism is not cost-free: it benefits individuals who wish to identify themselves with ancestral cultures, to search for their genealogical "roots," or to affiliate with ethnic communities at the expense of those who, like Richburg, do not, will not, and cannot identify.

CULTURAL PRESERVATIONISTS VERSUS ASSIMILATIONISTS: THERE IS NO FREE RIDE

The hard question of ethics—perhaps the only serious question in ethics—is adjudicating between individuals with conflicting interests. Getting what I want prevents you from getting what you want; expanding the scope of choice for some people imposes constraints on others. I want to drive as fast as I can; you do not want to share the road with lunatics like me who represent a real and present danger to you. The state in its wisdom intervenes and regularly slaps me with tickets, fines, and sessions at traffic school. I whine and grumble but know in my heart that the state is right in this matter: my freedom to zoom down the freeway with the gas pedal floored impinges on the freedom of sensible motorists to enjoy safe, reasonably stress-free commutes. By imposing restrictions on me, overall freedom is expanded. I deserve what I get.

There is no free ride when it comes to multiculturalism either. Some people want to live in a salad bowl, but others want to live in a melting pot. Some members of ethnic minorities want to join the mainstream; others want to maintain their cultural traditions. We cannot assume that all or most would choose the latter course if they were free to do so and we cannot assume that accommodating those who prefer to maintain these traditions would be cost-free.

There is in fact a conflict of interests between cultural preservationists and individuals who wish to assimilate. Ethnic communities have their stakeholders: self-appointed "community leaders" who make their living by representing the supposed interests of their constituents to journalists and politicians and immigrants who cannot cope with the language or customs of the receiving countries. They include also members of visible minorities who, because they are not accepted within the larger society because they are inescapably tagged with their ethnic affiliations and face discrimination, retreat to ethnic enclaves or decide that since they cannot join mainstream society they will do what they can to beat it. Stakeholders have an interest in jacking up the costs of exit in order to preserve the integrity of their communities. These exit costs, however, impose constraints on individuals who want out. Whichever way multiculturalism breaks, there will be winners and losers.

Multiculturalists assign cultures to individuals in virtue of kinship and bloodlines and assume that people *like* the cultures thus assigned. They support the right of individuals to identify with their ancestral cultures. Some black Americans indeed want to identify with African culture and are glad that multiculturalists support their right to do so. Richburg, however, a living, raging counterexample, does not like "his" assigned African culture; the "right" to identify with it is of no use to him because he wants no part of it and does not want to be identified with it. And, apart from blood-and-soil notions of race and identity, there is no reason to imagine that Richburg should find himself, or even a missing piece of himself, in Africa.

It would be good if assimilationists like Richburg and cultural preservationists could both get what they want, but that is not feasible. According individuals some of the "rights," multiculturalists affirm, enlarges the liberty of cultural preservationists at the expense of others. In the United States, for example, the *Yoder* court decision, which gave Amish parents the right to pull their children out of school after eighth grade, severely curtailed the freedom of Amish children who, without even a high school education, had few prospects outside of the Amish community. Most conflicts of interest are not so stark. The fashion for Afro-Centrism that Richburg deplores did not impose any serious material constraints on his career. Nevertheless, when members of a "visible" minority "do ethnic," their behavior affects the way in which all members of the group are perceived and treated. If blacks make a fuss about their African roots, Richburg will be pressed to "find a piece of himself" in Africa.

There is no free ride. Policies that enable cultural preservationists to get what they want make it more difficult, or even impossible, for assimilationists to get what they want; policies that satisfy assimilationists set back the interests of cultural preservationists.

Livingstone and other multiculturalists who make the conventional defense do not recognize the costs of multiculturalism for members of ethnic minorities. Even if in the end we decide that the benefits to cultural preservationists outweigh the costs to assimilationists, these costs have to be recognized and counted. Multiculturalism restricts individual liberty because it renders ethnicity, which is not a matter of choice, salient. Where multiculturalism is taken seriously it "scripts" ethnic identities. Members of ethnic minorities who play their assigned scripts are rewarded, while those who do not are deemed unrepresentative, inauthentic, or even "self-hating." The promotion of ethnic "authenticity" and the social pressure on "diverse" individuals, particularly members of "visible minorities" like Richburg, to play their scripts is a significant cost.

Livingstone and other conventional multiculturalists fail to recognize these costs because they construe culture as an innocuous matter of cuisine and costume and of practices that do not impose restrictions on anyone. They see culture in terms of St. Patrick's Day, Kwanzaa, and Cinco de Mayo celebrations, of chomping chorizo in Chula Vista and gagging on lutefisk in Lake Wobegon—Stanley Fish's "boutique multiculturalism." So, writing from within the British context, Livingstone claims: "Multiculturalism merely asserts that the right of a person to live their life as they wish includes the cultural dimension. If they wish to live in the most (supposed) classically of 'English' styles—tea at 4 pm, eating fish and chips or going to an English pub—they should be able to do so. Likewise, if they want to live a more Jamaican lifestyle or to organise their life more around Buddhism or Judaism."[4]

We should ask: what does Livingstone imagine those of us who are critical of multiculturalism propose? In the interests of promoting multiculturalism, my children were made to read a variety of "cultural" literature during their school careers, including the paradigmatic "cultural" novel *Bless Me, Ultima*, a tale of growing up Hispanic in the American Southwest, in which the protagonist is humiliated on his first day of school when he reveals a tortilla in his lunchbox. My kids were given to understand that multiculturalism affirmed the right of

Hispanic Americans to eat tortillas and speak Spanish without social opprobrium. What, I wondered, did their teachers and other promoters of this "cultural" literature think it was to *reject* multiculturalism? One suspects that they imagined a policy of forcing ethnic minorities to conform to the tastes and practices of the majority in cuisine and language enforced by the Tortilla Police raiding people's homes to see to it that they ate white bread and spoke English.

Critics of multiculturalism such as myself have no interest in pursuing this program. We hold rather that individuals identified as ethnically "diverse" should not be *expected* to speak ancestral languages, maintain cohesive ethnic communities, or live "more Jamaican lifestyles" than the general public. The problem with multiculturalism as it has played out is that *permission* to live a Jamaican or otherwise "culturally diverse" lifestyle has turned into the *expectation* that members of ethnic minorities would live at least mildly diverse lifestyles or, minimally, take pride in their ethnic identities. This expectation cramps Richburg and other assimilationists. What appears to be a pure expansion of liberty imposes burdensome constraints because multiculturalism imposes role obligations. These obligations sit lightly on us if we are white. We can choose how ethnic we want to be. We can even choose the ethnic identity with which we identify, citing real or mythical ancestors from a variety of European countries, and change our ethnic identity as we please. We are not pressed to affirm ethnic identities nor are we prevented from shedding them on pain of being declared self-hating or inauthentic. We can take up genealogy as a hobby or admit that we have no real connection to our ancestral cultures and no interest in them beyond occasional, idle curiosity. Members of visible minorities in the United States do not have that luxury and, where multiculturalism is taken seriously, no one does.

It is that absence of choice about the "community" to which you belong and the extent to which that affiliation figures in what is taken to be your "identity" that liberals find objectionable, because liberalism at its core is, unsurprisingly, about liberty. Liberalism affirms the supreme value of freedom, including the freedom to "invent oneself," to affiliate with the communities we find congenial, to make as little or as much as we wish of our ancestry and kinship, and to be "treated as individuals"—a cliché because it is something that is widely favored. Diversity as such imposes restrictions and burdens on the "diverse."

THE PRICE OF DIVERSITY

Diversity has its price and imposes role obligations even if they are trivial and even if they are imposed with the best of intentions and reasonably compensated. Black History Month, journalist Debra Dickerson complains, "makes life a bitch for blacks. All that pesky thinking about how to take advantage of an opportunity that's condescending, if well-intentioned, at its core."

Ethel Morgan Smith, a black professor at a white university, sketches an evocative pastiche of what it's like to be required to represent your race when you least expect it. She muses:

> During February, my mailbox is overflowing. Most of the mail wants me to represent "my people" for some worthwhile organization in February and February only. . . . I also get numerous calls. A pleasant woman from the arts council needed someone to attend her luncheon book-club meeting at her house. One of my colleagues, whom I haven't even met, gave her my telephone number. Her group is thinking of including a black writer on its reading list next year. I accept her pleasant invitation. It doesn't conflict with my calendar. I can be black that Wednesday.
>
> Come January, we'll all start sending her words around again, even as we scour our in boxes for last-minute solicitations and fill our send boxes with indignant forwards of "come be black for me" invites from white people we've never met. The ones we forward and mock are those from people who expect us to come be black for free. The others, the paying ones, we hoard and reply to promptly. . . . Another black friend whose children attend a swanky Manhattan

private school was sweetly asked to explain Kwanzaa at a holiday
school assembly.[5]

In addition to imposing what Anthony Appiah calls "scripts" on
members of ethnic minorities—even if only by way of invitations to "be
black" for book club meetings or to explain Kwanzaa at holiday assemblies—multiculturalism encourages the preservation of cohesive ethnic
communities within the context of a cultural "salad bowl" from which
exit is difficult or unfeasible. Prima facie the salad bowl seems to be a
good thing: we cherish our Chinatowns, Amish communities, and Indian
reservations and we enjoy the ethnic character of urban neighborhoods
as a welcome relief from the bland homogeneity of suburbia. Many of us,
however, do not appreciate the costs of exit required to maintain these
communities. Leaving the reservation is not so easy—if it were, the
ethnic communities we visit as tourists might disappear or subside into
urban theme parks like Colonial Williamsburg or the Greektowns and
Little Italys in most major cities, maintained by suburbanites who com-
mute to run family restaurants. Authenticity has its costs, and those costs
are borne by the immigrants and members of ethnic minorities who contribute to that "rich mosaic" others find appealing.

Living in these places can be perfectly rotten. History and literature abounds with stories of liberation, in which individuals leave the
village, the ghetto, the small town, the ethnic enclave, or the Old
World, escaping from family, clan, and tribe to the anonymity of the
city where they can "invent themselves" or to the New World where
all things are possible. Individuals who take this freedom for granted
worry about anomie and romanticize those restricted worlds, which
they admire from a distance, through the mist, or enter and leave at
will, as tourists. Those of us who have been there and done that, and
who have escaped, are not impressed.

Finally, multiculturalism suppresses the recognition that, by any
reasonable standard, some cultures are better than others insofar as they
provide greater scope for individual choice and are more conducive to
human flourishing. As noted earlier, we have all been carefully taught

that such sentiments are ethnocentric and naive. *We*, of course, would not want to be confined to our huts or home compounds like the indigenous women in the nameless non-Western culture McWhorter describes. We were taught, however, that *they* liked it that way because it was *their culture*. "Their culture" was a universal trump card and automatic conversation stopper because, in some quarters at least, enculturation was supposed to create a preestablished harmony between what people wanted and what they got. *We* wouldn't want to live *that way* because *our* values, preferences, and desires were formed by *our* culture; they *liked* living that way because *their* values, preferences, and desires were formed by *their* culture. It was only uneducated people, who didn't know how diverse human societies and customs were, or religious people, who believed the natives should be Christianized and made to wear pants, who thought otherwise.

According to the professional version of this account, the very idea that people should have scope for choice and if possible get what they wanted was itself a Western fetish. In traditional societies, people had few options and, when it came to the work they did and the roles they played in the family and community, no scope for choice. Women did what their mothers did; men did what their fathers did. Everyone played his assigned role and all, we were assured, were happy living in communities, which insofar as they had not been contaminated, were stable, smoothly functioning, organic wholes. Would members of such societies choose to live differently if they realized there were other possibilities and if other options were available? Perhaps. Nevertheless, we were warned, the availability of other options and the knowledge that other ways of life were possible, were themselves contaminants that undermined traditional societies and the well-being of their members. The very idea that well-being was a matter of satisfying informed preferences was itself a parochial Western notion. There was no legitimate cross-cultural standard to support our "value judgment" that we, who had a wide range of options, were better off for that than those women confined to their houses, cooking and caring for their children because that was all they knew.

This account is unfalsifiable: nothing can count against it. Do members of traditional societies prefer Western dress, crave Western junk food, and clamor for Western freedom? They do, but that is because their cultures have been contaminated by the knowledge of what is possible. Do natives who have tried it both ways prefer life in the West to life in their traditional communities? They do: legions spend their savings and all they can borrow, trek for hundreds of miles, and risk their lives crowded in leaky boats to make landfall in the West; few if any return to their native villages voluntarily. But what reason do we have for imagining that they are better off for getting what they prefer beyond our own indefensible, ethnocentric Western notion that getting what one wants is a good thing? Do we believe that we are better off than members of traditional societies? Certainly, because we have been enculturated. Do members of uncontaminated traditional societies, like the women McWhorter describes, believe that they are better off than we are? Certainly not, because the life they live is all they know, so they cannot make any comparison—but if we were to explain to them the differences between the lives they know and our lives so that they could compare, that would itself contaminate them, so it is a question that cannot even be asked!

Against doctrines like this no direct argument is available. The best we can do is to note that we in the West have been reluctant to "impose our values" on others precisely because we value freedom and believe that people should get what they want. To "impose" values is to force them on people, to constrain people and prevent them from getting what they want. There is, however, something logically peculiar about the idea of "imposing" freedom on people or "forcing" them to get what they want.

Raised on Margaret Mead's sunny South Sea fantasies, we didn't feel the force of this logical peculiarity because we imagined that people in traditional societies were *more* free than we were: they weren't forced to punch the clock, dress for the office, keep to schedules or, we thought, observe sexual taboos. They lived, so we imagined, peaceful, happy lives, in tune with nature, in harmony with one another, without competition, stress, or frustration. The discovery that traditional societies were not like that, that their members had fewer opportunities than we did and were far less free, was disconcerting.

MULTICULTURALISM IN THE WEST

The focus of this book, however, is not on those exotic foreign lands where women are sequestered and veiled, where children have their genitals sliced off, where tribes engage in ethnic cleansing and clans conduct vendettas. My concern is with the West, where immigrants from those places and members of indigenous minorities figure in the cultural mix and only peripherally on foreign parts. Until 9/11 and 7/7, the Madrid train bombings and riots in French immigrant suburbs, we in the West—and in the United States in particular—thought that we did multiculturalism right. We didn't do ethnic cleansing or vendettas, female genital mutilation, honor killing, or virginity tests. We did ethnic costume and cookery with ethnic communities, represented by "community leaders," contributing to the rich mosaic.

Current events gave us a turn. Native-born French citizens in the immigrant suburbs were burning cars, and lads from Bradford with broad local accents were blowing up London busses. In the United Kingdom, Jack Straw urged a ban on Islamic face veils, and Americans, convinced that the day laborers who loitered outside their local Home Depot stores looking for construction jobs were out to get them, clamored for a Berlin-style wall along the Mexican border. Quite apart from these worries, the media display of immigrant ghettos in Europe, where youths burned cars, and blighted neighborhoods in New Orleans, as segregated as they were in the days of Jim Crow, gave us pause. Multiculturalism and identity politics, radical forty years ago, had become a new orthodoxy, and ethnic pride celebrations were woven into the fabric of civic life, but hadn't done much to improve the lives of minorities. In fact, the new orthodoxy just promoted the same old thing: segregation.

Growing public awareness of failed multiculturalist policies freed Americans to scrutinize multiculturalism and identity politics—a program based on the notion that members of traditionally disadvantaged groups should be accorded recognition "on the basis of the very grounds on which recognition has previously been denied . . . *qua* women, *qua* blacks, *qua* lesbians . . ."[6] An increasingly conservative government in the Netherlands tightened up immigration policies and required prospective immigrants to watch a film showing gay men kissing and half-naked women on the beach as a test of their readiness to participate in liberal Dutch culture. In the United Kingdom, Tony Blair announced that immigrants had a duty to integrate. It became socially acceptable, and even fashionable, to recognize that multiculturalism had social costs.

Most critics of multiculturalism, however, failed to recognize that it was primarily members of ethnic minorities who paid the price and, even more importantly, that if immigrants and minorities had a duty to integrate, members of the larger society had a duty to make integration feasible. There is an important difference between assimilation and acculturation noted by social scientists: "Individuals of a foreign or minority culture learn the language, habits, and values of a standard or dominant culture by the cultural process of acculturation. The process by which these individuals enter the social positions, as well as acquire the political, economic, and educational standards of the dominant culture is called assimilation. These individuals, through the social process of assimilation, become integrated within the standard culture."[7] Assimilation requires cooperation and, to many members of ethnic minorities—particularly the children of immigrants—it had become clear by the turn of the twenty-first century that acculturation would not get them full political, economic, and social integration into the majority culture. It should hardly be surprising that a vocal, visible minority—most through symbolic gestures but some through violence—declared that since they could not join us they would beat us.

NOTES

1. Pascal Bruckner, "Enlightenment Fundamentalism or Racism of the Anti-Racists?" Signandsight.com, http://www.signandsight.com/features/1146.html (emphasis in original).

2. Ken Livingstone, "To Defend Multiculturalism Is to Defend Liberty," *Independent*, January 3, 2008, http://comment.independent.co.uk/commentators/article2021228.ece.

3. Keith B. Richburg, *Out of America: A Black Man Confronts Africa* (New York: BasicBooks, 1997).

4. Ibid.

5. Debra J. Dickerson, "Race Matters," Salon.com, http://www.salon.com/opinion/feature/2006/12/04/black_history_month.

6. Cressida Heyes, "Identity Politics," in *The Stanford Encyclopedia of Philosophy*, Fall 2002 ed., edited by Edward N. Zalta, http://plato.stanford.edu/archives/fall2002/entries/identity-politics.

7. Gail King and Meghan Wright, "Diffusionism and Acculturation," University of Alabama Web site, http://www.as.ua.edu/ant/Faculty/murphy/diffusion.htm.

Chapter 4

THE DIVERSITY TRAP

*Why Everybody
Wants to Be an X*

How am I supposed to feel French when people always describe me
as a Frenchman of Algerian origin? I was born here. I am French.
How many generations does it take to stop mentioning my origin?

—Nadir Dendoune

Ethnicity is both *ascribed* and *immutable*. Our ethnic affiliations are
assigned to us at birth, and we cannot change them. Under the
multiculturalist regime, they are in addition *socially salient* and
scripted. They engender expectations about our beliefs, preferences,
character traits, behavior, and impose "scripts" dictating what we
ought to believe and prefer, how we ought to behave, and what sorts
of people we ought to be.

We want to be ourselves, free from the constraints such ethnic
scripts impose. We also want to be seen for what we are in the deepest
sense—what we have *made* ourselves and choose to be. Multiculturalism thwarts those desires.

ETHNICITY AS AN ASCRIBED STATUS: LOCKED IN AND LOCKED OUT

The fact that we regard individuals who attempt to choose ethnic identities as imposters or, at best, as fellow travelers, indicates that ethnicity, as we understand it, is an *ascribed* status. It is something you are born into rather than an achievement or choice. Typically, in addition to being an ascribed status, ethnic identity is also an immutable characteristic: you cannot lose ethnic identity, opt out, or even be kicked out. So Spinoza, cursed and formally excommunicated by the Jewish community in Holland, remains in most histories of philosophy a great Jewish philosopher. Likewise Madeleine Albright, after discovering late in life that her grandparents were Jewish, is puzzled about what, if anything, she should do about the fact that she is "not really Catholic," if, indeed, she wonders, it is a fact.

Ascribed characteristics impede desire-satisfaction and in the case of Elizabeth Stern, author of *I Am a Woman—and a Jew*, undermined what she felt was her authentic identity:

> In his memoir, *Secret Family*, Thomas Stern tells his readers of his reaction upon learning, in 1925, of his mother Elizabeth Stern's forthcoming book, *I Am a Woman—And a Jew*, which has since become one of the classics of immigrant autobiography.
>
> In our living room, I told Elizabeth, "I think you shouldn't publish that book! It isn't true. It twists our family. It makes us what we are not."
>
> Elizabeth screamed, "I have to publish my book! It makes me what I want to be. It shows our family as I want people to see us."

Stern's autobiography was a fiction. Born in Pittsburgh, the illegitimate child of a Welsh Baptist mother and a German Lutheran father, she claimed to have been born in Skedel, Poland, and to have immigrated to the United States with her parents as a child. It is not clear, however, that Stern was motivated by an interest in exploiting a false identity for literary purposes or financial gain. Placed in a Jewish foster family when she was seven, where she remained until she was seventeen, Stern eventually married another illegitimate child who, like her, was raised in a Jewish foster family. Both claimed to be Jewish, and their son, who records a childhood of "ethnic confusion," writes that the family "spent years moving between the Lutheran world of his natural grandfather, a prosperous merchant, to the home of his Welsh grandmother, to the Orthodox Jewish world of his foster grandparents."[1]

The ascribed and immutable character of ethnic identity blocked Stern's desire to adopt what she felt was her authentic identity. It did not, however, prevent her or her husband from passing themselves off as Jews. If she had yearned after an alternative *visible* racial identity, matters would have been considerably worse. While John Howard Griffin succeeded in passing as black while researching *Black Like Me*, most individuals cannot effectively cross color lines. Most are not only blocked from choosing racial identities—they are blocked from choosing to *seem* like members of other races and from constructing plausible alternative autobiographies like the one Stern created for herself.

Role-playing games have wide appeal because they provide us with the opportunity, at least in Second Lives online, to invent ourselves. In fictitious virtual worlds we can escape the constraints of sex, race, and circumstance, invent ourselves, affiliate with the groups we choose, and play the roles we prefer. Stern's fictitious autobiography, the limiting case of such self-invention, reveals a troubling feature about rhetoric of "authenticity" associated with ascribed ethnic identities. "Authenticity," as conventionally understood by multiculturalists, prohibits self-invention. It blocks us from playing the roles we prefer, from being seen as we want to be seen, and from being ourselves in the deepest sense—the persons we choose to be.

There is no mystery about why Elizabeth Stern chose to pass herself off as Jewish. To mask her illegitimacy, which eighty years ago was stigmatized, she had an interest in identifying her foster family as her family of origin. More importantly, however, the Levins, whom she claimed as her birth parents, had raised her. They *were* her family, and, to the extent that they had a distinctive cultural identity and history, she shared that cultural identity and history. Even if she was compelled to fabricate the details to identify with that culture and history, in an important sense her autobiography was authentic.

Elizabeth Stern—née Morgan aka Elizabeth Levin and writing under the pseudonym of Leah Morton—wrote an autobiography that was, as reviewer Theodore Dalrymple notes of a more recent pseudonymous but explicitly fictional work, *Down the Road, Worlds Away*, "a fraud that was no fraud."[2] It was a work that, while falsifying details of the author's biography, was true to the author's experience, but it was nevertheless denounced as a fraud.

Like Stern's fictionalized autobiography, *Down the Road, Worlds Away*, a collection of young adult short stories published pseudonymously under the name of Rahila Khan, is generally regarded a literary hoax. Published in 1986 by Virago Press, marketed as a collection of "twelve haunting stories about Asian girls and white boys . . . about the tangle of violence and tenderness . . . in all their lives," and lauded as a book that "seemed to fulfill one of Virago's laudable objectives, that of publishing the work of a diverse group of contemporary feminist authors," *Down the Road* was pulped soon after publication when Virago discovered that its pseudonymous author was in fact the Reverend Toby Forward, a Church of England vicar.

Apart from writing pseudonymously, Forward never attempted to pass himself off as either Asian or female, still, the details of his biography were strikingly similar to the fictitious Miss Khan's. In the words of Theodore Dalrymple, "the great advantage that . . . [he] enjoyed over his publishers and critics was that he knew what he was talking about and they didn't."

> His critics probably assumed that, as a vicar of the national church in seemingly terminal decline, he was an otherworldly scion of the English country gentry in its last gasp, who could therefore be expected not to know much about anything, and was at best a figure of fun . . .
>
> The Reverend Toby Forward, as it happens, is not the scion of

privilege, even of privilege in decline; his biography in outline followed that of Rahila Khan's very closely. He was born in Coventry in 1950, and did live for many years in the cities of the English Midlands. He did marry in 1971, did have two daughters, did start to write in 1986, and did live in Brighton at the time the book was published. . . .

Both his parents, who were working class, left school when they were fourteen years old. They lived in slum areas of the unlovely cities of the Midlands, and he himself went to schools in which half the pupils were of Indian or Pakistani descent. His early life was lived in precisely the social environment depicted in *Down the Road, Worlds Away*: that is to say, in a society in which a nihilistic and entirely secular white working-class culture was thrown into involuntary contact with a besieged traditionalist Indian culture in which religion, particularly Islam, played a preponderant role.[3]

As Dalrymple notes in his review, Forward was able to enter empathetically into the lives of the British-Asian girls about whom he wrote. Indeed, he was a participant in their culture, and his fictions, which never purported to be autobiographical, were to that extent authentic. His authenticity and literary intent were, however, challenged by Virago because his editors assumed that gender and ethnicity carried with them an ethos and sensibility that disqualified Toby Forward from writing "authentically" about the lives of working-class British-Asian girls. That is to say, the editors at Virago and erstwhile favorable critics who did a volte-face on discovering that Toby Forward was a white male regarded ascribed gender and ethnic identities as *socially salient*.

ETHNICITY AS SOCIALLY SALIENT: WHY EVERYONE WANTS TO BE AN X

Where multiculturalism is more than a fiction, ethnicity is socially salient, and this is a state of affairs that most people would prefer to avoid.

A property is socially salient within a community to the extent that members of the community take it to predict or explain beliefs, character traits, tastes or other socially significant psychological characteristics. Social salience is a matter of degree: it depends upon how many other characteristics it is thought to predict or explain, how important they are, how many members of the community believe it has this explanatory or predictive power and the degree of conviction with which they hold this belief. . . .

The salience of a property does not arise from its visibility or noticability. Freckles are highly visible but wholly non-salient. In many communities, by contrast, some invisible ethnic origins, occupations and avocations are salient: people have notions of what Germans and Italians, lawyers, librarians and academics, stamp-collectors and soccer fans are like.

Finally, for some properties, which are salient to a given degree, the absence of these properties, or possession of other properties of the same category may be less salient or non-salient. People have notions about what used car salesmen are like; they don't generally have preconceived ideas about what veterinarians, geologists or copy-editors are like.[4]

The social salience of a personal characteristic for an individual is not a matter of individual choice. Where a property is nonsalient, individuals may choose the extent to which it figures as part of their social identity; where it is salient, individuals do not have that choice. Handedness is nonsalient. There are nevertheless a number of lefties who make a big deal out of it, and firms that produce lefty merchandise to cater to their special interest, including practical items like scissors and notebooks as well as novelty items like mugs, T-shirts, and bumper stickers proclaiming the virtues of left-handedness. Most left-handed individuals, however, do not make a hobby out of left-handedness, and no one else notices or cares about their handedness. Where a property is socially salient, by contrast, individuals cannot choose the extent to which it figures as part of their social identity. If you have that property, others will take it to be an important feature of your identity whether *you* think it is or not and regardless of any preferences you may have about the matter.

Characteristics that are more socially salient *dominate* properties that are less salient. Individuals will be taken to have more in common with others who share those characteristics than they do with people with whom they share less salient properties, regardless of whether these are the characteristics that are most important to them. The hierarchy of social salience in a given context functions like a hierarchy of sort rules for organizing data in tables and spreadsheets. I have a spreadsheet on which I keep grade records for different sections and sort on different data depending on my interests. When my primary concern is to keep different sections of the same class separate, I will sort first by section and then by alphabetical order; if my objective is to identify the best students, who will be offered jobs as tutors for the Logic Center, or to see how my overall grade distribution looks, my first sort will be by grade. In the same way, the most socially salient properties are those we invoke for the first sort.

Everyone has a wide range of personal characteristics, commitments, values, loyalties, and social affiliations, some of which are more important than others. Social sorting rules, however, may not reflect the relative importance an individual places on the various groups to which he or she belongs. My profession may be more important to me—and have more to do with my attitudes, commitments, and interests—than my gender, but in contexts where being female is more salient than being an academic, the first sort will be by gender. After Thanksgiving dinner I will go to the kitchen to clean up and chat with women who are doctors, housewives, secretaries, and stockbrokers while the menfolk, who are bricklayers, lawyers, salesmen, and also academics like me talk politics in the living room while watching football. Where a characteristic is socially salient, the sort it prescribes overrides the way in which we, as individuals, sort ourselves out, as well as the hierarchy of our own values, what we believe to be most important about ourselves, and how we identify ourselves and wish to be identified.

Even where our characteristics are chosen and our affiliations are voluntary—and, indeed, even where they are highly valued—we are at best ambivalent about their social salience. No one wants to be a "typical lawyer" or a "typical middle-class suburbanite," and no one wants others to make assumptions about his character, tastes, interests, abilities, commitments, and beliefs or to explain his behavior on the basis of such socially salient characteristics. Where socially salient characteristics are ascribed, immutable, and visible, so much the worse: no one—but no one—wants to hear "just like a woman" or to deal with remarks about his "natural sense of rhythm." This is how clichés about the importance of "treating people as individuals" and "not putting them in boxes" cash out. We do not want our personal characteristics, particularly ascribed and immutable characteristics, to be socially salient. We do not want to have to fight our way out of boxes.

Almost everyone has known, at some time or other, what it is like to fight his way out of a box. If you are identified with any socially salient group, whether as a member of a racial or ethnic minority, a political liberal among conservatives, a woman in most social settings, a Christian in academia, or an atheist anywhere else, you face a swarm of tacit assumptions about your intelligence and abilities, beliefs, moral commitments and interests, lifestyle, and character and you have to fight to be seen for who you are and to be taken seriously. And sometimes no amount of effort will get you through.

Multiculturalism puts people whose racial or other ethnic characteristics are socially salient into boxes and imposes on them the burden of fighting their way out to establish their individuality. What is bad about minority status in a seriously multicultural context is not only that it is sometimes associated with undesirable characteristics but also the mere fact that it is socially salient. Indeed, even when the characteristics associated with an ascribed identity are socially valued, all other things being equal, most people still want out of the box.

The characteristics associated with some ethnic identities are highly valued. In the United States, for example, all the characteristics conventionally associated with being Asian or of Asian descent—intelligence, education, ambition, self-discipline, diligence, industriousness, and good citizenship—are highly valued by Americans. Likewise, remembering Elizabeth Stern's affirmation of her identity as "a woman—and a Jew," the characteristics associated with being female and being Jewish, which overlap the characteristics associated with being Asian, are largely positive. Yet readers still wonder why Stern would attempt to pass herself off as Jewish because, particularly in the early years of the twentieth century when she was writing, Jewish identity was highly salient. They are puzzled because *the salience of ascribed identities as such, whether they are associated with desirable or undesirable characteristics, is in and of itself undesirable.* In Stern's case, there were overriding considerations that induced her to assume this identity. However, most people would rather not be saddled with socially salient ethnic identities.

The advantage of being a member of the mainstream culture in any given social context is the privilege of possessing an ascribed identity that is nonsalient. Outside of contexts in which political correctness marks or enhances the salience of all social categories—including sex and ethnicity as well as sexual orientation, age, and disability—one of the privileges white Anglo males enjoy in the United States is the advantage of an identity that is nonsalient. Whiteness in America and Europe is nonsalient and, in effect, transparent: it is the absence of any salient ascribed identity and that, for most of us, is a consummation devoutly to be wished. In the United States, white privilege is a function of the asymmetry of social salience: because whiteness is nonsalient and transparent whites can be seen for who they are without making any special efforts.

Where whites are a privileged *minority* or appear only as wealthy tourists, whiteness is salient and is a positive advantage, albeit a mixed blessing. Waiters, shop assistants, and cab drivers will be accommodating and often embarrassingly servile, but children will stare and market stall keepers will charge them four to ten times the going rate for souvenirs. Like Elizabeth Stern, white settlers and tourists accept the costs of racial salience in exchange for other benefits. Where whites are a privileged *majority*, the advantages of being white are quite different and consist primarily in the benefits that come from the *absence* of a visible, socially salient ethnic identity. So, most of the items on Peggy McIntosh's entertaining list of white privileges are advantages whites enjoy where whiteness is nonsalient:

> I can swear, or dress in second-hand clothes or not answer letters without having people attribute these choices to the bad morals, the poverty, or the illiteracy of my race, I can speak in public to a powerful male group without putting my race on trial, I can do well in a challenging situation without being called a credit to my race, I am never asked to speak for all the people of my racial group. . . . If a traffic cop pulls me over, or if the IRS audits my tax return, I can be sure I haven't been singled out because of my race . . . I can be sure that if I need legal or medical help my race will not work against me, if my day, week, or year is going badly, I need not ask of each negative episode or situation whether it has racial overtone's.[5]

Multiculturalism enhances the salience of ascribed, immutable ethnic identities, and that is something most of us do not want. We do not want to be spokespeople for our race or to have our personal idiosyncrasies interpreted as racial characteristics. If we swear or dress in secondhand clothes, we would prefer others to put that down to personal crudity and slovenliness and blame us, rather than to have them explain our behavior as typical for members of our ethnic group—even if they excuse us on that account.

Multiculturalism is attractive as a fiction viewed from a comfortable aesthetic distance, but it is not something in which most of us care to participate, because we want our ascribed identities to be transparent. We all like to classify, to rehearse stereotypes rooted in race, ethnicity, nationality, class, and gender, but we do not want to be classified or boxed in ourselves. We want to be outside the system, asserting our peculiarities and our distinctive personalities, which cannot (we like to think) be captured by any classificatory scheme. So Paul Fussell, in his pop sociological *Class: A Guide through the American Status System*, divides Americans into nine social classes, chronicling their folkways, but provides readers with an escape route. In addition to the bulk of Americans in the system, he suggests, there are anomalous individuals whom he calls Xs and who, he claims, do not fit into the classificatory scheme at all.[6] It is likely that virtually all of Fussell's readers smugly identify themselves as Xs.

All other things being equal, everybody wants to be an X. All other things are not always equal, however, and some people may take on socially salient characteristics voluntarily in the way that Elizabeth Stern did or use ascribed socially salient identities to their advantage. Adolescents questing for identity, whether black or white, opt into hip-hop culture or—much to their regret in later life—get tattoos. White settlers buy white privilege in colonial or postcolonial societies at the cost of embarrassing visibility. Academics and "community leaders" capitalize on their minority status to get grants, jobs, and lecture fees. Some individuals who are stuck with immutable, visible socially salient characteristics simply decide that since they cannot disassociate themselves from salient group identities, they may as well capitalize on them. Most people, however, do not like being boxed in, and multiculturalism, because it promotes the social salience of racial and other ethnic identities, is contrary to their interests.

ETHNICITY AS SCRIPTED: THE TYRANNY OF AUTHENTICITY

In addition to promulgating doctrines about what members of various ethnic minorities are like, multiculturalism promotes normative claims about what they *ought* to be like in the name of "authenticity." It prescribes behavior and confers entitlement: outsiders cannot get in and insiders cannot get out.

Elizabeth Stern was outed as an "imposter," and the Reverend Toby Forward was asked by Virago Press to return his advance and pay the costs of printing for what his editors regarded as a distasteful hoax.[7] Because ascribed ethnic and gender were taken as necessary qualifications, not only for group affiliation but also for literary authenticity, both Stern and Forward were excluded from roles that they were otherwise well qualified to play. Under the auspices of multiculturalism, members of traditionally disadvantaged groups exclude white males and claim special sensibilities that members of the privileged majority "wouldn't understand"—largely, one suspects, in retaliation for their own exclusion from the mainstream.

That response is understandable and, after a fashion, fair to the extent that turnabout is fair play. No one charged political correctness when students at Gallaudet University, America's oldest and most prestigious institution of higher education for the deaf, demanded a deaf president. Even if some conservatives claim to believe that affirmative action privileges women and blacks, *no white Anglo male would seriously want to trade places with us.*[8] Most people recognize that, identity politics notwithstanding, women and minorities, like the deaf, are socially crippled and that cultural self-affirmation is, at best, only partial compensation for serious social impediments.

Being locked out of minority ethnic status is a trivial inconvenience compared to the disadvantages of being locked in. And currently for minorities the lock-in is enforced not only by the majority community's exclusionary practices but also by what Ford calls the "difference discourse" of multiculturalism:

> Because difference discourse often establishes lists and canonical accounts of group identity, it tends to favor traditional behavior over behavior that is novel or transgressive within the group. . . . In this respect, rights-to-difference include proscriptions and mandates, not only for those who would assert them and their contemporaries but also for future generations. . . . Every racial group (with the telling exception of whites) has a derogatory term for people who fail to exhibit their assigned racial culture: there are African American "Oreos," Latino "Coconuts," Asian-American "Bananas" and Native-American (you guessed it) "Apples."[9]

Decades ago, sociologist David Riesman described the plight of individuals who were "marginally marginal": middle-class blacks who "talked proper," "mannish" career women, and others who were doubly disadvantaged by being saddled with membership in socially salient disadvantaged groups and who were either unwilling or unable to act out what Anthony Appiah calls the "scripts" associated with group membership.[10]

Even in the 1950s when Riesman was writing, before multiculturalism, marginally marginal individuals faced social opprobrium and were regularly trapped in double binds. During that period, when the feminine mystique was in force, women were "marginalized" to the extent that they were de facto excluded from public life and the professions and locked into suburban domesticity or, if unmarried, into a narrow range of women's occupations. While this marginalization was not as oppressive as many contemporary feminists seem to imagine— there are worse things than being a middle-class suburban housewife—marginally marginal females who could not or would not play their prescribed "feminine role" were trashed. As Betty Friedan noted, the behavior and aspirations of such women were construed in the categories of psychological pathology as maladjustment, neurosis, self-hatred, or penis envy.[11]

In the wake of Friedan's exposé of the feminine mystique, the second wave of feminism effectively dismantled the pop-psychological theories that defined marginally marginal women as psychologically defective. But, remarkably, these psychological theories were refurbished and recycled by multiculturalists to beat up on marginally marginal "Oreos," "Coconuts," "Bananas," and "Apples," individuals who were said to be black, brown, yellow, or red on the outside but white on the inside and who were therefore held to be self-hating and inauthentic.

Like women, who were damned if they were suitably feminine but doubly damned if they weren't, minorities under the multicultural regime were caught in double binds because the scripts for members of racial and ethnic minorities quite often rehearsed racist stereotypes and prescribed behavior that was, in the larger social context, unacceptable. Naive members of racial and ethnic minorities regularly fell into traps by innocently following advice that they were not supposed to take seriously. At workplace "diversity workshops," minorities were encouraged to wear "ethnic" costume and supervisors were urged to be "sensitive" to their non-Western conceptions of time. Black employees who showed up late the next day wearing dashikis were reprimanded and sent home to change.

A few socially adroit individuals have been able to capitalize on multiculturalism by playing both sides of the net, acting out stylized versions of their ethnic scripts without deviating from the fundamental social requirements of mainstream society. For most, however, multiculturalism imposed additional social burdens and constraints. Ethnic minority roles were tightly scripted and imposed requirements on minorities that were more stringent than the relatively loose requirements for generic good citizenship. Even where ethnic roles were self-affirming and socially valued, they imposed norms and demands on individuals who, in virtue of unchosen, immutable characteristics, were expected to act out their assigned scripts. Anthony Appiah observes:

> An African-American after the Black Power movement takes the old script of self-hatred, the script in which he or she is a nigger, and works, in community, to construct a series of positive black life scripts. . . . What demanding respect for people *as blacks* or *as gays* requires is that there be some scripts that go with being an African-American or having same-sex desires: there will be expectations to be met; demands will be made. It is at this point that someone who takes autonomy seriously will want to ask whether we have not replaced one kind of tyranny with another. If I had to choose between Uncle Tom and Black Power, I would, of course, choose the latter. But I would like not to have to choose.[12]

The remarkable novelty of multicultural scripting was that it purported to benefit the very individuals whose ethnic identities were scripted. In addition, it was promoted by "community leaders" who claimed to have the interests of their constituents at heart rather than members of the privileged majority, thus aiming to keep minorities in their place. Their aim in any case was not to eliminate ethnic scripts or to debunk stereotypes but to valorize them.

While this was a new story for ethnic minorities, it was a very old one for women. For over two hundred years feminists, in the interests of helping women gain entrée to socially desirable male preserves, vacillated between arguing that women were like men so that their presence would make no difference, and arguing that they were unlike men so that their presence would make a change for the better, if only by introducing a needed element of "diversity." Should women get the vote? Yes, because they were as intelligent, rational, and capable of exercising political judgment as men—and, yes, because being kinder, gentler, and more conscientious than men, they would clean up political corruption and end war. Would it be desirable to have women in management positions? Yes, because they were as capable of doing the job as men—and, yes, because they had different "management styles" that would be good for business. For political purposes, feminists played both sides of the net and were not averse to exploiting stereotypes or telling "good lies" about male-female differences to achieve their goals.

The difference strategy that some feminists adopted was characterized as "radical" because it struck at what was taken to be the root of sexism: the idea that "women's way of knowing" and operating was inherently defective. This was an assumption that "radical" feminists claimed mere liberals, intent on getting women the chance to be guys, not only overlooked but tacitly accepted. Why would a woman want to be a guy unless she bought into the sexist notion that guyhood was superior, "radicals" asked? Radical multiculturalists and advocates of the politics of difference put similar questions to members of ethnic minorities who aimed at integration and assimilation: why integrate so that you can hang with white Anglos? What's so great about them? Why would you want to be accepted by them or be like them?

The answer, I have suggested, is that white Anglo guyhood is the most desirable identity because, in most American contexts, it is the least salient. Integration and assimilation liberate individuals from the burdens and constraints of identities that are salient and tightly scripted.

"Radicalism" is a safe, accommodationist strategy. Radicals in effect struck a bargain with sexists and bigots: we will accept *la différence* if you accept us as separate but equal; we will play gender and ethnic scripts if they are refurbished and improved. Radicals, however, did not understand the nature of white male privilege and overlooked the asymmetry of social salience. They assumed that there was a white Anglo male script on a par with all others but arbitrarily privileged, because it was the script associated with individuals who were in a position of power. They refused to recognize that white, Anglo, male identity, unlike other ethnic identities, was nonsalient, and that it was not differently scripted so much as it was less tightly scripted than the identities associated with less privileged groups.

Because white Anglo males were privileged, they were able to buy their way out of socially salient identities and tight scripting. In spite of peripheral attempts to promote a men's movement focused on bonding rituals and drumming, white males are rarely, if ever, pressed to manifest authenticity. Whether under the old regime or the new multiculturalist dispensation, it is members of disadvantaged groups—women and minorities—who are stuck with tightly scripted role obligations. And, whether they are imposed by members of the privileged elite in the interests of keeping disadvantaged minorities in their place or by multiculturalists intent on promoting ethnic self-affirmation and punishing "Oreos," "Coconuts," "Bananas," and "Apples," these scripts impose a burden on members of ethnic minorities. Multiculturalism burdens and constrains the very people who are its intended beneficiaries.

MULTICULTURALISM AND FREEDOM

Multiculturalism restricts individual freedom. Because it renders characteristics that are ascribed and immutable, salient and because it imposes scripts on individuals in virtue of them.

No one is completely free to invent himself. There are countless characteristics that are ascribed and immutable, including sex, race and ancestry, height, handedness, and sexual orientation. The aim of liberals, for whom individual freedom is of paramount importance, is to minimize the extent to which such unchosen characteristics affect the way in which people's lives go—the way in which they are perceived and treated, the way in which they are supposed to behave, and the range of options open to them. Multiculturalism, because it promotes the salience of race and ancestry and scripts ethnic identity, is therefore inconsistent with liberalism.

There are three reasons why this obvious fact has rarely been noticed or appreciated.

First, we confuse serious multiculturalism—plural monoculturalism—with hybridity, the innocuous stuff of "multicultural faires." What freedom is constrained, we ask? You can be as ethnic as you like. You can research your genealogy, get into ethnic cookery and ethnic folk dancing, or you can ignore the whole thing. No one's making you do anything.

This is true for most white, middle-class Americans precisely because their ethnicity is *not* salient. It is not true for members of visible minorities and it is not true for anyone in tribal territories in the United States or elsewhere. You cannot decide how big a deal you want to make of being Sunni or Shiite in Iraq or of being Italian in northern New Jersey. In tribal territories ethnicities are dense on the ground—everybody *is* something and what you are is a big deal whether or not you want it to be.

Second, under the influence of communitarianism, we imagine that ethnic identity is an expression of individual identity rather than a constraint. Communitarians and other critics of liberal individualism are fond of pointing out that our values, interests, and desires do not come from nowhere: they are formed by enculturation and socialization in the community in which we are embedded. Culture, on this account, is not a constraint on the self but an expression of the self, which is formed within a culture.

In response, liberals do not deny the causal origin of our values, interests, and desires in culture, but they do note that there is no guarantee of a preestablished harmony between individuals' interests, aspirations, and cultural expectations. Even in traditional societies, where members are fully enculturated, there are misfits and malcontents. Studying the Arapesh of Papua New Guinea, whose culture encouraged gentleness, cooperation, and a variety of traits we think of as characteristically feminine for both men and women, Margaret Mead (who *liked* the Arapesh) discovered that there were Arapesh who found these cultural expectations burdensome and the Arapesh way of life boring. More importantly, multiculturalism imposes expectations and role obligations on individuals who have not been enculturated into their ascribed ancestral cultures. So Keith Richburg legitimately objects to the expectation that he will find "a little piece of himself" in Africa, where some of his ancestors had lived four centuries earlier.

Multiculturalists gain sympathy by being highly selective about the stories they tell, and, until recently, these were the only stories that most of us heard. We heard innumerable stories about Indian children shipped to boarding schools where they were not allowed to speak their native languages and immigrants who were forcibly "Americanized." We rarely heard stories of individuals who wanted to assimilate to the dominant culture but were thwarted—perhaps because multiculturalism had become the dominant ideology or perhaps because these stories are so commonplace that they were not newsworthy.

Reading a book on the worldwide pattern of language and language-change, I recall one story of a ten-year-old French boy of Moroccan origin who pretended that he could not understand Arabic. The language, he claimed, was much too hard. His interviewer flushed out his deception by asking him how he was able to do the shopping for his mother, who spoke no French. Did she write down a list for him? How did they communicate? It isn't difficult to understand this child's motivation: he just wanted to be a regular little French kid and to be seen for what he was. There are likely thousands of commonplace stories like this of individuals who are burdened by ethnic identities that do not express their values, interests, or aspirations, whose ascribed cultural identities do not express who they are but impose constraints.

Finally, the multiculturalist program gained traction because Americans in particular came to assume that the chief problem faced by members of traditionally disadvantaged minorities—and women—was inequality rather than separateness as such. In *Brown v. Board of Education*, the landmark 1954 case that ended school segregation, the Supreme Court ruled that separate was "inherently unequal." This was a reasonable response to the sham of separate but equal accommodation under Jim Crow, but it left open the counterfactual question: would separate accommodations be acceptable if they *were* equal?

This question was rarely addressed, and by the late twentieth century the emerging consensus was that what mattered was inequality rather than separateness or difference. Increasingly, in the interests of achieving equality for women and minorities, activists supported separatist schemes that they believed would promote equality. Some of these projects were downright silly. So, in the Episcopal Diocese of San Diego during the 1990s—the pan-Anglican "Decade of Evangelism"—the bishop proposed the establishment of ethnically identified congregations, including plans for planting a black church, to attract traditionally underrepresented minorities to the Episcopal Church in order to promote church growth. The bishop dropped his plans for the segregated black church when he learned that, unlike Hispanics, blacks were not a *growing* minority in the area and so would not contribute significantly to church growth. That was not, however, the end of the ethnic agenda. At the period's high-water mark, an ambitious priest divided her parish of perhaps one hundred souls into three ethnically defined "congregations," which she called the Apples, Bananas, and Mangos for blacks and whites, Hispanics, and Pacific Islanders, respectively. No one's mouth dropped open at the Diocesan Council meeting where she described her program, and no one suggested that the arrangement was either racist or patronizing, since it guaranteed that virtually every adult Hispanic and Pacific Islander could avoid black/white Episcopalian hegemony and serve on a vestry.

Speculatively, the quest for justice for traditionally disadvantaged minorities and women focused on inequality while ignoring segregation and separation because these concepts were framed in terms inherited from once-fashionable Marxist analysis: hierarchy and patriarchy, hegemony, class warfare, colonialism, subjugation, and oppression. Activists were uncomfortable with worries about stereotyping, segregation, and the constraints imposed by ascribed group identities because such concerns assumed what they saw as an unhealthy individualism, which undermined the solidarity of the oppressed.

In any case, for whatever reason, liberation movements in the late twentieth century focused on social equality, dignity, respect, cultural self-affirmation, and group rights rather than individual freedom and opportunity. Arguably this focus was fundamentally wrongheaded and detrimental to the interests of traditionally disadvantaged minorities. The salience of ethnic identity as such, I have argued, is in itself a bad thing even apart from inequality because it restricts individual choice.

NOTES

1. Leah Morton, *I Am a Woman—and a Jew (by) Elisabeth Gertrude Stern* (New York: Arno Press, 1969).

2. T. Dalrymple, "An Imaginary 'Scandal,'" *New Criterion* 23, no. 9 (May 2005).

3. Ibid.

4. H. E. Baber, "Gender Conscious," *Journal of Applied Philosophy* 18, no. 1 (2001).

5. Peggy McIntosh, "White Privilege: Unpacking the Invisible Napsack," Anarchist Black Cross Network Web site, http://www.anarchistblack cross.org/org/wp/peggy.html.

6. P. Fussell, *Class: A Guide through the American Status System* (New York: Summit Books, 1983).

7. Dalrymple, "An Imaginary 'Scandal.'"

8. For a discussion of the protest movement by Gallaudet students that resulted in the appointment of a deaf president in 1988 and for useful links

concerning deaf culture, see the Wikipedia article "Gallaudet University" at http://en.wikipedia.org/wiki/Gallaudet_College.

9. Richard T. Ford, *Racial Culture: A Critique* (Princeton, NJ: Princeton University Press, 2005), pp. 78–79, 87.

10. See, e.g., D. Riesman, *Individualism Reconsidered* (Glencoe, IL: Free Press, 1954).

11. See, of course, B. Friedan, *The Feminine Mystique* (New York: W.W. Norton & Company, 1961).

12. K. A. Appiah, "Race, Culture, Identity," in *Color Conscious*, ed. K. A. Appiah and Amy Gutman (Princeton, NJ: Princeton University Press, 1996), pp. 98–99.

Chapter 5

WHITE PRIVILEGE AND THE ASYMMETRY OF CHOICE

I started a part-time teaching gig last week at the University of California at Berkeley, and part of the paperwork . . . was a form that asked what my ethnicity was. . . . I'm half-Japanese, so I looked for a mixed-race box, but there wasn't one. I asked the woman who was doing the paperwork if I could put down that I was half-white and half-Asian, but she said, "No, you just have to choose one." Even though I knew I was probably bumming out some U.C. diversity honcho, I put an X in the box marked "white."

Why did I choose "white"? It was a matter of intellectual honesty. . . . [W]hen I am forced against my will to make a reductive choice, as I was at U.C., the most honest thing is to choose white. I do that not because I see whiteness as a positive identification, or as my identity, but for precisely the opposite reason: because whiteness is the marker of racial invisibility in America. . . .

Let me be clear. I am not talking about disavowing one's culture or background, acting "white," or any other external actions. I am simply talking about an inner freedom from a superficial definition imposed by others. . . . [W]ho wants to go around carrying the burden of being "Asian" or "black" all the time? It's a burden because it's a phantom, an abstract concept, that nonetheless weighs you down. To feel "Asian," for me, would be to embrace an entirely political definition of myself, one simultaneously empty and all-encompassing. I would become a caricature of myself, a spokesman for a "myself" entirely constructed by others. Having no racial self-identification is a utopian state because it allows you to escape this malignant mirror. In America, the white majority is fortunate to enjoy this.[1]

My college class voted to forgo graduation caps and gowns in order to start a scholarship fund for students from "the Chicago ghetto" with the money we would have used to rent them. Even though one professor noted that the savings on rented regalia wouldn't pay tuition and expenses at Lake Forest College for more than two weeks, it seemed the right thing to do at the time, and, we believed, our gesture sent a message of some sort.

Our graduation ceremony was a whirling mass of colorful costume: countercultural garb of every kind and a variety of multicultural outfits—African dashikis, Native American dress, generic ethnic costumes of unknown provenance, and even a sari. I hardly need to add that we were all white.

The appropriation of postcolonialist categories to make sense of racism and ethnic privilege in the global north, and in the United States in particular, fails to account adequately for the extent to which privilege is a consequence of the transparency of whiteness and the asymmetry of choice. Going native, at least temporarily, has always been an option for privileged white Americans, from anthropologists studying exotic cultures as participant-observers to journalists embedded with native families to report on their doings—and no one ever suggests that those who manage to go native permanently are inauthentic or self-hating. White privilege is the privilege of self-invention. Immigrants and members of ethnic minorities do not have that luxury. Even when they are not locked out of the mainstream by discrimination and economic disadvantage, multiculturalist notions of authenticity, role obligation, and group loyalty dog them.

GOING NATIVE AND PASSING

For middle-class white Americans, ethnic costume is a fashion option; multiculturalism, as my college classmates saw it, simply expanded the range of individual choice. For members of "visible minorities" ethnicity is not a matter of choice. "[S]ymbolic ethnicity has very little practical impact in the everyday world of the middle-class white American suburbanites who espouse it," writes political scientist R. D. Grillo, reflecting on pluralism and the politics of difference.

> For such Americans "ethnic" identity is highly flexible, and largely a matter of choice: evidence reported by Waters (1990: 40) shows the extent to which informants changed their ethnic identification between interviews a year apart. Within certain limits, says Alba, "whites are largely free to identify themselves as they will and to make these identities as important as they like" (1990: 295). This is manifestly not true of other Americans: "the ways in which ethnicity is flexible and symbolic and voluntary for white middle-class Americans are the very ways in which it is not so for non-white and Hispanic Americans." (Waters 1990: 156)[2]

The argument against multiculturalism so far trades on a controversial but plausible empirical conjecture, namely, that most members of minority groups would prefer to assimilate to the dominant majority culture. Until recently, however, almost all popular discussions of multiculturalism simply assumed that minorities preferred to preserve their own distinctive cultures. Liberal multiculturalists argued for cultural diversity in the interests of accommodating minorities' supposed desire to preserve their distinctiveness. Conservatives, in particular when they argued for exclusionary policies and restrictions on immigration, assumed that most members of ethnic minority groups either could not or would not assimilate.

So, in this vein, when young men of North African descent took to burning cars in French immigrant suburbs, conservatives tried to spin their activities as an expression of radical Islamicist sentiment. There was, however, no evidence that the youths rioting in the streets of immigrant suburbs were on jihad. In interviews with immigrants, their children, and their grandchildren, none complained about the decadence of French culture or expressed an interest in reestablishing the caliphate. They complained that, in spite of officially color-blind policies, they faced ongoing discrimination and that even after two or three generations they were not regarded as fully French. This is typical:

Some groups do advocate cultural separation for Muslims—but they do not speak for many. Far more common is the attitude of Noureddine Skiker, a youth worker near Paris: "I feel completely French. I will do everything for this country, which is mine." Mr Skiker's Moroccan origins mean a lot to him. But, like many youths in the suburbs, he sees no contradiction between being French and having foreign roots. The main problem is that many French people do, says writer Nadir Dendoune.

"How am I supposed to feel French when people always describe me as a Frenchman of Algerian origin? I was born here. I am French. How many generations does it take to stop mentioning my origin?" And crucially, the suburbs are full of people desperate to integrate into the wider society. "I do not know a single youth in my estate who does not want to leave," Mr Dendoune says.

Immigrants have been housed in estates around French cities. France's Muslim ghettos, in short, are not hotbeds of separatism. Neither do they represent a clear challenge to secularism—a doctrine all national Muslim groups profess to support. "We have no problem with secularism," says Lhaj Thami Breze, president of the Union of Islamic Organisations of France (UOIF). He argues that by establishing state neutrality in religious matters, the doctrine allows all religions to blossom. Islam has adapted to local laws—from Indonesia to Senegal—and is adapting to France, says Azzedine Gaci, who heads the regional Muslim council in Lyon.

This is not just the leaders' view. A 2004 poll suggested that 68% of French Muslims regarded the separation of religion and state as "important," and 93% felt the same about republican values.[3]

Until recently, when the media began paying attention to people of color with stature as "public intellectuals"—people like Amartya Sen, Salman Rushdie, Ayaan Hirsi Ali, and Anthony Appiah, who expressed reservations about multiculturalist assumptions—accounts of the plight of immigrants and ethnic minorities were highly selective. Journalists eagerly reported the views of the Arab "street," ignoring educated, cosmopolitan individuals in non-Western societies. Multiculturalists intent on giving "voice" to immigrants and other members of minority groups in the global north ignored voices like M. Dendoune's as inauthentic or atypical, while hanging on the words of culturally disaffected members of immigrant communities and the self-appointed "community leaders" who articulated their views.

When the British public was shocked to discover that the London bombings were carried out by native-born citizens with Northern accents, the press revealed that almost one-third of Muslims in the United Kingdom regarded British culture as "decadent." The press did not seem to think it worthwhile to note that more than two-thirds of British Muslims did not regard British culture as decadent, or that among Muslims, males were twice as likely as females to regard British culture as decadent. Perhaps even more significantly, the press did not think it worthwhile to provide data about the percentage of British *non-Muslims* who regarded British culture as decadent.

Reporting on the controversy over the ban on Muslim headgear in the public schools, bien-pensants featured protesters but did not note that most Muslims did not protest or that many Muslim women favored the ban. Outside of France Samira Bellil's account of growing up in immigrant housing projects, *Dans l'enfer des tournantes* (The Pure Hell of Gang-Rape), was not translated and got little attention, and the protest movement *Ni Putes Ni Soumises* (Neither Whores nor Submissives) was ignored. No one noticed, or wanted to notice, the fact that some immigrants and a significant number of their children, in particular women, did not like their ancestral cultures and wanted out.

The idea that members of ethnic minorities might want out was one that multiculturalists found deeply disturbing. The assigned scripts for members of ethnic minorities prohibited behavior deemed to be "inauthentic": "passing" and even serious critiques of the minority culture were taboo. So, in her reflections on critics' response to the reissue of Nella Larsen's 1929 novel *Passing*, Margo Jefferson noted that "a certain taint" clung to Larsen's reputation: "Larsen is accused by some white and black critics of literary passing, thanks to a prose style that draws little from black ritual, folklore or vernacular. Nor do her characters speak in black vernacular; like many privileged African-Americans, they speak mostly standard English, tossing in bits of black slang."[4]

As Jefferson suggests, privileged insiders enforce no-exit rules that prohibit disaffiliation by members of disadvantaged minority groups: "culture's power brokers are often most at ease when outsiders do and say nothing that might allow them to be mistaken for insiders."[5] When it comes to no-exit rules there is an asymmetry: while passing "up" is condemned, passing "down" is almost always represented as meritorious. We applaud Eppie's decision to stay with Silas Marner because she "was not raised to be a lady," but when Pinky, in the eponymous 1949 film, who has been passing as white while at a northern nursing school, announces her intention to return to the North and marry a young white doctor, we know she will have to be punished. And punished she is, bullied into doing nasty jobs earmarked for black women: nursing an elderly white lady and working as a washerwoman alongside her black grandmother. She redeems herself only by rejecting her white suitor and resolving to stay in the South to "help her people" by establishing a clinic and nursery school.

Remarkably, multiculturalists accepted and promoted this asymmetry. Middle-class whites were applauded when they dabbled in minority cultures, including white working-class culture, or went native, but members of less privileged groups were denounced as inauthentic, disloyal, or psychologically damaged if they adopted the folkways of the privileged majority. While multiculturalists were vocal in condemning the faults and foibles of white, middle-class American culture, criticism of other groups' cultural practices, whether by outsiders or insiders, was taboo. Conservatives who were quick to notice this asymmetry and to take note of the patronizing sentimentality behind multiculturalists' prohibition on "blaming the victim," lampooned the silliness of "boutique multiculturalism" and condemned what they took to be a double standard, privileging women and minorities over white males.

But the double standard did not privilege women and minorities. Rather, it locked in the asymmetry of social constraint. Members of the privileged majority could roundly condemn conventional white middle-class culture, reject academic gowns in favor of the regalia of real or imagined non-Western cultures, condemn mainstream cultural practices they found personally objectionable, and drop out. Members of disadvantaged groups, however, could not critique their ascribed cultures, reject practices associated with these cultures that they disliked or that were alien to them as individuals, or opt out of them without being accused of disloyalty or inauthenticity. Those who were critical of their ascribed cultures or who wanted out were deemed disloyal, psychologically defective or, at the very least, unrepresentative.

Given this doctrine, multiculturalists' assumption that members of ethnic minorities preferred to preserve their ancestral cultures was unfalsifiable. Any members of ethnic minorities who felt otherwise were either ignored or written off. Treated fairly as an empirical claim, however, the suggestion that all or most members of ethnic minorities want to preserve their ancestral cultures within the integrity of distinct ethnic communities is clearly false. In the United States every cohort of immigrants has followed the same pattern: a bilingual first generation, an assimilated second generation with an imperfect or minimal knowledge of the ancestral language, and a monolingual, English-speaking third generation, intermarried and culturally indistinguishable from the general population. When assimilation is feasible for immigrants and their descendents, most choose to join the dominant culture. Friends of multiculturalism, however, ignore the choices of most immigrants and their children and, even more importantly, the social circumstances and policies, including those established in the interests of multiculturalism, which undermine their ability to assimilate.

PREFERENCE AND CHOICE

Preference is not simply choice, but there is no reason to believe that the choice of many immigrants to the United States, most of their children, and all of their grandchildren to assimilate to the dominant culture does not faithfully represent their preferences. There is, indeed, some reason to believe that the choice of some immigrants and a few of their children to live in ethnic enclaves may *not* represent their preferences. All other things being equal, an immigrant might prefer to join the mainstream, but all things are not equal. The costs and risks of life outside the immigrant community are high. Outside, the language is difficult and the customs are unfamiliar; outside, there is no social network or family circle and the natives are not particularly friendly. We cannot infer from the choices of some immigrants and their children to stay within ethnic enclaves that they are motivated by an interest in preserving ancestral cultures rather than an understandable desire to operate under conditions where they are fluent in the language, familiar with the customs, and socially connected. Both multiculturalists and conservative nativists underestimate the difficulty immigrants have in negotiating alien social environments, the costs of exit from ethnic enclaves, the extent of ongoing discrimination against people of color, and the extent to which well-intentioned government policies make it difficult for minorities to join the mainstream.

Even where assimilation is feasible, the prospects for many immigrants within the larger culture are grim. The Reverend Toby Forward, writing as Rahila Khan, described the "unlovely cities" of his childhood where "a society in which a nihilistic and entirely secular white working-class culture was thrown into involuntary contact with a besieged traditionalist Indian culture in which religion, particularly Islam, played a preponderant role." If immigrants have to choose between maintaining traditional cultures imported from the old country and assimilating downward to a generic underclass, mired in the "culture of poverty," they have compelling reasons to resist assimilation for themselves and their children.

Sociologist Alejandro Portes notes that immigrants to the United States face the same choice:

> Children of immigrants do not grow up to be low-paid foreign workers but U.S. citizens, with English as their primary language and American-style aspirations. In my study with Rubén G. Rumbaut of more than 5,200 second-generation children in the Miami and San Diego school systems, we found that 99 percent spoke fluent English and that by age 17 less than a third maintained any fluency in their parents' tongues. Two-thirds of these youths had aspirations for a college degree and a professional-level occupation. The proportion aspiring to a postgraduate education varied significantly by nationality, but even among the most impoverished groups the figures were high.
>
> The trouble is that poor schools, tough neighborhoods, and the lack of role models to which their parents' poverty condemns them make these lofty aspirations an unreachable dream for many.... Assimilation under these conditions does not lead upward into the U.S. middle class but downward into poverty and permanent disadvantage.... No matter how ambitious parents and children are, no matter how strong their family values and dreams of making it in America, the realities of poverty, discrimination, and poor schools become impassable barriers for many.... The emergence of a "rainbow underclass" that includes the offspring of many of today's immigrants is an ominous but distinct possibility.[6]

All other things being equal, I might prefer to join the dominant culture, but all other things are far from equal, and receiving countries do not do a very good job of making things more equal for immigrants and their children.

Government policies, often influenced by the ideology of multiculturalism, quite often promote segregation and make it more difficult for immigrants to assimilate. When European countries, coping with mass immigration from Africa and the Middle East, built projects in remote suburbs to house newcomers, they effectively segregated them from native populations. When the Swedish government, in the interests of accommodating immigrant cultural practices, waived or modified regulations that applied to native-born citizens for immigrants, it effectively thwarted the desires of those who wished to assimilate. When the French government, committed to assimilation, refused to adopt policies to counteract ongoing discrimination, it made it more difficult for immigrants to join the mainstream. Shortly after the 2005 riots in French immigrant suburbs, *BusinessWeek* reported that in spite of France's laudable aim of encouraging the complete assimilation of immigrants, its color-blind policies, which ignored the color-consciousness of native French employers and failed to address ongoing discrimination, impeded its stated objective:

> France has long opposed affirmative action on the grounds that— since the constitution requires everyone to be treated equally, and since everyone is fully French—no such programs are needed. A beautiful idea, but it ignores the reality of the ghettos, which impede assimilation. One result is that unlike Britain, the Netherlands, and Germany, France has no Muslims in its Parliament.
>
> The government, insisting on a color-blind policy, refuses even to collect data on racial and ethnic backgrounds, which makes it difficult to attack discrimination, even though nearly everyone agrees it is prevalent. In a study last year to test employment discrimination, University of Paris researchers sent out résumés from fictitious job applicants to more than 200 French employers. A résumé with a classic French name received more than five times as many positive responses as one with a North African name, though both listed identical qualifications. "France has been in a state of denial for a long time," says Zaïr Kedadouche, who serves on the government's High Council for Integration.[7]

Immigrants who want to integrate into the social and economic mainstream are effectively locked out. And quite often it is precisely immigrants and minorities who regard policies that promote the cohesion of distinct ethnic communities and cultural preservation as objectionable.

Consider the internationally notorious case of Fadime Sahindal, the daughter of Kurdish immigrants and victim of an "honor killing" in Sweden. After her death, it was members of immigrant minorities who were most critical of government policies intended to accommodate immigrants, which they charged denied them equal protection under the law:

> "The message this should send to Swedish people, especially the Social Democrats who have been in power for 40 years, is that the system isn't working," said Dilsa Demirbag-Sten, a former government advisor on integration affairs whose Kurdish family came to Sweden from eastern Turkey when she was 7. She accuses authorities of arrogance in their view that certain rights and freedoms accorded Nordic residents, such as gender equality and protection from forced marriage, are not necessarily applicable to immigrants. . . . Swedish law allows girls from immigrant families to marry as young as 15, while marriage for Swedish citizens is permitted only at 18 or older. That de facto bow to immigrant cultural practice is expected to be legislated out of existence as momentum gathers in a national campaign to prevent forced marriage.[8]

It was immigrants and minorities who objected most strenuously to policies that promoted the cohesion of ethnic groups and effectively segregated them from the native population:

> "There are places just outside of Stockholm where the entire population is foreign. These people aren't living in Sweden at all," said Keya Izol, head of the Federation of Kurdish Associations in Sweden, referring to towns and suburbs such as Botkyrka, a 30-minute drive from central Stockholm. . . . "It is a mistake to have too many people from the same town or village or clan together," Izol added. "It is the habit of exiles to want to protect their way of life, and in such places they hear no Swedish, they see no Swedish television and they have no jobs that bring them in contact with Swedish people."[9]

Not everyone wants the same thing, and, arguably, the fundamental problem of ethics is precisely adjudicating between the desires of individuals with conflicting interests. Danish justice minister Erling Olsen notes that in Scandinavian countries experiencing the social pressures of recent mass immigration: "We have been too slow to integrate the older generation and too fast in integrating the younger one's."[10] As a consequence, members of the first generation, locked out of the mainstream and without a stake in the larger society, clamor for cultural preservation:

> "People who come to such a level of despair that they can kill must feel cornered in this society," said Annick Sjogren, a sociologist directing an integration program in Botkyrka, where more than 80% of the 30,000 residents are immigrants and refugees. "They aren't used to women being equal to men or nakedness being taken as natural instead of sexual or the idea that you can choose your own partner. They get scared and become defensive and much more fundamentalist than they would be at home."

Different people want different things, and there will always be people who want to "protect their way of life" or live within cohesive minority communities—in particular, those who are effectively excluded from participation in the larger society. There is no reason, however, why the desires of individuals who, for whatever reason, want to maintain cultural distinctiveness should be privileged over the desires of individuals who want to assimilate, and there are compelling reasons why the desires of individuals who want to join the dominant culture should be accommodated.

First, as a matter of empirical fact, there are simply many more of these individuals. Most people do not want to be locked into ghettos or "put in boxes." They do not want to be stuck with ascribed ethnic affiliations that are socially salient and scripted and, when they are not being coached, bribed, or bullied by advocates of cultural diversity, they say so. Second, it seems highly likely that even more would profess a desire to assimilate if it were feasible and if the costs of exit from their ethnic communities were not prohibitive. Ethnic "imposters," like Elizabeth Stern, are newsworthy because they are rare. Most individuals prefer to disassociate themselves from socially salient, scripted identities and join the mainstream.

This, then, is the most compelling reason to reject multiculturalism: most people don't want it.

WHEN DOES "DIVERSITY" END?

Perhaps the most puzzling feature of multiculturalism is its failure to address M. Dendoune's important question: "How many generations does it take to stop mentioning my origin?" When does an immigrant become a fully assimilated, unhyphenated member of the dominant culture? The official French answer was "As soon as he touches French soil," even though the French government, in denial, refused to take effective measures to bring that about. The Swedish government's answer was "after the first generation," but its culturally sensitive policies in some cases produced disastrous intergenerational conflict. In the United Kingdom, the answer seems to have been "it depends on the individual, and it depends on where he comes from." In Japan the answer was "never."

The *Australian*'s Tokyo correspondent, Peter Alford, remarks that, in Japan, "though most people are delighted for you to visit, they feel more comfortable to know you plan to go away at some stage."

> Before my wife found work, she took full advantage of Minato's cheap language classes, yoga lessons, free day trips and guided walks. Returning from the seaside at Kamakura, Kathy marvelled to the volunteer guide beside her in the bus, a bright-eyed old gentleman, about the generous spirit we found in Minato. "Well," he said, "we want you to learn about our country and to enjoy yourself during your stay in Japan."
>
> He emphasized, gently, the words "during your stay." The subtext was clear: And then you will go home, please. . . . This may not

be a universal view in Japan, but I think it's close. . . . Our office manager Hiroshi Osedo once said he saw it as part of his duties to steer correspondents away from becoming Japanised. Hiroshi has spent more than 30 years working with foreign reporters and most become lifelong friends. But in his experience, Japanised Westerners don't work out: they are like cats trying to bark or dogs attempting to climb trees.

Only once have I been taken completely off balance on this matter. At an embassy reception last year, a diplomat pushed me towards an amiable, professorial-looking fellow: "Here's someone you should meet, he's got interesting views . . .". He was indeed an academic, one of Japan's little band of Australian studies scholars. He was very disappointed by the Howard Government's hostility to state-sponsored multiculturalism.

I said I thought the government view was that multiculturalism discouraged new Australians from assimilating. But yes, he said, that's the purpose of multiculturalism (I'm paraphrasing). We should study Australia's multiculturalism for when Japan needs large numbers of immigrants.

Now he had my attention. I'd never heard any Japanese talk about mass immigration in terms of if, let alone when. Yes, we should use multiculturalism policy to help immigrants maintain their own ways and languages.

In Japan? Yes, so that when they have finished their work here, they and their families can be sent home without experiencing any difficulties. He finished with a flourish: "I call it economic multiculturalism. What do you think?"[11]

This is multiculturalism, taken seriously and pushed to its logical conclusion.

Mercifully, most advocates of the cultural diversity in the United States do not take multiculturalism seriously. They imagine a cultural salad bowl in which participation is temporary, voluntary, and, in the end, largely symbolic. Immigrants will settle in ethnic neighborhoods, maintaining their language and distinctive customs for a generation or two before dispersing to make way for the next group of new arrivals, leaving a few of their number behind to man the restaurants. Their descendents in the suburban diaspora will, within limits, be as ethnic as they choose, though it will be counted as virtue if they make some effort to connect with ancestral cultures, and they will be expected to express pride in their ethnic heritage—or at the very least, not to deny it.

The burden such expectations impose is in most cases trivial and irritating rather than seriously harmful: blacks will be expected to be black for community groups during February, and children will occasionally be asked to concoct ethnic dishes for their schools' multicultural faires. Nevertheless, members of traditionally disadvantaged groups who fail to exhibit ethnic pride will be punished.

Consider the unfortunate boob George Allen who, during the run-up to midterm elections in 2006, destroyed his political career and single-handedly delivered the US Senate to his political opponents with the word—if indeed it was a word—*macaca*. At the height of Macacagate, Allen was exposed . . . as a Jew. No one imagined that this revelation of Jewish ancestry would damage Allen, least of all E. J. Kessler, who, writing for the *Jewish Daily Forward*, "outed" him.[12] The charge was "passing": Kessler, in consultation with experts in Sephardic genealogy, discovered that Allen's mother, an exotic Francophone from Tunisia, was Jewish, and conjectured that Allen himself must have known:

> This might complicate life for Allen, a practicing Presbyterian who besides running for re-election this year in Virginia is often mentioned as a possible Republican 2008 contender. Political analyst John Mercurio of National Journal's noted tip sheet, The Hotline, said that any complication "would depend largely on how this information was revealed."
>
> "If it was discovered that Allen knew this family history, but attempted to keep it under wraps for whatever reason, it could do great harm to any political campaign," Mercurio wrote in an e-mail. "He'd face serious questions, in the wake of the Macaca incident and his history with the Confederate flag, of whether he's both racially prejudiced and anti-Semitic. Given the intensely pro-Israel

sentiment that exists in this country today, that could be a huge political liability—but on the other hand, if this is something he dis-
covers and promptly reveals about himself, and does so with a *sense
of pride in his family history*, I don't think he'd face much backlash
at all." [emphasis added][13]

Allen, who could have achieved some degree of damage control
by showing a suitable "sense of pride" in his Jewish heritage—and
might even have turned it to his advantage—predictably blew it. The
rest, as we know, was history. In any case his sin—venial compared to
his proclivity for racial slurs and penchant for collecting Confederate
memorabilia—was not his Jewish ancestry but his failure to acknowledge and take pride in it. Like Pinky, Allen was punished not for being
a member of a traditionally disadvantaged minority but for refusing to
"identify" with it.

At this point, once again, we note the asymmetry of privilege. If
Allen had had a family connection to some privileged group—if it
turned out, for example, that his ancestors were members of the British
aristocracy—he would not have been required to publicize or express
a "sense of pride" in his family history. If his mother had belonged to
a neutral, nonsalient ethnic group that was not traditionally disadvantaged—if she had been Swiss, Icelandic, or Belgian—there would
have been no "outing." No one would have worried that Allen was
keeping his heritage "under wraps" and no one would have punished
him for failing to exhibit a sense of pride in his ethnic origins. Even
under the American plan, however, where ethnic identity is largely
nominal, members of socially salient ethnic groups are under special
role obligations, if nothing more than the duty to acknowledge and
identify with ancestral cultures. Allen was supposed to have included
information about his Jewish ancestry in his biography or, failing that,
to have expressed "pride" in it once it came to light just as, we recall,
Richburg was supposed to have "found a piece of himself" in Africa.
These are not intolerable burdens, but we should still ask why any such
obligations, however trivial or symbolic, should be imposed at all.

For groups on which more stringent obligations are imposed, the burdens are heavier. Janet Halley notes that when land on Indian reservations is held in common in the interests of maintaining culturally cohesive communities, individuals' options are very seriously constrained.

[A]s the Dawes Act experiment demonstrated, converting reservation land to individual Indian ownership allowed white buyers and lessors to make confiscatory deals and then to move into the midst of Indian tribes, diversifying the cultural milieu in a way that was, and continues to be, devastating for tribal cultural continuity. What happens when, in contrast, land is held in common? . . . Typically it will mean that most tribe members are left not with less alienable property, but with none. Economically, this means not merely difficulty in finding collateral, but complete abstention from the surrounding market economy. And at this point Kymlicka's failure to take note of culture's constraints becomes visible: he has not mentioned the "purpose" of promoting cultural interdependence and cohesion by blocking—for people with acute material needs—the exit marked "sell or lease your land and move away from the tribe."[14]

Where multiculturalism is taken seriously across the board, as in the scheme envisaged for a future Japan dependent on immigrant labor, all members of minority groups will be "helped" to maintain their native culture and then be "sent home." No matter how long they stay, such "guest workers," and presumably their native-born children, will remain guests—honored guests, guests who are treated courteously and paid decent wages but who nevertheless will always be guests.

Multiculturalists rarely address M. Dendoune's question. Apart from the Japanese Australian studies scholar, whose program is clear, it is hard to understand how multiculturalists intent on cultural preservation and diversity imagine the future decades or centuries hence. Will "miscegenation" be discouraged in the interests of preserving cultural diversity or will individuals who were themselves ethnically diverse be obliged to track their genetic heritage and give all ancestors their due, back to the Angles, Saxons, Jutes, Danes, and Norman

French if necessary? Will genetically hybrid individuals be allowed to choose their cultural affiliation from among their ancestral cultures or will they be expected to track their cultural heritage matrilineally, patrilineally, or according to some other special convention?

Minority ethnic communities eventually dissolve if they are not bound together by isolation, high-exit costs or exclusion from a dominant culture in which members are not welcome. Unless they are sent home when their jobs are done, guest workers usually stay in receiving countries. Unless they are "helped" to maintain their ancestral language and ways, their children or grandchildren join the dominant culture, even if only at the low end, merging with the indigenous underclass.

Maintaining the cultural salad bowl is difficult and costly, both to members of minority groups whose options must be constrained in order to preserve their cultural distinctiveness and maintain their cohesive communities, and to the dominant community that must "help" them and, if necessary, adjudicate interethnic disputes. It is not impossible to maintain a culture that is seriously multicultural, consisting of cohesive ethnic communities that coexist but do not coalesce. The millet system in the Ottoman Empire was such a system. But millet systems are expensive in human terms as well as in administrative costs, and it is hard to see why we should be willing to pay for such an arrangement unless we believe that immigrants and members of minority groups, regardless of their interests or desires, cannot, will not, and should not assimilate.

"Economic multiculturalism" is feasible. The United States could run a pure "bracero" program employing short-term contract workers from developing countries. The question is whether this is the *only* immigration program we as Americans should support. It would also be feasible, if costly, to run a millet system. The question again is whether we, either as potential citizens of the millets or members of the larger society, want it, whether such a system is consistent with our fundamental values, and whether the benefits, if any, of this system outweigh the costs.

I do not think that economic multiculturalism is cost-effective, consistent with our most fundamental values, or morally decent. Many immigrants are not interested only in making a quick buck: they want to live here, raise their families here, and become Americans. We should take their desires and interests seriously. We have enormous wealth—we can afford to share it. We have an excellent culture—and we can afford to share that, too.

NOTES

1. Gary Kamiya, "Black vs. 'black,'" Salon.com, http://www.salon.com/opinion/kamiya/2007/01/23/race_in_america/index.html.

2. R. D. Grillo, *Pluralism and the Politics of Difference—State, Culture, and Ethnicity in Comparative Perspective* (Oxford: Clarendon Press; New York: Oxford University Press, 1998), p. 226.

3. "Ghettos Shackle French Muslims," BBC News, October 31, 2005.

4. Margo Jefferson, "On Writers and Writing: Authentic American," *New York Times*, February 18, 2001.

5. Ibid.

6. http://www.prospect.org/print/V13/7/portes-a.html.

7. "Crisis in France," BusinessWeek.com, November 21, 2005, http://www.businessweek.com/magazine/content/05_47/b3960013.htm.

8. Carol J. Williams, "The Price of Freedom, in Blood," *Los Angeles Times*, March 7, 2002.

9. Ibid.

10. Ibid.

11. http://www.theaustralian.news.com.au/story/0,20867,20994885-28737,00.html.

12. E. J. Kessler, "Alleged Slur Casts Spotlight on Senator's (Jewish?) Roots," *Jewish Daily Forward* online, August 26, 2006, http://www.forward.com/articles/alleged-slur-casts-spotlight-on-senator's-jewis/.

13. Ibid.

14. http://www.bostonreview.net/BR22.5/halley.html.

Chapter 6

COMMUNITIES

Respecting the
Establishment of Religion

The legitimate powers of government extend to such acts only as are injurious to others. But it does me no injury for my neighbor to say there are twenty gods or no God. It neither picks my pocket nor breaks my leg.

—Thomas Jefferson

For individuals who are assigned salient, tightly scripted identities and second-class status within mainstream society because of visible racial characteristics and those who find it difficult to participate because they are unfamiliar with the language and social practices, retreating to an ethnic enclave may provide significant benefits. Immigrants who are locked out of participation in the larger society may be patriarchs in their own families, with the power of life and death over their children. Underclass youths who have no prospects outside the ghetto and little chance of legitimate employment may occupy leadership roles within street gangs and take on lucrative positions in the underground economy. For them, a system of semiautonomous communities within the geographical boundaries of nation-states—ghettos, communes, reservations, immigrant housing projects, or millets on the Ottoman model—may provide a desirable alternative to integration.

Most such communities, however, are fragile. Individuals for whom exit is feasible quite often choose to leave so, in order to maintain the community, cultural preservationists may jack up exit costs and impose constraints on those who want out. Often, in order to minimize the attrition rate, cultural preservationists require the official or unofficial collaboration of the state.

Should the state promote cultural preservation, even at the cost of supporting policies that restrict the individual liberty of community members who might prefer to leave? This question is especially pressing where the communities are religiously defined, as are, for example, Muslim communities in Europe and Amish communities in the United States. The state must weigh its interest in defending freedom of religion against the claims of individual liberty.

THE MILLET SYSTEM

Salience and scripting are context dependent: within homogeneous ethnic enclaves, the ethnic identities of individuals who are tagged as Other and boxed in by the larger society become transparent and less tightly scripted.

This phenomenon is familiar to women who have gone to single-sex schools or who have been Girl Scouts. In all-female groups, women get to be guys—and that is a heady, liberating experience. In single-sex schools, girls fill the ecological niches that, until recently, were reserved for boys—as student government leaders, jocks and nerds, class clowns, and loudmouths. While there are settings in which the preponderance of women pumps up femininity—one thinks of therapy groups or Oprah audiences—the appeal of many all-female settings is precisely that they liberate women from femininity and from the expectations and constraints associated with being female.

So, for example, Margaret Rossiter in her history *Women Scientists in America* notes that in spite of the popular perception that women's colleges had weak or nonexistent science programs in 1940, the ending date of her first volume, most American women in the sciences were "either students or grandstudents" of a group of women scientists who had taught at the Seven Sisters around the turn of the twentieth century. These women's colleges freed women from the female script imposed by the larger society during the period and enabled them to enter professions that were strongly identified as male preserves.

The liberation of women from conventional expectations and role obligations in all-female settings has little to do with sexuality as such. Many individuals whose ascribed identities are salient and scripted enjoy retreating, at least occasionally, to homogeneous group subcultures where they can, at least temporarily, shed their Otherness and escape their scripts. Deaf people who, within the larger society are assigned the handicapped script, participate in deaf community organizations and events where they can escape the handicapped role assigned to them by hearing people. Dwarves join the Little People of America. It seems likely that almost everyone who is saddled with a visible, salient, scripted identity has at some time enjoyed the sense of liberation that comes from participating in a group where he is "normal" and does not have to fight his way out of the box.

Now it is possible to maintain a multicultural society while accommodating the desire of ethnically diverse individuals to live and work in settings where they can maintain distinctive cultural practices and where their ethnic identities are not salient by maintaining a system of semiautonomous ethnic enclaves. Historically, the paradigm—and perhaps the most successful version of such an arrangement—was the Ottoman millet system. The Ottoman Turks, to accommodate Christian and Jewish minorities who enjoyed an inferior but protected status as dhimmi under Islamic law and who could not be forced to convert to the state religion, established a system of autonomous communities, or millets, for Jews, Greeks, Armenians, and other, smaller non-Muslim minorities within their empire. Because these groups were spread throughout Ottoman territory and because minority communities figured prominently in most major cities, territorial autonomy was not feasible, so community membership under the millet system was, of necessity, a matter of personal status.

Ethnic groups, clustered in homogeneous villages and urban neighborhoods, enjoyed considerable autonomy. Each millet, composed of individuals who lived and worked in an archipelago of these enclaves, was supervised by a leader, typically a religious patriarch, who reported directly to the Ottoman sultan. The millets set their own laws, collected and distributed their own taxes, and maintained their own courts. Although the millet system was abolished by Attaturk— since in the secular nation-state he envisaged, the rationale for maintaining it disappeared—its legacy, in congeries of unassimilated, balkanized ethnic groups in the Balkans and other former territories of the Ottoman Empire, persists. Posed with the problem of accommodating a variety of culturally distinct ethnic minorities, a number of countries within the former territory of the Ottoman Empire and elsewhere, whether informally or formally through systems of "personal law" for members of various religious/ethnic groups, maintain comparable arrangements.

In the aftermath of the London bombings and French riots, some critics of multiculturalism were quick to note that European countries in which there were growing communities of Muslim immigrants were in effect sponsoring millet systems. In France, housing projects in immigrant suburbs enjoyed an unofficial semiautonomous status: police tolerated chronic low-level violence, drug dealing, and gang rape and generally kept out. Not surprisingly, when one resident was asked whether he regarded himself as Algerian or French, he responded that he did not consider himself either—he belonged, he said, to his cité.

Nevertheless, the millet system as such is not necessarily undesirable and may in fact be the most satisfactory arrangement for some authentically multicultural societies. Under the millet system, minorities live and work in ethnic enclaves where they can maintain distinct cultures. There is no reason why the primary cultural unit in which individuals socialize and transact business should be the nation state, defined by territorial integrity, rather than some nonterritorial community defined by the religious commitments, ethnic identity, or other characteristics of its members. Indeed, the Internet and other technological advances would make it much easier to run a millet system now than it was for the Ottoman Turks.

In America, as well as European countries that have experienced mass immigration, a millet system of sorts is a reality in tribal areas. Most major cities boast Chinatowns and Little Italys as well as ethnic neighborhoods populated by blacks and recent immigrants, and in many older cities ethnic organizations are active. In rural areas there are Indian reservations for Native Americans, whose status is in many respects comparable to that of ethnic minorities under the Ottoman regime, and communities of Amish, a semiofficial millet, who are exempted from some state regulations and left largely to police themselves.[1] And then there is the Mafia.

There are, however, practical considerations that militate against the millet system. First of all, it is not clear that it is a viable arrangement in modern Western societies where it is not feasible for most educated middle-class people, even with good Internet access, to conduct their business from within ethnic enclaves. Second, many if not most people do not want to live in ethnic enclaves, and the policies needed to maintain these enclaves for individuals who want to live in them make exit difficult or impossible for those who want out. The millet system works best for individuals who are happy to live in the ancestral village and work the family farm or help with the family business. It does not serve the interests of most middle-class professionals who need to go to university and continue on through graduate and professional programs and who will spend their professional lives working for large firms or other organizations and need to be geographically mobile to pursue their careers. We may be enchanted by visions from the *Arabian Nights*, of cities that include the Street of the Carpet-Weavers, the Street of the Potters, and the old Jewish Quarter, or charmed by Amish communities exhibiting their traditional farms, crafts, and foodstuffs for tourist consumption, but most of us would not want to live in any of these places. To get the quality of education, the professional opportunities, and the range of activities we want and expect, we cannot be restricted to these ethnic enclaves.

In addition, ethnic enclaves more often than not become what economist William Easterly, writing on global development, calls "poverty traps"—vicious circles that lock nations, regions and neighborhoods, ethnic groups, and families into poverty.[2] In the affluent United States, remarkably, there are counties—in eastern Kentucky, the Mississippi Delta, and perhaps even more surprisingly in Texas, New Mexico, Arizona, and elsewhere in the West—with poverty rates above 35 percent. These areas, Easterly suggests, stay poor because human capital investments don't pay off for individuals who live there.

> Suppose a country starts out poor, with everyone having low skills. Ms. X is deciding whether to make the sacrifices necessary to get trained as a doctor. If she gets a medical education, she will have to forgo working at an unskilled job that she could get immediately. She will not be able to support her aged parents or her young siblings for the duration of her medical training. But after she becomes a highly skilled physician, she can earn more. She will be able to support her parents and siblings even better after a few years of privation. But how much will her earnings increase after she becomes a doctor?
>
> We are back to where we were before. How much her earnings increase depends on how successful she is at matching up with other skilled workers—say nurses, pharmacists, and bookkeepers. The likelihood of a profitable match depends on how much education everyone else is getting. Her problem after getting skilled is going to be to find other people of comparable skill. . . . This is her bottom line: go to school if average nationwide skills are already high; don't go to school if average nationwide skills are low. Her decision rule is sensible for her but disastrous for the nation. The nation with low average skill is going to be stuck with low average skill because no single individual is going to find it worthwhile to go to school.[3]

The picture is not, of course, quite as bleak as Easterly's a priori economic analysis suggests. Some individuals in poor countries do break out of poverty traps—however, in most cases they do so by immigrating to wealthier countries. The brain drain only exacerbates the vicious circle that Easterly describes.

Comparable vicious circles, as Easterly notes, operate at every level of aggregation. Ambitious individuals leave small towns for the big city, Indians who do not want to spend their lives selling beads or working in casinos leave the reservation, and successful restaurateurs move out of the ethnic neighborhoods where they do business and into the suburbs. It is striking to note that immigrants virtually never improve the poor city neighborhoods where they first land: they move out to make way for successive waves of poor immigrants. These neighborhoods become gentrified only when middle-class outsiders move in. Where the costs of exit are not prohibitive, those who can get out, do.

THE COSTS OF EXIT

In one respect, the brain drain phenomenon is counterintuitive. If the labor market were perfectly efficient, we should expect individuals with education and training to migrate to areas where their skills were in short supply rather than to places where they face stiff competition. Even more so, we should expect native sons and daughters, trained as doctors, nurses, or educators, to return to the village or reservation, the neighborhood or ethnic community after they are qualified, where they could enjoy the proximity of family and childhood friends and perhaps even, like Pinky, the moral gratification of "helping their people."

But they don't. And so, in order to keep ethnic enclaves from disintegrating and, in particular, in order to keep young people and talented individuals who have attractive prospects elsewhere from leaving, such communities must impose exit costs on their members.

It is easy to see why cultural preservationists need to impose these costs. First, as Easterly notes, pursuing one's profession requires "matches" with other educated individuals who have complementary professional skills. Without incentives and disincentives, educated people, whose skills the community needs, will leave. Second, and perhaps more importantly, most people have a taste for choice, which few small communities or ethnic enclaves can provide. Big box stores boom while mom-and-pop businesses fail because, even apart from the lower prices they offer, these larger stores provide consumers with a wider range of choices. Megachurches grow while small congregations stagnate for much the same reason: they provide consumers with a wider range of programs, services, opportunities for volunteer work, and other religious products.[4] Many people want the option of occasional retreat to small, homogeneous groups—that is itself yet another choice—but most also want the option of nonparticipation, and relatively few want to be locked into such groups permanently. They do not want to live under the millet system.

Because, like remote villages, ethnic enclaves do not offer the professional opportunities that provide incentives for individuals to pursue education and training or the choices and amenities that would induce ambitious individuals to stay, they become poverty traps. Accustomed to thinking of poverty as an urban phenomena with, perhaps, outlying poverty areas in Appalachia and the Deep South, we may be surprised to see large regions of poverty on Easterly's map in Arizona, New Mexico, Montana, and the Dakotas until we remember that these are remote rural areas where the archipelago of Indian reservations that comprise the Native American millet are clustered. People like to visit these places, but almost no one wants to live there.

Even though the persistence of such ethnic enclaves has entertainment value for tourists, policies that protect and promote the persistence of these communities constrain their members and may make the cost of exit prohibitive. As Janet Halley noted, policies that make it possible for members of indigenous minorities to maintain the cultural integrity of such communities set back the interests of individuals who want out. Exit from Amish communities, which in the eastern United States have tourist appeal comparable to that of Indian reservations in the West, can be even more difficult. Nadya Labi in *Legal Affairs* writes:

> To the hordes of tourists who travel to Pennsylvania Dutch country each year to go to quilting bees and shop for crafts, the Gentle People, as the Amish are known, represent innocence. They are a people apart, removed in place and arrested in time. They reject the corruptions of modernity—the cars that have splintered American communities and the televisions that have riveted the country's youth. The Amish way of life is grounded in agriculture, hard work, and community. Its deliberate simplicity takes the form of horse-drawn buggies, clothes that could have come from a Vermeer painting, and a native German dialect infused with English words. . . . The Amish want to be left alone by the state—and to a remarkable extent, they are. They don't fight America's wars or, for the most part, contribute to Social Security. In 1972, noting their "excellent record as law-abiding and generally self-sufficient members of society," the Supreme Court allowed the Amish to take their children out of school after eighth grade.[5]

Without secondary education or marketable skills, the prospects of Amish who wish to leave their communities in the outside world are grim. Moreover, from the time individuals formally join the church through baptism in their late teens, defection entails shunning by the entire community, including the defector's immediate family. It is hardly surprising that the majority of Amish remain within their communities; what is surprising is that a significant minority, in some communities as many as 37 percent, leave.[6]

Life within traditional Amish communities is, under the best of conditions, tough, monotonous, and constrained. Moreover, when things go awry, the community closes ranks to resist interference by the "English," as they did in a number of cases where children were abused and sexually molested by fathers and other family members. For their part, social workers and police, respecting the autonomy of the Amish millet, were reluctant to interfere:

Anna, who is the eighth of nine children . . . was often in trouble. Her father was in poor health, because he refused to take insulin for his diabetes, but he knew how to give a good beating. Sometimes he used the strap, a foot-long piece of rubber common in Amish homes; at other times, he took Anna "to the woodpile" and hit her with a piece of wood.

When Anna turned 11, she told me, her 19-year-old brother began molesting her, stopping just short of intercourse. When he moved away, another 17-year-old brother started raping her. . . . Anna wanted help, but she didn't think she would get it from her church. So she began dropping hints about the abuse to English neighbors. When they didn't pick up on her cues, she got bolder. In 2001, while cleaning house for her family's landlord, Anna used the phone to call a battered women's shelter in Mt. Vernon, Ohio. The counselors on the other end of the line didn't take her seriously. But after a month of calls, the shelter alerted Children and Family Services Division of Knox County.

When a social worker visited Anna's home, Anna told her about the sexual abuse. She also reported that her parents were moving the family to Pennsylvania. Laurie Roberts, one of the social workers on Anna's case in Ohio, said she was taught in training that sexual abuse among the Amish is pervasive, and seldom reported. (The problem is significant enough that the counties near Knox publish a pamphlet to educate the Amish about sexual abuse.) Yet the county left Anna in her home. . . . Anna tried to run away. But when her parents figured out where she was and called the woman who was sheltering her, Anna was sent home. Fannie began locking Anna in her room. The family moved to Tione'sta, Pa., where Fannie tried to get her daughter declared mentally ill. She took Anna to a doctor who found that Anna's eardrum had collapsed from blows to her head and seemed doubtful that the damage had been caused by buggy accidents as he'd been told. Fannie next tried a massage therapist, Barbara Burke. Noticing scars on Anna's legs, Burke called Children and Youth Services in Clarion County. On a later visit, Burke massaged Anna's father while CYS secretly interviewed Anna in the basement. The agency later visited Anna at her home. But it didn't take her into protective custody. (CYS declined to comment.)

When Fannie found out about the CYS visit, she and Anna went with 13 other kids to the home of John Yoder, an Amish dentist. . . . Yoder shot some novocaine into her upper gum. She shook her head and told him that two of her lower teeth had cavities. He shot the lower gum, and asked Fannie which teeth should go. Anna's mother answered, "Take them all," and Yoder pulled—along the upper gum, along the lower gum, until every tooth was gone. "After he had pulled the last tooth," Anna remembered, "my mom looked at me and said, 'I guess you won't be talking anymore.'"[7]

Like Fadime Sahindal, a victim of honor killing in Sweden, Anna discovered that she could not count on authorities outside of her community to protect her. Eager to respect the cultural practices of her community and the autonomy of the millet, they were reluctant to interfere.

Anna's case, like Fadime's, is extraordinary. Most Kurdish immigrant fathers do not murder their daughters and most Amish mothers do not punish their children by having all their teeth taken out. Nevertheless, policies in Sweden and the United States intended to respect cultural practices and group rights undermine the rights of individuals, deprive them of protection under the law, and make it difficult for them to extricate themselves from cultural enclaves.

The rationale for the *Yoder* decision cited by Labi, which affirmed the right of the Amish to remove their children from school after eighth grade in virtue of their communal self-sufficiency and good behavior, subordinated individual interests to community autonomy. The court, in effect, declared that since the Amish did not cause trouble or cost the taxpayers money, they could do as they pleased. This set a double standard not only for practices but also for principles concerning the rights of individuals.

The state passes laws and imposes regulations on members of the larger community in order to protect individual rights. The state establishes a school-leaving age to support the interests of children in achieving a level of education that will enrich their lives as adults and provide them with a reasonable range of career options—not merely to see to it that they won't be disruptive or burden the taxpayer. By contrast, when it comes to members of formal or informal millets, the state adopts a hands-off policy so long as the activities of their members do not have any adverse effect on the larger community.

It is this double standard with respect to individual rights that immigrant associations in Sweden and groups like *Ni Putes ni Soumises* in France complained about. Short of honor killing or street riots, the authorities tolerated practices that set back the interests of minorities: group sovereignty trumped individual rights. Indeed it is not the relatively rare, striking examples of abuse that make the case against such millet systems but the lesser lives to which the system relegated their members as a matter of course. Children of fifteen could be and often were married off to relatives old enough to be their fathers or grandfathers. Immigrants lived in housing projects run by gangs of thugs who were allowed to engage in constant low-level violence so long as it didn't spill over. Liberal governments protected the individual rights and liberties of white, native-born citizens but adopted a policy of containment when it came to immigrants and people of color.

Once again there is a compelling argument against the millet system: most people don't want it. It is hard to see why the desires of relatively few individuals who benefit from the system should trump the preferences of the majority who want out.

RESPECTING THE ESTABLISHMENT OF RELIGION

The Amish pose special difficulties because they are a religiously defined community and claim to need special accommodations on religious grounds. However, the right to free exercise of religion is not absolute. While some religious groups have obtained exemptions from military service and the right to engage in some otherwise illegal practices—for example, the Native American Church enjoys the right to engage in the sacramental ingestion of peyote—the state does not accommodate religious practices that are seriously harmful to others.

Arguably, as the initial quote from Jefferson suggests, the right to religious freedom should be understood as a special case of John Stuart Mill's "Harm Principle," according to which state restrictions on individual liberty are warranted only in the interests of preventing harm to others. Mill writes:

> That the only purpose for which power can be rightfully exercised over any member of a civilized community, against his will, is to prevent harm to others. His own good, either physical or moral, is not sufficient warrant. He cannot rightfully be compelled to do or forbear because it will be better for him to do so, because it will make him happier, because, in the opinion of others, to do so would be wise, or even right. . . . The only part of the conduct of anyone, for which he is amenable to society, is that which concerns others. In the part which merely concerns himself, his independence is, of right, absolute.[8]

Adult Jehovah's Witness may refuse blood transfusions, which they oppose on religious grounds, for themselves but not for their children. According to the Harm Principle, religious believers have the absolute right to martyr themselves but do not have the right to martyr their children.

Jefferson, living at a time in American history when Puritanism was a spent force and fundamentalism was not yet on the horizon, assumed that religion was, or would soon become, completely harmless. Writing in 1822 he remarked: "I trust that there is not a young man now living in the United States who will not die a Unitarian."[9] Less sanguine than Jefferson, we note that some practices defended on religious grounds are dangerous or harmful. If, however, religious freedom is, as I suggest, a special case of the Harm Principle, the question we need to ask in deciding whether these practices should be allowed is *how* dangerous or harmful they are and whether the dangers and harms are outweighed by the benefits, including the satisfaction of adherents' desires to engage in religious practice.

The Harm Principle is permissive: it prohibits state restrictions on actions that are not dangerous or harmful to others and allows prohibitions on those that are. However, it does not require that *all* actions that are in any way or to any degree harmful or risky be prohibited. We agree that assault with a deadly weapon is sufficiently harmful to be prohibited by law; most of us agree that insults, name-calling, ridicule, and culturally insensitive remarks are not sufficiently harmful to be prohibited. We agree that depriving children of adequate medical care is sufficiently harmful to license state intervention; most of us, however, agree that ordinary religious indoctrination, the regime of Sunday School, catechism, and churchgoing is not sufficiently harmful to warrant interference. Most people I know went through this program and are now firm atheists—as sociologist Peter Berger suggested, children inoculated with a weakened form of Christianity are forever immune to the real thing. The few who were not, are now convinced Christians. We enter the free marketplace of ideas, live, learn, leave home, and enter worlds very different from our childhood homes.

In *Wisconsin v. Yoder*, however, the US Supreme Court ruled that Amish parents, in addition to providing ordinary religious training, could pull their children out of school after eighth grade to make sure that they were not exposed to "worldly learning" that might undermine their religious beliefs or tempt them to leave their home communities. The Court's assumption was that this practice was not sufficiently harmful to children to warrant state interference and, indeed, that exposure to the alien values and practices of "English" society would be contrary to their interests:

> Formal high school education beyond the eighth grade is contrary to Amish beliefs, not only because it places Amish children in an environment hostile to Amish beliefs with increasing emphasis on competition in class work and sports and with pressure to conform to the styles, manners, and ways of the peer group, but also because it takes them away from their community, physically and emotionally, during the crucial and formative adolescent period of life. During this period, the children must acquire Amish attitudes favoring manual work and self-reliance and the specific skills needed to perform the adult role of an Amish farmer or housewife.[10]

Nowadays middle-class parents fall all over themselves to get their children into the most prestigious colleges and even the best possible preschools so that they will have the widest possible range of desirable career options as adults. It is hard to understand how in this case the Court could have imagined that the interest in religious liberty outweighed harm to children by restricting their career options to farming, homemaking, or menial work they might be able to get outside the Amish community with an eighth-grade education should they decide to leave.

Advocates for the Amish, however, argued that attending high school would be seriously harmful to Amish children and would undermine the Amish community.

> William B. Ball, defense lawyer for the Amish, said, "The State makes no bones about its desire to enter the minds of these young people, expose them to worldly education, fill up their minds with state packaged learning, alien to the Amish way, threatening the privacy of their psyche and threatening painful personality restructuring by placing them in a high school with stress upon competition, ambition, consumerism, and speed . . . the state is violating the free exercise of the Amish religion by interfering with the whole fabric of Amish worship life that permeates the whole of their ceremonial community and daily farm living, stopping parents from nurturing their children in the Amish faith, preventing the Amish youth from following their religious faith and farm vocations, and violating their right of communal association."
>
> Ball said if the U.S. Supreme Court does not stop this invasion by the state "it will sound the death knell for an old, distinctive and innocent culture."[11]

Ball and other Amish supporters repeatedly deplored the state's attempts to "enter the minds" of Amish children and "fill" them with alien ideas, but they never noted that Amish parents and other members of the community were continually entering the minds of Amish children to fill them with the doctrines and values of their sect. While

English schools "intruded" in this regard, Amish parents "nurtured." Public schools offered "packaged learning"; the Amish "ceremonial community" incorporated children into the fabric of communal life. English life stressed competition, ambition, and consumerism; Amish life supported children's religious faith and "vocations."

In fact what a high school education would have offered Amish children was a chance to try "English" life and make informed decisions about their futures as well as the skills and credentials to enter mainstream society on reasonable terms. Ball's rhetoric suggested that mere *exposure* to "worldly education" was an intrusion into Amish children's psyches that could result in "painful personality restructuring"—a psychobabble trump card. Stripped of rhetorical flourishes, the worry was that if Amish children had a clear idea of what life outside the community was like and the wherewithal to choose it, most would leave—sounding "the death knell for an old, distinctive and innocent culture."

Most Americans were deeply averse to cultural extinction for much the same reason that they were keen to avoid the extinction of species and loss of wilderness. Understandably, they wanted to live in a world where there was diversity, color and interest, variety and richness—not a world paved over, without wilderness or waste, industrialized, standardized, and packaged, populated by predictable suburban commuters crunching numbers in office cubicles. That is an almost universal desire. Most Americans were also Romantics, which is to say, they had little imagination and no empathy. Whether slumming in urban ethnic neighborhoods, reading Margaret Mead's South Sea fantasies, or visiting Amish country during tourist season, they saw only the aesthetic surface. They bought Amish crafts, ate Amish fudge, and enjoyed the unspoiled countryside, but they could not imagine daily life behind the scenes on an Amish farm—the back-breaking labor, drudgery, tedium, emptiness, constraint, and brutality. They could not imagine what it was like to be Anna.

Americans cherished what they saw as the "innocence" of Amish communities and wanted to preserve them but did not count the costs.

In fact, only Justice Douglas, the sole dissenter on the Court, recognized that Amish child-rearing practices might be harmful to children:

> While the parents, absent dissent, normally speak for the entire family, the education of the child is a matter on which the child will often have decided views. He may want to be a pianist or an astronaut or an oceanographer. To do so he will have to break from the Amish tradition. It is the future of the student, not the future of the parents that is imperiled by today's decision. If a parent keeps his child out of school beyond grade school, then the child will be forever barred from entry into the new and amazing world of diversity that we have today. The child may decide that that is the preferred course, or he may rebel. It is the student's judgment, not his parents', that is essential if we are to give full meaning to what we have said about the Bill of Rights and of the right of students to be masters of their own destiny. If he is harnessed to the Amish way of life by those in authority over him, and if his education is truncated, his entire life may be stunted and deformed.[12]

It is hard to understand how the other justices could have missed this or why the American public has never been in the least disturbed by the costs of exit Amish communities impose on their members, who have few prospects outside of the community and who are severely penalized if they leave as adults. Remarks in the decision by the Wisconsin Supreme Court, which had earlier heard the case and ruled in the parents' favor, may be illuminating: "To the Amish, secondary schools not only teach an unacceptable value system," said the court, "but they seek to integrate ethnic groups into a homogenized society, resulting in psychological alienation from their parents and cause great harm to the child."[13]

This is the familiar multicultural story, the assumption that assimilation is harmful to members of ethnic subcultures, so that even if Amish children, after exposure to "worldly learning," *choose* to leave their communities, they would be making a *bad* choice. The court assumed that schools' attempts to "integrate ethnic groups into a homogenized society" would cause harm, indeed *great* harm to children and that it was reasonable to take the risk of stunting and deforming their lives in order to avoid "psychological alienation" from their parents. This claim is unsubstantiated and, in fact, remarkable. The children of every immigrant group to the United States have integrated into the larger "homogenized" society and many have, as a consequence, suffered some degree of "psychological alienation" from their immigrant parents. There is no reason to think that they have suffered "great harm" as a consequence—it is not even clear what sort of great harm they are supposed to have suffered. There does not seem to be any reason to imagine that Amish children who leave their communities would do any worse or to privilege the religious interests of their parents over their own interests in having a wider range of life and career options than their community could provide.

In any case, we should note that in *Yoder*, even though the Court cited the First Amendment, religious freedom was a red herring. The question was whether allowing Amish parents to take their children out of school after eighth grade would be sufficiently harmful or socially disruptive to warrant coercive state action. The Court ruled that it would not—on *secular*, multiculturalist grounds. Amish religious commitments figured as little more than a guarantee that Amish parents would control and indoctrinate their children so that they would not become socially disruptive. The stability of the Amish community over three centuries and their long-standing practice of taking care of their own likewise guaranteed that even without the credentials or skills to get decent jobs they would not require public assistance or other social services that would burden the taxpayer. Apart from Justice Douglas's brief remarks, the Court did not address the question of whether being "harnessed to the Amish way of life" was a harm. Indeed, in this regard it tacitly concurred, on secular, multiculturalist grounds, with the illiberal values of the Amish, highlighting the extent to which multiculturalism is incompatible with liberalism.

MULTICULTURALISM IS INCOMPATIBLE WITH LIBERALISM

The Amish do not merely reject modern social arrangements or gadgetry: they repudiate the fundamental doctrine of liberalism that individual freedom and self-gratification are of supreme importance and that nothing else is of value except to the extent that it enlarges the scope of individual choice and promotes desire-satisfaction. Consequently, they did not regard a program that would restrict their children's career options or the drudgery, discipline, and constraint of the Amish way of life as harms. The Court concurred.

This leaves open the fundamental question of how liberals ought to deal with illiberal cultures, in particular those whose illiberality is a feature of their religious commitments. On the minimalist interpretation I have suggested, the constitutional guarantee of religious freedom is nothing more than a rule of thumb for applying the Harm Principle: a recognition that religious belief and most religious practices are harmless and therefore ought not to be regulated by the state. On a stronger reading, however, the establishment clause also affirms state neutrality when it comes to religious doctrines and may not make any law on the assumption that they are either true or false. This constraint seems plausible and innocuous when it comes to central religious doctrines concerning the existence and nature of God. It is clearly not within the competence of secular legislators or judges to address theological issues involved in working out the doctrine of the Trinity or the divinity of Christ. More importantly, these metaphysical matters have no consequences for social policy.

For many religious believers, however, religion is not just a matter of metaphysics but also a package of moral precepts, values, and doctrines concerning the character of the Good Life. And many would certainly reject the liberal contention that individual freedom is of paramount importance and that Good Life is a life that maximizes desire-satisfaction. If the Supreme Court had ruled against the Amish on the grounds that their program harmed children by restricting their options for self-gratification, it would have rejected a fundamental

Amish religious commitment, contrary to the strong reading of the establishment clause. It would have taken the position that the Amish view of the Good Life as one of harmony, humility, hard work, and discipline was simply wrong.

This, I suggest, is one very good reason for preferring the minimalist interpretation of the establishment clause according to which it is merely a rule of thumb for applying the Harm Principle. Liberals in my sense of the term are not namby-pamby relativists who hold that all value systems are equally good or equally to be honored: we hold that individual freedom in the interests of desire-satisfaction is the supreme value. If others think differently, they are wrong. If they prefer to live according to alternative values or to enter voluntarily into arrangements that restrict their own freedom or impede their self-gratification, that is their business. According to the Harm Principle, the state may not interfere with people in order to prevent them from harming themselves. If they attempt to impose such restrictions on others, however, that is the state's business insofar as one of the state's most important jobs is preventing people from doing harm to others.

This is where the conflict between liberalism and multiculturalism comes into sharp focus. Small communities that are outside of the cultural mainstream are fragile. Most members of such communities will leave if it is feasible and if they have reasonable prospects outside the community, as the Amish well understood. To maintain such communities, cultural preservationists must provide disincentives to exit that, to some extent, restrict individual freedom and impede desire-satisfaction. Liberals oppose the imposition of such restrictions on individual freedom. Cranking down the costs of exit from such communities, however, *will* likely "sound the death knell" for Amish communities and other traditional societies.

Multiculturalism is not cost-free but neither is liberalism. Liberal policies if pursued consistently would likely mean the end of Amish communities, Indian reservations, and a variety of small cultural enclaves that add richness, variety, and interest to the world in which we live. That is a loss. But as always, we weigh the costs and benefits.

A minority of cultural preservationists within these communities will be big losers. A great many other people who would like to visit *real* Amish communities, Indian reservations, and ethnic enclaves, who will not be satisfied with mock-ups and theme parks, will be mildly disappointed—and get on with their lives. But a great many members of these communities who would prefer to integrate into the "homogenized society" beyond their communities of origin will win big. We may be able to compromise, negotiate, and tweak policy, but in the end, the interests of assimilationists and cultural preservationists conflict and there is no free ride. In the end we may have to make do without the communities and ethnic enclaves that add richness, variety, and interest to the cultural mosaic at the expense of their members.

NOTES

1. See, e.g., Nadya Labi, "The Gentle People," *Legal Affairs* (January/ February 2005). "The Amish," she writes, "want to be left alone by the state—and to a remarkable extent, they are. They don't fight America's wars or, for the most part, contribute to Social Security. In 1972, noting their 'excellent record as law-abiding and generally self-sufficient members of society,' the Supreme Court allowed the Amish to take their children out of school after eighth grade."

2. W. Easterly, *The Elusive Quest for Growth* (Cambridge, MA: MIT Press, 2002). See especially chap. 8, "Tales of Increasing Returns: Leaks, Matches, and Traps," pp. 145–69.

3. Ibid., pp. 159–60.

4. Jane Lampman, "Megachurches' Way of Worship Is on the Rise," *Christian Science Monitor*, February 6, 2006, http://www.csmonitor.com/2006/0206/p13s01-lire.htm.

5. Labi, "The Gentle People."

6. Thomas J. Meyers, "The Old Order Amish: To Remain in the Faith or to Leave," *Mennonite Quarterly Review* (1993).

7. Ibid.

8. John Stuart Mill, *On Liberty*, http://www.bartleby.com/130/4.html.

9. Letter from Thomas Jefferson to Dr. Benjamin Waterhouse, Monticello, June 26, 1822, http://lachlan.bluehaze.com.au/lit/jeff17.htm.

10. "Wisconsin v. Yoder," Wikipedia entry, http://en.wikipedia.org/wiki/Wisconsin_v._Yoder.

11. Reverend William C. Lindholm, "U.S. Supreme Court Case: Is There Religious Freedom in America—for the Amish?" Holy Cross Livonia Web site, http://www.holycrosslivonia.org/amish/case.htm.

12. "Wisconsin v. Yoder," Cornell University Law School Web site, http://www.law.cornell.edu/supct/html/historics/USSC_CR_0406_0205_ZD.html.

13. Lindholm, "U.S. Supreme Court Case."

Chapter 7

MULTICULTURALISM AND THE GOOD LIFE

W ell-being, on the account assumed here, is simply a matter of being able to get what we want. The more of this effective freedom we have, that is, the greater the scope of our real options, the better off we are. On this account, liberal societies with their roots in the Enlightenment—where positive freedom is valued and most citizens have a relatively wide range of options—are more conducive to well-being than traditional societies—where individuals' lives are determined largely by sex, tribe, class, caste, and other unchosen characteristics. Individuals in traditional societies are badly off because they have little scope for choice even if they are content with their lot.

Multiculturalism undermines well-being because it assigns what Anthony Appiah calls "scripts" to individuals on the basis of unchosen characteristics and so restricts choice. Members of ethnic minorities are therefore worse off in multicultural societies where their ethnic identity is salient, their roles are scripted, and their options are more restricted by cultural preservation policies than they are in societies where assimilation is expected and facilitated.

Currently, the account of well-being assumed here has been under fire. Before going any further, therefore, we need to examine it more closely and defend it against objections.

CAN WE HAVE TOO MUCH OF A GOOD THING?

Having choices is good, but we can have too much of a good thing. Critics argue that getting what we want is in some cases bad for us and that expanding the range of options we enjoy may make us worse off. First, they suggest that having a wide range of options may confuse and befuddle us so that we cannot make a reasonable decision and that the cost of deliberation may leave us on net worse off than we would be if our options were restricted. Second, they argue that our preferences may be "deformed" so that satisfying them will not benefit us and may, indeed, make us worse off. Finally, they note that some individuals make choices that restrict, or eliminate, their future options and that intuitively leave them very much worse off. I shall consider each of these objections in turn and in the sections that follow, I will suggest responses.

The first objection originates in the literature on *bounded rationality* inspired by Herbert Simon's work in the 1950s, subsequently discussed by Jon Elster, and most recently popularized by Barry Schwartz in *The Paradox of Choice*.[1] Herbert, Elster, Schwartz, and numerous other writers note, correctly, that for agents who are not ideally rational and informed, choice itself has costs and the availability of abundant options can set back their interests. In a range of cases, the costs of search and deliberation may be prohibitive, and reasonable people may do best by adopting "satisficing" rather than maximizing strategies, that is, by going for good enough rather than aiming to get the very best. The availability of a wide range of options, for example, an extensive menu of competing plans for utilizing Medicare drug benefits, imposes heavy costs on individuals who are compelled to compare and choose. In some particularly striking cases, as Elster notes, the availability of options creates irresistible temptations that individuals wish to avoid. In such cases, rational individuals opt into arrangements that restrict their choices: they enter monasteries or sign themselves into fat farms in order to avoid temptation, or they ask their families and friends to stop them if they attempt to buy useless junk on impulse, order fatty food at restaurants, or buy cigarettes.

The moral of this story is that increasing people's options may not always make them better off and, indeed, that reasonable individuals may intentionally choose to lock themselves into social arrangements that restrict their options. Multiculturalists, considering the circumstances of individuals in liberal societies, who can choose from among a wide range of careers, affiliations, and lifestyles, wonder whether they are better off than members of traditional societies who are not burdened with extensive costs of deliberation and search. Citizens of liberal societies suffer from anomie; young people with a wide range of career options become confused and many make poor choices. Within traditional societies, paths are marked out for individuals: if individuals follow them—as they must—these paths enable most to satisfice.

Communitarians suggest further that many of the ascribed characteristics and unchosen social affiliations that liberals regard as constraints and impositions on the self are, rather, components of the self. As Charles Taylor notes, following Aristotle, man is a social animal and indeed a political animal.[2] The network of social affiliations in which we figure is not external to us but essential to who we are. Likewise, Alison Jaggar and other feminist critics of liberalism argue that the "liberal theory of human nature" according to which individuals are social atoms, inherently without social location, takes as its model privileged white males in affluent societies while denigrating the lives and persons of members of traditional societies and women who live "embedded" lives.

On this account, well-meaning attempts to liberate individuals from the social roles and affiliations that inform and guide their lives is akin to what, in the past, members of the counterculture engaging in politically motivated shoplifting described as "liberating" consumer products from the shelves of commercial establishments. Members of traditional societies who are "liberated" from the roles they play in virtue of sex, family membership, tribe, and circumstance and from the network of social affiliations in which they are embedded are not freed from external constraints but, rather, deprived of components of their essential selves and mutilated.

The second objection comes from the literature on *adaptive preference*. Martha Nussbaum and others who worry about this phenomenon take issue with the suggestion that well-being is nothing other than being able to get what one wants. Our preferences, they never tire of reminding us, do not come from nowhere: they are formed by our social circumstances. Unfavorable life circumstances may "deform" our preferences. Thus Nussbaum describes Vasanti, who stayed for years in an abusive marriage because of "desire-deformation" induced by intimidation, contempt, and neglect. Nussbaum writes that

> [l]ike many women, she seems to have thought that abuse was painful and bad, but, still, a part of women's lot. . . . The idea that it was a violation of rights . . . and that *she herself* had rights that were being violated by his conduct—she did not have these ideas at that time, and many, many women all over the world still do not have them. My Universalist approach seems to entail that there is something wrong with the preference (if this is what we should call it) to put up with abuse.

Multiculturalists, likewise, looking to the analysis of racial self-hatred suggested by Franz Fanon and canonized in the literature of identity politics, suggest that members of disadvantaged groups suffer from desire-deformation because they "internalize" racist or sexist ideologies. On the received view, blacks straighten their hair because their desires have been deformed by racist notions about the aesthetic superiority of Caucasian physical characteristics, and women diet because their preferences have been deformed by patriarchal ideology. Satisfying preferences with such tainted origins, they hold, does not contribute to well-being.

The last objection arises from the long-standing and universal recognition that life is full of hard choices. You can't have it all, and in some cases people want things that cut off a great many other options for them. Some individuals, with what most of us consider perverse tastes, want healthy limbs amputated—a preference that, if satisfied, will severely restrict their ability to satisfy other desires they may have or develop—and there are suicides who relinquish the possibility of any future desire-satisfaction. In what is perhaps the most bizarre example of this phenomenon, several years ago a German man killed and ate a willing victim who had entered into a voluntary cannibalism pact negotiated through the Internet.

> The man apparently shared a last meal of flambéed penis with his willing victim before carving him up and freezing the man's remaining body parts to eat later. . . . Police arrested the man after he posted an Internet advert seeking another male volunteer to satisfy his appetites. . . . "There are tapes," said a spokesperson for the police, who were combing the suspect's elegant, half-timbered home in the picturesque town of Rotenburg-an-der-Fulda, near Kassel, yesterday. They had already found deep-frozen human flesh and bones, as well as video recordings of the exceptionally bizarre crime.[3]

These are limiting cases of a more common phenomenon. Some individuals *prefer* to live "embedded" lives in traditional societies where their options are restricted. Others, living in liberal societies, *choose* to act out the scripts attached to their assigned roles that restrict choice. Are they better off for getting what they want, worse off because the states of affairs they choose restrict their options, both, or neither?

Each of the three objections suggested here deserves to be taken seriously. In the end, however, the fundamental thesis stands: the more options we have, the better off we are. Life is indeed full of hard choices, for individuals in the conduct of their daily lives and for social planners who must adjudicate between the conflicting desires and interests of many individuals. Both must rank and weigh preferences and, in deciding which course of action to follow, consider also the risks and probability of success in achieving their goals. Sometimes we choose to restrict our own options because we discover that the process of deliberation and choice is itself too risky or costly; sometimes we choose states of affairs that restrict choice. These are, however, themselves choices and ones that we are better off for having.

In the sections that follow, I respond to the objections noted above in turn.

MAXIMIZING AND SATISFICING:
THE CHINESE MENU PROBLEM AND THE PARADOX OF CHOICE

Drawing on the work of Daniel Kahneman and Amos Tversky in behavioral economics and the results of empirical research by psychologists, market researchers, and decision scientists, Barry Schwartz argues that "we would be better off if we embraced certain voluntary constraints on our freedom of choice, instead of rebelling against them" and other conclusions that "fly in the face of conventional wisdom that the more choices people have, the better off they are."[4]

In the cases that concern Schwartz, there are typically a plethora of options that confuse, befuddle, and, occasionally, incapacitate consumers facing a bewildering array of products. Paradoxically, Schwartz notes, the more choices consumers have, the less likely they are to be satisfied. Furthermore, becoming informed and coolly deliberating only makes things worse, as rational choosers, aiming to maximize preference-satisfaction waste time, effort, and resources on research and deliberation.

Schwartz notes, however, that even faced with the same range of options, consumers adopt very different strategies when it comes to deciding which to pursue.

> Maximizers need to be assured that every purchase or decision was the best that could be made. . . . The alternative to maximizing is to be a *satisficer*. To satisfice is to settle for something that is good enough

and not worry about the possibility that there might be something better. . . . In the end . . . [maximizers] are likely to get less satisfaction out of the exquisite choices they make than will satisficers. . . .

When Nobel Prize-winning economist and psychologist Herbert Simon initially introduced the idea of 'satisficing' in the 1950s, he suggested that when all the costs (in time, money, and anguish) involved in getting information about all the options are factored in, satisficing *is* in fact the maximizing strategy. In other words, the best people can do, all things considered, is to satisfice.[5]

What this means is that Maximizers are irrational. They have simply adopted a bad strategy for securing preference-satisfaction and, more often than not, they fail. Their problem is not the range of options available to them—Satisficers faced with the same alternatives do splendidly—but the way in which they deal with their options.

To understand what is going on, it is crucial to recognize what the objects of choice for consumers actually are. They are not discrete, spatiotemporally bounded consumer products, canned goods, cars, or boxes of laundry detergent but states of being and doing that include such intangibles as leisure and comfort. When a Maximizer comparison shops, reads labels, and checks out consumer magazines to get the best possible product at the lowest possible price, he is choosing a state of being and doing that includes not only the possession of the product he eventually buys but the trips to stores all around town, the time and effort spent reading consumer magazines, and the process of deliberation. The price he pays also includes substantial opportunity costs. Even if he succeeds in choosing the product that he would prefer, all other things being equal, all other things are in fact *not* equal, and he might have done better overall to have grabbed a merely satisfactory product early on without research or comparison shopping and spent his time doing more interesting things.

Most consumers are not adequately informed, and so their choices do not reflect their "true" preferences. They imagine that they are choosing among jeans or brands of potato chips rather than among states of being and doing. They do not realize that their time is worth something; they have never heard of opportunity costs and do not get the idea that minor differences between available options may not be worthy of serious consideration. While the availability of many options may contribute to their well-being, their own ignorance makes it impossible for them to convert their resources into preference-satisfaction. Arguably, there is nothing in cases like this that seriously undermines the suggestion that having the widest possible range of options for getting what one wants is what matters for well-being.

First, it is not the availability of many options but their intrusive visibility that makes life miserable for Maximizers. My word processor includes a huge range of "tools" for formatting, viewing, editing, and inserting objects in text, but only a few of these appear in menus, and defaults make it easier for me to satisfice. Most users believe that they are better off with software that includes lots of options that they will never use: they happily pay a substantial premium for these products. Few are befuddled or stressed by the range of options because good software is set up to make reasonable choices effortless.

While *knowing* all my options can do damage, *having* options does not. Similarly, lacking options—even if I am unaware of my predicament and do not know what I am missing—makes me worse off. So, Martha Nussbaum's account of the lives of rural underclass women in India, which plausibly suggests that women whose lives she chronicles are badly off even if they do not know what they are missing, is compelling.[6] Having options is good, even if having them in our face at all times may be undesirable; lacking options is in and of itself bad, whether we feel the shoe pinch or not.

Second, even where the scope of choice is confusing, it is easy enough to make it more manageable. In advance of deliberating about my options, I can set parameters: I can decide that when choosing from the menu at a Chinese restaurant I will consider only the items marked "hot" (my usual strategy), or I can ask the waiter to choose for me. At the supermarket, I can decide as a matter of policy to buy the cheapest product of its kind to save money or the first one I spot on the shelf to save time. Since I know that satisficing is more conducive to preference-satisfaction than attempting to maximize, I can rationally make the decision to satisfice.

Many Maximizers cannot bring themselves to make such decisions or to abide by them. They compulsively read every item on the menu and comparison shop until they drop. They suffer from weakness of will. The availability of endless possibilities makes it impossible for them to get the option they would choose if they were rational and fully informed—the state that yields the greatest benefits *on net after the costs of search and deliberation are subtracted*. This is weakness of will: congenital Maximizers, even if they know better, just cannot resist the temptation to keep searching and deliberating when a wide range of products are on offer.

Weakness of will is quite a separate issue from the Paradox of Choice, and the fact that Maximizers often succumb to temptation in such circumstances does not undermine the thesis that the more options we have to satisfy our desires the better off we are. To see this we need to distinguish between those wants whose satisfaction contributes to our well-being, those desires we have to the extent that we are rational and fully informed, and what may be called "feely temptations." We all know about feely temptations and quite often succumb to them. And much of the time we succumb not because we want desire-satisfaction but because we want, what Philip Pettit usefully calls, *desire-relief*: we just want that irritating, distracting, gnawing feely temptation to go away.

I smoke solely in order to avoid irritating feely temptations that distract me from doing anything productive, like writing this book. My problem, however, isn't too many options—including the option of buying and consuming cigarettes—but *too few*; in particular, I do not have the option of not smoking without feeling irritated and distracted. If I could get the bit of my brain that produces that feely temptation zapped, I'd do it: I am after desire-relief. My personal "utility function," which ranks states from those I most prefer to those I least prefer, looks like this:

Don't smoke but don't feel irritated   →   3

Smoke and don't feel irritated   →   2

Don't smoke and feel irritated   →   1

The numbers at the right represent the amount of "utility" or well-being these states deliver for me. I am best off not smoking but not feeling irritated, the state I prefer, and least well off not smoking and having nicotine fits. But my preferred state is not an option, and, since avoiding irritation and distraction is currently more important to me than avoiding the expense and risk of smoking, I settle for second-best: I smoke so that I will not feel irritated or distracted. My problem is that I have too few options; I cannot get my most preferred state.

Now consider a consumer faced with a list of options so extensive that deliberating about each one and comparing them would be more trouble than it was worth. Either the consumer is a compulsive Maximizer suffering from the feely temptation to deliberate about each item or he isn't. If he isn't, there's no problem: he can adopt a procedure for making his choice without wasteful deliberation. He can adopt a randomizing procedure—eeny-meeny-miney-moe, roll the dice, or throw the dart; he can ask someone else to decide for him; or he can adopt a satisficing stopping-rule—as soon as I get to one that's OK, I'll take it. The extensiveness of the option list is no problem for him.

The compulsive Maximizer does have a problem, however, his problem is not too many options but too few. He just can't resist the temptation to deliberate and compare, even though it vexes him. Moreover, he knows that if he doesn't go through the whole compulsive routine, he will agonize afterward about whether or not he made the best choice. He needs medication. But so far there does not seem to be anything on the market to zap the feely temptations from which compulsive Maximizers suffer. So, the compulsive Maximizer's problem is like the addicted smoker's. He just can't zap the feely temptation to compare and deliberate; the only way he can relieve that desire is by succumbing, even though he would prefer to relieve the desire without giving in to it. Like me, the addicted smoker, he settles for second-best because first-best is not available.

Too many options therefore aren't a problem either for the rational chooser or the compulsive Maximizer, and the so-called Paradox of Choice does not undermine the intuitive thesis that the more options we have, the better off we are.

ADAPTIVE PREFERENCE AND TAINTED ORIGINS

Multiculturalists worry that the desire of some members of ethnic minorities to assimilate have tainted origins. According to the received view, some of our preferences are a result of cultural conditioning and, when it comes to the desire to assimilate to the majority culture, that is a consequence of "internalizing" cultural assumptions about its superiority to minority cultures.

Now suppose something like this story is true. Our preferences, as multiculturalists remind us, don't come from nowhere, and it does seem highly likely that many are caused by our cultural circumstances and upbringing. I like dogs. I talk to my Lab much more than I talk to most of my colleagues and I kiss him every morning when I come downstairs. I also have a variety of other preferences when it comes to social interaction: I prefer to stand about five feet away from anyone I'm talking to, and if they get any closer I will back up, pushed by some invisible, ethereal barrier, until I am pinned against the wall or pushed out the door. These are culturally Anglo-Saxon attitudes. By the same token, it may very well be true that some blacks' preference for straight hair and most women's intense desire for slimness, including my own, are caused by racist and sexist ideologies embedded in our culture.

But so what? Moralists have been preaching for quite a long time that if we only knew where some of our preferences came from—if we realized that their sources were tainted—we would recognize that satisfying these preferences was not good for us and repudiate them. I do not see why. I do in fact strongly suspect that my desire for slimness is caused by sexist attitudes embedded in my culture and I *know* that my desire for glitzy gadgets has been caused by my exposure to advertising, but I do not see why this should make any difference. These are things I want, it doesn't matter to me why I want them, and, I believe, I shall be better off for getting them because I want them regardless of where those wants came from. I cannot understand why the source of my wants should make a difference in the extent to which their satisfaction contributes to my well-being.

I might repudiate tainted wants, or at least refrain from satisfying them, as a symbolic gesture or political act in the spirit of Jonathan Swift, who, as an Irish nationalist, famously advised his countrymen to "burn everything English except their coal." But this is quite another thing. If the Irish had followed Swift's advice, they would have made a statement that the English might have taken seriously and they might even have induced the English to make political concessions. But the Irish would not have been better off for repudiating their desire for English goods—they would, indeed, have sacrificed personal well-being in the interests of pursuing a political agenda. By the same token, I might repudiate my desire for glitzy gadgets as an act of protest against piggish American materialism of which I disapprove, but forgoing this tainted stuff would not make me better off. Acting on principle almost always makes us worse off.

The cases Nussbaum considers, however, are quite different. Most readers recognize that Vasanti, and the other women whose stories she tells, are badly off. However, Nussbaum does not produce any evidence to show that the lives they live are the lives they *prefer*, and, indeed, her stories strongly suggest that Vasanti and the others wish that things were otherwise but believe, with justification, that they can't do any better.[7]

Nussbaum's construal of Vasanti's motivation is speculative. If, however, speculation is in order, we might, with equal justification, understand Vasanti's decision as the result of a utility calculation given a reasonable assessment of her options and the probabilities of various outcomes. Vasanti recognizes that, given her circumstances, staying in an abusive marriage is her best bet if she wants to have a home and basic necessities. Even if she would rather avoid getting beaten, she is prepared to take on that cost in order to avoid her least preferred outcome—homelessness and destitution. This is Vasanti's utility function:

Home and basic necessities + no beatings $\rightarrow$ 3

Home and basic necessities + occasional beatings $\rightarrow$ 2

No home + begging in the street + no beatings $\rightarrow$ 1

Vasanti does not have a preference for abuse: she prefers having a home and being beaten to not having a home and not being beaten because she is more averse to homeless and destitution than to abuse. Unless there is more to the story than Nussbaum reveals, there does not seem to be any reason to assume that Vasanti was in a "slumberous state induced by years of contempt and neglect" or that her acquiescence is a consequence of "preference-deformation." Vasanti is a rational chooser who settles for second-best in circumstances where she has very few options.

Like Nussbaum, most privileged observers not only grossly overestimate the options deprived individuals have, they do not understand that disadvantaged individuals cannot afford to assume risk, so that exit strategies we should regard as reasonable for ourselves are, for them, tantamount to "shooting the moon." Consider Saida, an Afghan woman who decided to marry off her daughter at the age of twelve instead of sending her to school. "Saida, 27, received no formal education. . . . Saida says her eldest daughter Nahid, 12, is getting ready for her betrothal to a 26-year-old farmer and does not have much time to spare for morning instruction. . . . Saida teaches her girls the really important things—how to cook, sew and soothe a husband's ego. 'Teaching my daughters how to make their husbands comfortable is the most important thing,' she says, 'because if a husband is not comfortable, then the woman's life is hell.'"[8]

This is a rational decision, given her assessment of the options girls in Afghanistan have and the probability of success in achieving various goals. It is unlikely that any lower-class Afghan girl, or boy, will become a teacher, doctor, or engineer. Statistically, the overwhelming likelihood is that a girl will eventually marry and be totally dependent on her husband's good will for financial support and a decent life. Afghan mothers know that they don't make the rules and can't change them. Saida recognizes that it is highly unlikely her daughters will be able to achieve any degree of financial independence or have lives significantly different from her own. She believes that making a husband comfortable is the most important thing, because she knows that the only other alternative her daughters will have is *failing* to make their husbands comfortable—and suffering the consequences. Saida may or may not like her culture, but that is immaterial because she cannot do anything about it.

Saida calculated correctly that the educational option was too risky. Playing the odds, she recognized that it was not only highly unlikely that investing in education would pay off but that the opportunity costs were high. By passing up a favorable marriage deal, Nahid could end up much worse off. And without the skills and attitudes required of an Afghan wife, once married, her life might be very bad indeed. Below is a diagram of the game of Hearts, which is comparable, in its formal features to the game Saida was playing.

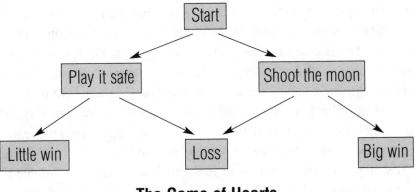

The Game of Hearts

In the game of hearts, (1) the probability of getting a little win by playing it safe is higher than the probability of getting a big win by shooting the moon, and (2) the probability of getting a loss if you shoot the moon is higher than the probability of getting a loss if you play it safe. Few players "shoot the moon"—go for the big win—not only because success is unlikely but because going for the big win substantially diminishes their chances of getting a little win and puts them at risk of losing outright. This was the game that Saida was playing, with the cards stacked against her. There is no reason to think that she prefers the role of a traditional, subservient Afghan wife to what we should regard as more desirable alternatives, either for herself or for her daughter, or that she suffers from "preference-deformation." Saida knows that she cannot extricate herself and believes with very good reason that attempting to get a better life for Nahid would be far too risky. She is a rational chooser.

Would Vasanti, Saida, Nahid, and the rest be better off getting what they want? Certainly. But what they want is remote from what they've got or can get. They have few options, and if they had more, they'd be better off. They are badly off precisely because, like most people, they *cannot* get what they want. Their problem is not that their preferences are "deformed": their problem is that they cannot satisfy their preferences given the circumstances of their lives, and they are, consequently, badly off.

When people get what they want, they're better off for that, regardless of where their wants come from. When they're badly off, like Vasanti, Saida, and Nahid, it's precisely because they can't get what they want and have to settle for the least worse alternative.

HARD CHOICES

The hardest cases for the account of well-being as preference-satisfaction are those in which individuals, who have a wide range of options, prefer courses of action that make them, by our lights, irremediably worse off. These cases are striking and newsworthy because they are rare. A willing victim responds to an Internet ad and enters into a cannibalism pact; a number of otherwise sane individuals clamor to have healthy limbs amputated. Surely, we think, they would be worse off for getting what they want.

This may be so. But we need to consider *why* we think it is so. When a person has a limb amputated, he irreversibly cuts off a wide range of options for himself; when an individual enters into a death pact, he cuts off *all* his options. It is debatable whether we believe that having more options is better because we regard them as insurance against the possibility that we will change our minds about what we want, because we believe that having many options is something most people want, or because we believe that having options is in and of itself a good thing. Without deciding that philosophical question, we nevertheless note that we intuitively believe that all other things being equal the more options people have, the better. Nevertheless, some goals are more important to us than others, so we also *weigh* our options. In some cases, the importance of one object of desire, the pearl of great price, may be so great that we are prepared to forgo a wide range of options to get it.

If this is correct, then it seems possible, though unlikely, that an individual who satisfies his desire to have a healthy limb amputated may be better off for it. In most cases, when we get what we want, we close off options for ourselves. We do this every time we spend money to buy goods and services. We satisfy our desire for the products we buy at the cost of diminishing our options for buying other items. Money is, paraphrasing Mill, the permanent possibility of preference-satisfaction, and so spending it to satisfy our preferences diminishes our possibilities.

I am stingy because I am a possibility hog; I like having the possibility of getting stuff more than I like actually having the stuff. When I pick up friends from the international terminal, I read the board of departing flights with pleasure, knowing that I have a high enough limit on my credit card to go to any of these exotic places, most of which I have no interest in visiting. Even if I don't want to go to a place, the fact that I *could* go makes me better off because it satisfies my desire to have possibilities. There are also some places I'd like to go to which I haven't gone because, strangely, I want to have the possibility of going to these places more than I want to go to them. I live frugally because I like money, that is, possibility, better than stuff.

Other people prefer stuff to money and willingly sacrifice the options that come from having money to get the stuff. Given their preferences, they are better off for getting what they want even given the cost in possibilities. That may be the way it is with otherwise sane individuals who want healthy limbs amputated. They are aware that as amputees they will have fewer options than they would if they were able-bodied, but they are nevertheless so keen to get their arms or legs off that they are prepared to forgo these options. There's no accounting for tastes, and, if this is indeed what they want, they are better of for getting it. This is, however, a rare taste: most people want more possibilities and so are better off with a wider range of options.

By the same token, there is likely a minority of individuals who prefer, all other things being equal, to spend their lives in traditional societies or ethnic enclaves where their options are restricted. Like individuals who want healthy limbs amputated, given their preferences, they may be prepared to sacrifice a great many possibilities in order to buy the way of life that they, as a matter of brute taste, prefer. And they may be better off for getting what they want. I have suggested, however, that there are far fewer of these individuals than we imagine and also that cultural preservation policies that support their interests burden a great many individuals who do not share their tastes.

CULTURAL PRESERVATIONISTS AND ASSIMILATIONISTS

Leaving aside the question of numbers, there is likely at least a minority of individuals who prefer to maintain their ancestral ways, either within traditional cultures or within ethnic enclaves in multicultural societies. Individuals who choose to live in traditional societies, like those who yearn to have healthy limbs amputated, choose to restrict their options. Traditional societies are different from liberal societies in the most fundamental ways. They are different in the value they place on playing one's assigned role, their understanding of the family, their view of outsiders, and the way in which they should be treated as distinct from the way in which they believe individuals who are members of their family, tribe, or clan ought to be treated. They are different in the way gender, age, and a variety of other ascribed characteristics determine the choices people have, the duties assigned to them, and the lives they live. These societies are not like the United States, Canada, Europe, or Australia but poorer or like Western societies in different costume with different food on the table, different dances and ceremonies, different domestic architecture, different games, and different ways of being polite. They are seriously Other, and their Otherness consists in the dearth of options for individuals and the prohibitive costs of exit.

There are individuals who prefer to live in such traditional societies. There are also members of liberal societies who prefer to live in ethnic enclaves and play roles assigned on the basis of sex, race, ethnic origin, and circumstance to satisfy their tastes.

Within liberal societies there are also many more people who want to see members of traditional societies and ethnic minorities playing these roles. Most of us have a gut-level aversion to the prospect of a world entirely transformed into an affluent American suburb—even if we ourselves prefer to live in affluent American suburbs. We want there to be hunter-gatherers in the Amazon jungle, Bedouins in the desert, and Lapps following the caribou. We, privileged white Anglos, want there to be traditional societies and ethnic communities for our entertainment. We want to go slumming to view the blacks, mountain people, and white ethnics. We want there to be Indian reservations and Amish communities so that we can visit them during tourist season, enjoy the local color, and buy their beads, blankets, homemade preserves, and patch quilts. We want exotic cultures in foreign parts to survive so that we can study their folkways, enjoy *National Geographic* documentaries about them and, if we are adventurous, visit them in the course of eco-safaris. Theme parks and mock-ups are not the same thing. We want places like this to exist and we want to think that they are nice places to visit even if we ourselves would not want to live there.

Getting what we want, I have argued, is good for us. But we can't all get what we want. Within traditional societies and ethnic enclaves, there is a conflict of interests between cultural preservationists and assimilationists. There also is a conflict of interests between romantic tourists keen on cultural preservation who do not want the world turned into a simulacrum of an affluent American suburb, and indigenes, who would prefer to live the lives of affluent American suburbanites. Life is indeed full of hard choices and we can't all get what we want. Multiculturalism is troubling because in a range of cases cultural preservation projects accommodate the interests of romantic tourists at the expense of members of minority groups who would prefer to escape the "rich mosaic" that privileged observers enjoy.

NOTES

1. See H. A. Simon, *Models of Man* (New York: Wiley, 1957), J. Elster, *Ulysses Bound: Studies in Rationality, Precommitment, and Constraints* (Cambridge: Cambridge University Press, 2007), and Barry Schwartz, *The Paradox of Choice* (New York: HarperCollins, 2004).

2. Charles Taylor, *Philosophy and the Human Sciences: Philosophical Papers 2* (Cambridge: Cambridge University Press, 1985), p. 90.

3. "German Cannibal Kills, Devours Gay Volunteer in Bizarre Pact," *Star* online, December 13, 2002, http://www.thestar.co.za/index.php ?fArticleId=27568.

4. Schwartz, *The Paradox of Choice*, p. 5.

5. Ibid., pp. 78–79. Schwartz includes in his book a psychological survey that readers can take to determine where they fall on the maximizing-satisficing continuum. After giving the survey to "several thousand people," he notes that the high score was 75 and the low was 25. At 27, I am, proudly,

a deep Satisficer: my standards are low, I have never had any problem making decisions or seriously regretted the decisions I made, and my only serious professional goal was to get tenure.

6. Martha Nussbaum, *Women and Human Development* (Cambridge: Cambridge University Press, 2000).

7. For a more extensive discussion, see my article "Adaptive Preference" in *Social Theory and Practice* (January 2007).

8. Richard Lacayo, "About Face for Afghan Women" *Time* magazine, January 17, 2002.

Chapter 8

THE CULT OF CULTURAL SELF-AFFIRMATION

What do young Islamic radicals and mohican-styled punks have in common?

Young people are more tolerant than their elders, aren't they? Absolutely not. When I was 16 or 17, I went through a very religious phase and attended a charismatic evangelical church. . . . So while other youngsters rebelled against flabby conventional society by smoking pot or becoming Goths or joining the Socialist Workers Party or indulging in petty crime, my rebellion (which meant a lot less pleasures of the flesh) was to devoutly follow a very hardline conservative morality. . . . Thankfully, we grow up: silly extremist views and outlandish lifestyles give way to the reality of 9–5, the property ladder and finding a mate.

So that's why I don't feel terribly alarmed by the Policy Exchange survey of young Muslim opinion that was reported in today's Times. We learn that young Muslims in Britain hold much more extreme, radical Islamist views than their parents—a third polled said they wanted to live under Sharia law, three-quarters preferred women to wear a hijab (though, of course, three-quarters of young Muslims don't wear them), and 13% said they admired al-

Qaeda. That should not be a surprise. Young people love being angry and love outraging the bourgeoisie. And if you are a Muslim you can pick an off-the-peg radical identity that really upsets mainstream culture. It sounds flippant but the veils that young Muslim girl wears are, to me, no different to the punk's Mohican in the late 1970s: a way of saying "f*** off."

This may be overly optimistic but I suspect that the vast majority of these young Muslims's views will mellow and the following generation will find some other way of upsetting their elders.[1]

VEILS, OPPOSITIONAL IDENTITIES, AND ADOLESCENT FASHION STATEMENTS

Back when I was in college, there was a brief adolescent fad for "maxi coats"—winter coats that went to the ankle like those women had worn a century earlier. They gave little, round girls like me a long, graceful line, and were in midwestern winters very practical. Even back in New Jersey, where winters, though mild by midwestern standards, were still formidable, I spent my childhood packed into immobilizing snowsuits and winter coats with matched "leggins" before graduating to tights. It was cold, and girls could not, of course, wear pants to school.

Adults hated maxi coats. Paging through the town newspaper in the library, I read a lengthy article on the hazards the long coats posed to health and safety. It included comments by a local pediatrician who warned parents that young girls who wore maxi coats, particularly in combination with the high boots that were also fashionable, could easily slip on the ice or trip on the hems and break their legs.

During the late '60s, adults hated everything associated with youth culture. They hated our music, our politics, our antiwar demonstrations, our incense and Indian print bedspreads, our hair, and, most especially, they hated the way we dressed. They hated maxi coats that concealed too much in winter, halter tops that revealed too much in summer, and jeans all year round, because they regarded the way we dressed as a sign that we rejected their most fundamental beliefs, values, and ambitions for us, their children. Our clothing was an emblem of an oppositional, countercultural identity that marked us as hippies.

It was hard to avoid being a hippie if you were in your teens at that time, because unless you dressed to the teeth—skirt, pantyhose, and makeup—adults assumed you were making a political statement. And, sometimes, we were. But sometimes we weren't. Before I left for college, my mother took me to Meyer Brothers in downtown Paterson— where she had been outfitted with her college wardrobe—to get the safe skirts and sweaters I would, she believed, wear as a coed and my first real grown-up suit. Once I discovered that I could go to class in jeans, I packed these wardrobe items away and never wore them again. I wasn't making a political statement: I was just a slob. As Freud is supposed to have said: "Sometimes a cigar is just a cigar."

But sometimes it is not. When I was feeling seriously oppositional, I sliced the legs of my jeans to the knee and sewed in alien fabric to make them bell-bottoms—more countercultural than ordinary dungarees. A friend, whose father had given him a Brooks Brothers charge account for his college wardrobe, got his underwear at Brooks Brothers but bought his jeans at the local thrift shop where they could be gotten preworn, prepatched, and instantly countercultural. Viewing the South Side of Chicago during our field trip, we saw some of our black counterparts wearing platforms and huge Afros, carrying suitcase-sized boom boxes blaring soul music, displaying identities that were more oppositional than anything we could ever achieve. It hardly mattered. There was a culture war on, and whether we wore bell-bottoms or straight-leg jeans, pumped up Afros or ironed hair to achieve a Native American look, as I did, enraged adults were convinced that we were making a statement. And sometimes we were.

Nowadays, right-thinking adults are more reticent about attacking adolescents' countercultural fashion statements, particularly where religious rights and cultural sensitivity are at issue. So, in 2004, when France's ban on "ostentatious religious symbols" in the public schools came into effect, the world sympathized with Lila and Alma Lévy, suspended from their Paris lycée, for refusing to remove their Muslim headgear. While some 70 percent of French citizens, including many Muslim women, supported the headscarf ban, the international liberal community did not know what to make of it. Should progressives oppose the headscarf ban as a violation of individual rights or support it in order to protect Muslim girls from familial pressure to cover up? Should feminists support the right of women to dress as they pleased or oppose veiling as a symbol of female subservience, which oppressed women? The Lévy girls and a number of other photogenic young women in hijabs were adroit at turning feminist arguments on their heads, explaining to delighted photojournalists that veiling was a free choice on their part in the interests of defending their bodily integrity and personhood in a society where women were regarded as sex objects.

No one dared to wonder out loud whether Lila, Alma, and the rest might not just be teenagers trying out a fashionable, oppositional identity. By the time the Lévy sisters had achieved their fifteen minutes of fame, most of us were aware of the social problems in affluent European countries with large immigrant populations. We knew that in France immigrants and their children were warehoused in high-rise housing projects in remote suburbs that ringed Paris and other French cities—no-go areas dominated by young men who made their living in the drug trade and engaged in chronic low-level violence. The year before, young women from the immigrant suburbs had taken to the streets in a "marche des femmes contre les ghettos et pour l'égalité"— French even I could understand—to protest their oppression at the hands of immigrant patriarchs and young thugs. It would have been culturally insensitive, and even indecent, to trivialize the legitimate concerns of Muslim women.

Lila and Alma, however, were not girls from the projects, and their father, a lawyer, fully supported them. Maitre Lévy, even more forthcoming to the press than his girls, told the BBC:

"I have a historical identity as a Jew, but not a religious one. I am an atheist."

Mr Levy has leapt with a passion to the defence of Lila and Alma—and of the right of all girls who wear the headscarf—to an education like everyone else. He accuses the government of using his daughters as cannon-fodder as it tests the ground ahead of a possible new law on religious insignia in schools. And he excoriates what he calls the "ayatollahs of secularism," hardliners of left and right who he says are preaching a new doctrine of intolerance— sowing the seed of even greater alienation and anger in France's high-immigration suburbs . . .

Mr Levy said his daughters had come under no pressure from radical Muslims, and remained as open-minded and as tolerant as they were brought up to be.[2]

Meanwhile in the United Kingdom, the case of Shabina Begum slowly ground its way through the courts to its denouement at the hands of the Law Lords in early 2006. Shabina, at age thirteen, had challenged her school's uniform policy by demanding the right to wear the *jilbab*, a long black robe covering all but her hands, feet, and face. The hijab was no problem at Denbigh High School in Luton, where 79 percent of students were Muslim and the headmistress, herself a Muslim, had devised a uniform option consisting of a modest *shalwar kameez* in school colors with optional matching headscarf in consultation with local Muslim clergy who sat on the board of governors. After four years at home studying from her school chums' notes and a disappointing performance on her A-levels, Shabina lost her case and emerged from Britain's highest court in her *jilbab*, under a slim maxi coat.

Is veiling in the West a countercultural fashion statement? Brendan O'Neill, writing recently in the *Guardian*, suggests it is:

Recently, I was strolling through Selfridge's in London when I saw something strange. At a make-up counter in the women's department, four young Muslim women dressed in the hijab, the veil that covers the head and hair but leaves the face on view, were trying on various shocking shades of lipstick and blusher, gaily chatting and giggling as they did so. "This shade makes my lips look fuller," said one, pouting in front of a mirror. Her friends agreed. "It's a must-buy," they chirped.

The hijab is meant to symbolise modesty and chastity. Yet here were four young veiled women, in their late teens or early twenties, painting their lips and reddening their cheeks, prettifying their faces for everyone to see. Even more strikingly, one of them had the word Fendi emblazoned in silver lettering across her black hijab—Fendi being the Italian fashion house best-known for its shoes, bags and furs, and which is beloved of those Sex and the City women. This was Muslim garb as high fashion.[3]

O'Neill bravely continues:

This all reveals something telling about young British women's choice to wear the veil: very often, they seem to be motivated more by vanity than modesty. The aim is to stand out and become a talking point, rather than to hide meekly away from an apparently rapacious culture. When a woman donned the burka in Taliban-ruled Afghanistan she became just another blue sheet drifting through the streets, indistinguishable from all the other women; a nobody, a non-person, just as the Taliban desired it. But when a woman in Britain puts on the hijab or niqab or burka, she immediately stands out from the crowd and turns heads.

It is the Islamist equivalent of becoming a goth and going out in public with jet black hair and garish black make-up: you know people will gawp at you and wonder about you. That is partly why you do it. Those who claim that young British Muslims' penchant for putting on the veil shows the rising influence of radical Islamism, of outdated, archaic beliefs, are missing the point. The fashion for the veil is very contemporary indeed, comparable to young working-class lads who wear hooded sweaters that shadow their faces, or middle-class girls who wear huge bug-eye sunglasses: it is a fashion item intended to indicate outsider status, because there is nothing cooler than being an outsider.[4]

Maybe. Sometimes a cigar is just a cigar—and sometimes it isn't. Most people can tell the difference. There are likely thousands of immigrant women in the United Kingdom and elsewhere in the West who are accustomed to wearing the hijab and who would feel naked in public without it who do not shop at Selfridges for makeup and designer headscarves. But there are also, one suspects, hundreds of girls for whom such attire is an expression of radical chic, like the Goth getup of the recent past or the Afros and bell-bottoms my cohort wore when we were their age.

As an American, I don't react viscerally to Islamic dress because in the United States, Muslims are not a significant minority as they are in the United Kingdom and Western Europe, nor are they identified as an underclass. I can, however, understand the visceral response Europeans must have when I reflect on my own reaction to underclass black and Hispanic youths doing ethnic. In curmudgeonly middle age, I can now appreciate Bill Cosby's rage at underclass minority youth affirming oppositional identities that do them in even more decisively than Shabina Begum was done in by her four-year lawsuit and lousy A-levels:

Ladies and gentlemen, listen to these people. They are showing you what's wrong. People putting their clothes on backwards. Isn't that a sign of something going on wrong? Are you not paying attention? People with their hat on backwards, pants down around the crack. Isn't that a sign of something or are you waiting for Jesus to pull his pants up? Isn't it a sign of something when she's got her dress all the way up to the crack—and got all kinds of needles and things going through her body. What part of Africa did this come from? We are not Africans. Those people are not Africans; they don't know a damned thing about Africa. With names like Shaniqua, Shaligua, Mohammed and all that crap and all of them are in jail. . . . Just forget telling your child to go to the Peace Corps. It's right around the corner. It's standing on the corner. It can't speak English. It doesn't want to speak English. I can't even talk the way these people talk. "Why you ain't where you is go, ra." I don't know who these people are. . . . Everybody knows it's important to speak English except these knuckleheads. You can't land a plane with, "Why you ain't . . ." You can't be a doctor with that kind of crap coming out of your mouth.[5]

Maybe I shouldn't have that reaction. But I do, and I have that reaction for the very same reason that the people over thirty whom I didn't trust when I was in college went ballistic about our Afros and bell-bottoms. They are expressing an oppositional identity, and I don't like it.

CONSEQUENCES OF CULTURAL SELF-AFFIRMATION

There are a variety of reasons why some Muslim women wear veils. The important question is whether Islamic dress is socially disruptive and, if so, why. Jack Straw, in a carefully crafted policy statement, claimed, disingenuously one suspects, that he was uncomfortable dealing with women who wore full face veils because he could not see their faces or read their expressions. Even worse, following Straw's remarks, politicians throughout Western Europe pressed to have *niqibs* and burkas, as well as ski masks and other gear that hid their wearers' faces, banned in the interests of public safety. Terrorists and even ordinary criminals, they claimed, could escape detection by donning Islamic female dress.

Straw did, however, come clean about the real reason for discouraging the more striking forms of Islamic dress, namely, that they made ethnicity more salient and promoted the idea of Muslims as alien and threatening. They made a "visible statement of separation and difference . . . [that] was bound to make better, positive relations between the two communities more difficult." *Niqibs*, burkas, and even the *jilbab* without face veil that Shabina favored, looked striking and weird, promoting the perception of Muslims as frightening and Other. Simple headscarves, particularly in areas with large immigrant populations, were not, as the French claimed, "ostentatious" and did not turn heads any more than the tidy, crocheted skullcaps some observant Jewish males attached to their hair with bobby pins. Women walking around in jet black tents made children cry, stopped traffic, and were in every way quite another thing. Regardless of why women wore these outfits, they sent the message that Islam was fanatical and strange and that Muslims were alien and would not integrate—the last thing anyone wanted in circumstances where ethnic tensions were already inflamed.

Should some of the more spectacular forms of Islamic dress be made illegal—or at least discouraged? The civil libertarian argument, appealing to rights of free speech, religious freedom, and self-expression, overlooks the fact that when self-expression takes the form of cultural affirmation—particularly if it is perceived as an expression of an oppositional identity—it has fallout for "innocent parties" who are identified with the cultural group in question. Because whiteness is transparent in the United States and Europe, I can behave badly without reflecting adversely on others. Members of traditionally disadvantaged "visible" minorities, by contrast, do not have that moral luxury because their ethnicity is salient. When black youths wear their pants "down around the crack," there is fallout for all blacks, however minimal, because being black is still a socially salient characteristic. And when underclass blacks, even though they are now a minority, "do black"— when they name their kids Shaniqua or Shaligua or speak in ways that Bill Cosby can't even manage: "Why you ain't where you is go, ra" and the like—they contribute to the continued salience of black identity.

The relevant moral questions are: to what extent does the cultural self-affirmation of some members of a group have consequences for other members of the group and are those consequences so significant as to override rights to free speech, religious freedom, and self-expression? These rights are not absolute. Notoriously, the right of free speech does not license individuals to shout "fire" in crowded theaters and, as the Law Lords noted when they ruled against Shabina Begum, while freedom of religion is absolute when it comes to individuals' beliefs, it does not license all and any public *expressions* of religious belief. Shabina could believe what she pleased—she just could not go to classes at Denbigh High School out of uniform.

We cannot dismiss the consequences of cultural self-affirmation. The question is one of *how* disruptive or divisive a particular form of cultural self-affirmation is, *how* adversely it affects assimilationist members of the cultural group with which it is identified, and whether, in any given case, the freedom of cultural preservationists to express their cultural or religious identities outweighs the interest of assimilationists and the public at large. That is, in part, an empirical question: what are the consequences of tolerating a minority of veiled Muslim women, a minority of underclass youths "doing black," or a minority of any traditionally disadvantaged group who by their appearance or behavior reinforce stereotypes and make a "visible statement of separation and difference"?

In "Eli, the Fanatic," a story of Philip Roth's set shortly after World War II, Eli, a lawyer, is asked by a contingent of neighbors to do something about a Jewish religious school established in town by a refugee rabbi and his flock. The neighbors, like Eli, are Jewish and they worry that the presence of the rabbi and his people—European immigrants with limited English who are strangely dressed and serve as visible symbols of perennial Jewish victimhood—will discredit them in the eyes of their Gentile neighbors. Eli, unwilling or unable to zone them out, gives the rabbi a selection of his gently worn old clothes as a hint. And, by way of exchange, the rabbi leaves his black, foreign suit and hat at Eli's door. Eli, on an impulse, tries on the costume and goes outside, trying to imagine what it would be like to take his place in the world as quite a different person.

Within seconds the phone rings. One of his neighbors, in a state of agitation, tells Eli, "I was just looking out of my window and *there's a Jew on your driveway!*"

Should Eli's Jewish neighbors have been worried? Probably not. When we first moved to New York we were amazed to see Hassidic Jews in their characteristic black hats and coats walking through the streets and riding on the subway. We were even more amazed to see that no one found their presence surprising or paid any attention to them. We got used to them very quickly ourselves. No one imagined that they reflected in any way on other Jews—they were a species unto themselves. But Eli's neighbors couldn't have known which way things would break—whether local Gentiles would view them as more foreign, more Other because of their association with the refugees at the religious school or regard the refugees as a species unto themselves.

Now suppose there were women in *niqibs* and burkas in your town at about the density of Hassidic Jews in New York City. Would you think that Muslims generally were weird and had strange ideas about how women should dress or would you regard these veiled women as members of a strange little sect, like the Amish, whose beliefs and practices didn't reflect on members of the mainline church? Would their presence inflame Islamophobia and provoke violence by nativist thugs or would the visibility of identifiably Muslim women going about the ordinary business of life, shopping, pushing strollers, and chatting outside the schoolyard send the message that Muslims were just folks like the rest of us? One suspects that Jack Straw's view that hijabs were OK but *naqibs* were not was a judgment call on this, an educated guess that headscarves were familiar and acceptable to the general public but that face veils and the more striking forms of Islamic female dress would be perceived as oppositional and so exacerbate interethnic tensions.

GROUP RIGHTS—AND WRONGS

We cannot know for certain which way things will break. What is important to understand is that public expressions of cultural identity are not private acts—actions that have no significant consequences for anyone but their voluntary participants. Regardless of the intention with which they are done, such acts "make a statement"—a statement that in some circumstances will be widely perceived as oppositional and that will effect the way in which others identified with the culture are perceived and treated. In some cases, whether we like it or not, we act as representatives of groups with which we're affiliated and, arguably, have a duty to avoid behaving in ways that discredit or harm other members of the group.

As an opener to *Racial Culture*, Richard Thompson Ford cites the extraordinary case of Renee Rogers, an African-American flight attendant who sued American Airlines for enforcing a grooming policy that forbade her from wearing cornrows, a hairstyle she claimed was "reflective of the cultural, historical essence of the Black women in American society." Rogers claimed that the policy violated her civil rights under the Thirteenth Amendment and under Title VII of the Civil Rights Act. "Roger's briefs," Ford notes, "evoke Malcolm X in support of the political importance of the cornrow hairstyle for blacks."

> But should anti-discrimination law protect politically controversial, if racially salient, behavior advanced through the vehicle of physical grooming? Suppose some black women employed by American Airlines wished to wear cornrows and advance the political message they ostensibly embody, while others thought cornrows damaged the interests of black women in particular and reflected badly on the race as a whole (given the cultural politics of black America in the mid-to-late 1970s, there almost certainly were such black women employed by American Airlines and even more certainly there were such black women among its customers). . . .
>
> Rogers and her supporters might object: "what business is it of other black women whether *we* wear braids—no one will be forced to wear them." But this individualistic account of the stakes of the case flatly contradicts the proffered rationale for conceiving of the hairstyle as a legal right: cornrows are the 'cultural essence,' not of one black woman but of black *women*. If this claim is to be taken seriously then cornrows cannot be the cultural essence of only those black women who choose to wear them—they must be the cultural essence of *all* black women. And in this case *all* black women have a stake in the rights claim and the message about them that it will

necessarily send—not only those who support the political and cultural statement conveyed by cornrows, but also by those who oppose that statement.[6]

Rogers lost her case, but it is remarkable that she got a serious hearing. It is even more remarkable that Shabina and the Lévy girls, teenagers who objected to their schools' dress codes, were taken seriously.

When Shabina, at thirteen, showed up at school out of uniform, she was sent home to change, and that was as far as her case would have gotten if she had not played the religion card. Like Rogers, Lila, Alma, and Shabina won public sympathy by playing both sides of the net. On the one hand their supporters made out that their behavior was harmless: a matter of self-expression that had no significant consequences for anyone else. On the other hand supporters claimed that such behavior was specially protected on cultural or religious grounds—in which case it was not merely matter of self-expression that had no significant consequences for anyone else but a matter that had import for other Muslims. Ford is surely correct in suggesting that some black women would have found Rogers's hairstyle offensive, and in Shabina's case the headmistress of Denbigh High School testified that quite a few other Muslim girls came to her office to express their concern that if Shabina won her case they would be forced to adopt more "modest" Islamic dress—something that they did not want to do.

The serious question this poses is whether membership in ethnic or religious groups confers special rights or privileges that override ordinary civic or professional obligations. In the Rogers case, and in the discussion surrounding Islamic veiling, there was no suggestion that American Airlines, the French government, or Denbigh High School had imposed dress codes or grooming requirements that were unduly restrictive or that violated the individual rights of employees or students as such. The claim was that these restrictions were discriminatory and violated special rights that individuals enjoyed in virtue of their religious convictions or racial identity, which should have exempted them from otherwise unobjectionable requirements.

It is also important to note that in each of these cases, cultural identity statements did not set members of a minority ethnic, racial, or religious group against the majority—they set members of minority communities with different interests, goals, and political agendas against one another. Ford continues:

> Even if we take it on faith that cornrows represent black nationalist pride as against the integrationist and assimilationist coiffure of chemically straightened hair, it's clear that a right to cornrows would be an intervention in the long-standing debate *among* African-Americans about empowerment strategies and norms of identity and identification. . . . A right to group difference may be experienced as meddlesome at best and oppressive at worst even by some members of the group that the rights regime ostensibly benefits. For the black woman who dislikes cornrows and wishes that no one—most of all black women—would wear them, the right not only hinders her and deprives her of allies, but it also adds insult to injury by proclaiming that cornrows are *her* cultural essence as a black woman.[7]

Once again, there is no free ride: there is a conflict of interests between cultural preservationists and assimilationists. Where interests conflict, if we are clear and honest about what is at stake, compromise and negotiation are always possible. And what were once symbols of oppositional identities have become mainstream and innocuous, like Beatles hits rearranged as Muzak and piped into elevators. No one cares about bell-bottoms or maxi coats these days, Afros are as quaint as hoop skirts, and if Oprah showed up in cornrows no one would turn a hair. The fact remains, however, that whatever the current symbols, advocates of group difference and integrationists have conflicting interests, and we cannot simply assume that multiculturalism expands freedom while assimilation imposes constraints.

THE IDEOLOGY OF DIFFERENCE

These days, dress and grooming codes are more relaxed than they were thirty years ago, when Rogers challenged American Airlines' cornrow prohibition, and I'm glad of that. It takes more now to achieve a seriously oppositional look than it did in my day, when jeans and tie-dyed T-shirts were enough to get adults frothing at the mouth. Nowadays it takes serious body piercing to get a comparable response.

At the same time, over the past three decades, identity politics went mainstream. It is because identity politics has become embedded in popular culture that we do not treat assimilationists' and cultural preservationists' interests as on a par. We reflexively assume that there is a prima facie case for cultural affirmation and difference—and that puts assimilationists on the defensive. "The black woman who dislikes cornrows and wishes that no one—most of all black women—would wear them" has to defend herself, and black Americans like Keith Richburg, who do not like or "identify with" Africa, are pressed to explain and justify themselves. Members of ethnic minorities who actively resist cultural identification are challenged: "Why shouldn't we assume that you have implicitly bought into white racist attitudes—that you are self-deceiving and self-hating?" No one, by contrast, challenges expressions of ethnic identification or cultural self-affirmation, at the least those of the more genteel sort. Black parents buy their kids *My First Book of Kwanzaa*, displayed seasonally at the supermarket checkout, and Asian college students sport "AZN" T-shirts. No one turns a hair.

The notion that ethnic self-affirmation, at least for nonwhites or non-Anglos, is normal and requires no defense and that assimilation by contrast requires justification is a novelty. A century ago, when blacks were not an ethnic group but an indigenous untouchable caste, Americans regarded ethnicity as a temporary impediment. Ethnic minorities were immigrant groups; immigrants would become "Americanized" as completely as they were able, and their children would be 100 percent unhyphenated Americans. That was the end of ethnicity, according to the official story, for the Germans and the Irish, then for Poles, Jews, and Italians. The process would repeat itself when the next wave of mass immigration came.

Back in Baltimore, when I was in grad school, there was a local politician with a long Polish surname whose given names were, remarkably, "American Joe." One imagines his jubilant immigrant parents, celebrating the birth of their first son in the New World: "A baby boy! Our first son born in America—100 percent American, a real American Joe!"

That was the way it was. But then things changed, not only for blacks whose status was regularized as an ethnic group on the model of European immigrant groups, but also for the grandchildren of European immigrants. Notoriously, what the second generation worked to forget, the third tried to remember—or reconstruct. By the 1970s, the ethnic revival was under way: the grandchildren of European immigrants set out to investigate their ancestral cultures, and Alex Haley wrote *Roots*. Ethnicity became part of the American experience: Ellis Island was incorporated into the American Great Trek saga, along with the *Mayflower* and the Oregon Trail, and *Roots* was televised as a miniseries. Thanks in large part to the miniseries, blacks became members of a normal American immigrant group, with an ancestral homeland, language, and culture—a Great Trek story even more dramatic than "Wagons Westward Ho" or "Steerage to Ellis Island," and, thanks to Ron Karenga, a national holiday in the form of Kwanzaa.

Coming from tribal northern New Jersey, I didn't care for these ethnic myths and cultural follies one bit. I'd seen the real thing. But, biting back gall, I recognized that they were harmless and that, in any case, if white Americans could tell stories, it was good that black Americans could tell them too. Domestic identity politics, however, also drew from the ideology of the global struggle against colonialism. As it happened, it was just at the time that Americans were fighting it out over the rights of minorities domestically that colonialism was collapsing and, within the Left, that the promotion of equal rights for minorities in the United States became inextricably linked with liberation movements on the world stage. Advocates of identity politics argued that there was a compelling analogy between the plight of disadvantaged minorities at home and colonized peoples abroad and that the remedies were similar.

The premise of anticolonial revolutions was that equal was inherently separate: colonized peoples could not achieve equality so long as their countries were dominated by imperial powers and, regardless of how benign a colonial regime was, "self-determination" was preferable. In addition to political independence, opponents of colonialism were, at best, ambivalent about the cultural influence of colonial powers and promoted indigenous cultures and languages. The ongoing struggle to achieve equality for disadvantaged groups in the United States was plugged into the anticolonial template so that self-determination and cultural preservation came to be seen as desiderata for ethnic minorities. During the latter years of the twentieth century the emerging consensus in the mainstream Left was that it was equality, not integration, that mattered and indeed that pushing for integration might even undermine the achievement of genuine equality.

First ethnic minorities, then women, and subsequently gays, the deaf, and the disabled were represented as colonized peoples, each with their own characteristic culture, under the thumb of white Anglo males who played the role of colonial oppressors. It became a commonplace that members of disadvantaged groups could not take down the master's house with the master's tools. According to the received view, people of color who promoted integration or advocated equal treatment on the grounds that whites and minorities were the same under the skin played the role of collaborators under colonial regimes. It was held that members of ethnic minorities, and, by extension, women, should not try to succeed on white Anglo male terms because to do so was to accept standards that were set by white Anglo males and skewed in their favor. Advocates of identity politics argued that the supposedly "neutral citizen of liberal theory was in fact the bearer of an identity coded white, male, bourgeois, able-bodied, and heterosexual."[8] Although these views were represented as radical, they were not uncongenial to conservatives who believed that blacks and women *could* not make it on white Anglo male terms and should not be encouraged to try.

At the same time, the political Right appropriated the rhetoric of integration and color-blindness to argue against a variety of regulations and policies intended to achieve equity for disadvantaged groups—most particularly affirmative action. It became a commonplace that traditional liberalism, concerned to achieve integration and a level playing field, was wedded to the idea that formal equality under the law was the only legitimate means to achieve fair treatment for women and minorities. Formal equality under the law, as represented by the Civil Rights Acts of the 1960s, had not come close to achieving that result—women and members of minority groups were still seriously disadvantaged—and so, critics concluded, identity politics were in order. Either you favored integration, sought to level the playing field so that members of disadvantaged groups could compete with white Anglo males on their own terms, *and* opposed government interference, or else you favored equal opportunity regulations and affirmative action policies in the interests of promoting cultural diversity *and* supported identity politics.

This was a false dichotomy that should have been transparent. It did not take much political sophistication to recognize that blacks and women were disadvantaged in large part by implicit bias and a daunting array of attitudes, customs, and policies that formal equality under the law could not fix. Nevertheless, it became dogma that favoring integration, color-blindness, and gender-blindness as *goals* meant rejecting color-conscious, gender-conscious proactive programs to counteract these attitudes, customs, and policies as a *means*.[9]

Given this history, by the late twentieth century it had become impossible for advocates of progressive policies to criticize multiculturalism without being branded as crypto-conservatives or worse. "Liberal" had become a dirty word on the left as well as on the right, being identified with libertarian opposition to proactive state intervention in the interests of promoting fairness for disadvantaged groups.

To oppose multiculturalism was, ipso facto, to oppose affirmative action. To oppose multiculturalism was to hold that formal equality under the law was enough. Moreover, because *multiculturalism* was ill defined and *culture* had come to be understood as a polite word for *race*, to oppose multiculturalism was to oppose genetic diversity. In short, for political liberals to oppose multiculturalism was to ally oneself with the Right.

The real sting of the grand multicultural myth to which these stories belonged in any case was not in *Roots*, but in Haley's *Autobiography of Malcolm X*, which channeled the zeitgeist at a slightly earlier stage of its development, before multiculturalism was fully domesticated. Touted as radical and countercultural when it was published in 1965, the book was itself quickly domesticated, and along with *Bless Me, Ultima*, became a standard coming-of-age book in high school English classes once *Catcher in the Rye* had become hopelessly dated. A Web search reveals not only a Random House teachers' guide but also a high Google listing for its SparkNotes companion. Malcolm had become as American as apple pie.

If the iconic moment in *Bless Me, Ultima* was the exposition of the tortilla, the episode from Malcolm's autobiography that all readers remember is Malcolm's first conk, the product of a painful hair-straightening process that leads him to conclude: "I know self-hatred first hand." And the episode is deservedly memorable because it encapsulates the cluster of ideas that constitute the canonical analysis of racial hatred and self-hatred embedded in popular culture. This cluster of ideas is both compelling and dangerous because it includes some claims that are both true and important and others that are false or questionable embedded in a medium that makes it difficult to pull them apart. It is worthwhile therefore to extract these claims for consideration.

Some features of Malcolm's account are true and indeed uncontroversial. Malcolm recognized that "respectable" blacks who refused to challenge the system of white privilege because they were able to work the system to get crumbs were deluded, and moreover that in working the system they helped to perpetuate it. This was an old story: we remember the episode in which respectable Uncle Tom, proud to be in a position of trust, rides off in a buggy to buy more slaves for his master. Beyond this, Malcolm's analysis and proposals for remediation were questionable. Merged with the mainstream of identity politics, the story can be reconstructed as follows:

The Story of Race

White culture includes a narrative of black inferiority. This narrative is pervasive and difficult if not impossible to extract: it permeates everything from the mainstream account of world history to canons of personal beauty and fashion. Blacks are unaware, deluded or self-deceived about the pervasiveness of racism. They buy into white culture to get the minimal benefits of second-class citizenship, itself a source of humiliation and so accept the narrative of black inferiority—which entails that they themselves are inferior. This is self-hatred. Some expressions of self-hatred are direct. If I straighten my hair I am implicitly accepting an aesthetic according to which Caucasian physical characteristics are superior. That aesthetic is a part of the racist package and by accepting it I take on the racist notion that I myself am inferior. Some expressions of self-hatred are less direct. If I buy into features of white culture that aren't explicitly or obviously racist, unaware that they are tainted if only by remote association, I still implicitly accept a package of racist doctrines according to which I am inferior.

To free myself from self-hatred and affirm my worth as a human being I reject the standards according to which characteristics associated with my race are deemed inferior and I reject features of white culture that are tainted. I affirm my personal worth by valuing characteristics associated with my race, by recognizing the achievements of other members of my race, by affirming the value of my ancestral African culture and by identifying it as my culture.

This story is the current "common sense" about race. It is not a radical view and it is not some doctrine peculiar to a politically correct minority: it is mainstream and orthodox—the conventional wisdom, so deeply embedded in popular culture that we do not notice it, much less challenge it. It is the story that puts those black Americans who dislike cornrows or refuse to acknowledge a connection to African culture on the defensive.

And it is false.

First, it assumes a "holistic" understanding of culture according to which apparently disparate features of culture are inextricably linked and racism is pervasive, so that in accepting what appear to be innocent features of the culture we unwittingly associate ourselves with a racist ideology. There is no reason to believe that cultures are locked together in this way rather than thrown together, messy, amorphous, and ever-changing congeries of beliefs, institutions, customs, and practices—like the English language "composed entirely of spare parts."

Second, even if some cultural product is ideologically tainted, there is no reason to believe that by using it I myself affirm or accept the ideology by which it is tainted. I don't use phrases like "that's mighty white of you" or talk about "jewing" someone down on a price, because this language is tainted and to most people offensive. But if I used them in my diary, whether or not I was aware of their origins, it would not follow that I accepted the racist or anti-Semitic notions by which they are tainted.

Third, the story assumes that if my preferences are a causal consequence of popular acceptance of racist doctrines or practices, then by acting on them or even simply by failing to repudiate them, I am accepting the racist ideology that is their source. I do not see why this should be so. I am well aware that my desire for thinness is a consequence of a sexist, patriarchal ideology. I've heard this a thousand times and I suppose I believe it. But I don't care. I reject this ideology, but I still want to be thin, a preference I have not satisfied but do not repudiate. By the same token I am sure that by now every black American knows that the preference for straight hair is part of an aesthetic that has its source in racism. They've heard it a thousand times a thousand times. Most don't care, and there is no reason why they should.

Fourth, "self-hatred" is not a matter of disliking some subset of one's personal characteristics—it is a matter of failing to value one's *self* and acting in ways that are contrary to one's interests. This is a pathology of individuals who feel guilty and ashamed for no reason, who believe that they are unworthy of respect, or who accept bad treatment because they do not believe that they deserve better. Serious self-haters typically can't pin their guilt, shame, or feelings of unworthiness to any personal characteristics—and that only makes them feel worse. There are lots of things about me that I don't like: I don't like being short, I don't like the lines around my mouth, I don't like my inability to do math or my lack of self-discipline—but I like myself just fine.

Fifth, even if I believe that all other members of my race are inferior or defective, it doesn't follow that I believe that I myself am. I may, wrongly, buy into the whole racist ideology but believe that I am a remarkable exception, or I may, rightly, recognize that other members of my race have been trashed by racism, ground down by poverty, and deprived of opportunities.

Sixth, I do not see how my assessment of my own worth is linked in any way to my views about the value of my ancestral culture. Culture is a historical accident: the quality of a culture doesn't reflect on the quality of its members and it certainly doesn't reflect on the quality of their descendents. There is no more reason to imagine that my ancestral culture reflects favorably or unfavorably on me than there is to believe that the character of the town where I was born reflects on me. I was born in a peculiarly unfavorable location, but I don't think I'm any the worse for it.

Finally, I do not see why anyone should identify with an ancestral culture to which they are linked solely by bloodlines, since culture is precisely what is *not* genetically transmitted.

The Story of Race is not only false: it is pernicious. Enhanced and generalized to describe the supposed experience of all minorities, it puts pressure on all nonwhite, non-Anglos to exhibit ethnic pride— which is as silly a notion as pride in the shape of one's big toe—to identify with ancestral cultures to which they have no cultural connection, and to satisfy a variety of role obligations on pain of being castigated as self-hating Oreos, Coconuts, Bananas, or Apples. It induces otherwise reasonable adults to take adolescents' oppositional fads seriously and to fund programs that ghettoize minorities, exacerbate interethnic tensions, discredit progressive policies, and do nothing whatsoever to address the real problems of poverty, poor education, and ongoing discrimination that minorities face.

It is time to stop telling this story, to stop teaching it to kids, and to stop using it as a basis for policy, time to expunge it from popular culture, from the schools, and the academy, and to stop taking it seriously. That, however, will not be an easy thing. Identification with minority ethnic groups is attractive to individuals in societies where mainstream national and cultural identity has worn thin. Moreover, once the Story of Race and other myths of its genre have become established, they are difficult to dislodge. As we shall see, multiculturalism *creates* identities and supports stakeholders who perpetuate it.

NOTES

1. Daniel Finkelstein, "What Do Young Islamic Radicals and Mohican-Styled Punks Have in Common?" Comment Central, TimesOnline, January 29, 2007, http://timesonline.typepad.com/comment/2007/01/young_people _ar.html.

2. Hugh Schofield, "Jewish Dad Backs Headscarf Daughters," BBC News online, October 1, 2003, http://news.bbc.co.uk/2/hi/europe/3149588 .stm.

3. Brendan O'Neill, "Veiled Meanings," December 21, 2006, *Guardian* online, http://commentisfree.guardian.co.uk/brendan_oneill/2006/12/the _vanity_of_the_veil.html.printer.friendly.

4. Ibid.

5. Bill Cosby, address at the NAACP on the 50th anniversary of *Brown v. Board of Education*, May 17, 2004, http://www.americanrhetoric.com/ speeches/billcosbypoundcakespeech.htm.

6. Richard T. Ford, *Racial Culture: A Critique* (Princeton, NJ: Princeton University Press, 2005), pp. 24–25.

7. Ibid., p. 25.

8. Cressida Heyes, "Identity Politics," in *The Stanford Encyclopedia of Philosophy*, Fall 2002 ed., ed. Edward N. Zalta, http://plato.stanford.edu/archives/fall2002/entries/identity-politics.

9. See, for example, Allison Jaggar's critique of "liberal feminism" in *Feminist Frameworks* and elsewhere. Jaggar announces—without argument—that the goal of liberal feminism, leveling the playing field for women, entails commitment to essentially libertarian political policies: according women equal rights under the law and letting the market work. Jaggar's work is a classic of feminist philosophy and is rarely challenged.

Chapter 9

IDENTITY-MAKING

He turned to the flyleaf of the geography and read what he had written there: himself, his name and where he was.

> Stephen Dedalus
> Class of Elements
> Clongowes Wood College
> Sallins
> County Kildare
> Ireland
> Europe
> The World
> The Universe

—James Joyce,
Portrait of the Artist as a Young Man

As a child, Joyce's alter ego Stephen knew exactly where he stood. And so I did, and do, not only in geography but also on a particular branch of a historical culture tree. This sense of one's place in the grand scheme of things is harder to come by these days, so identity-making has become big business. And multiculturalism remains attractive because it creates identity.

MANY MULTICULTURALISMS

> Happy families are all alike; every unhappy family is unhappy in its own way.
>
> —Leo Tolstoy

The Dutch Pillar System:
The Very Model of Modern Multiculturalism

Modern multiculturalism did not arise from the countercultural revolution in the United States during the 1960s or from the Canadian government's official recognition of its English, French, and "First Peoples" communities in 1971. It was born in the Netherlands during the seventeenth century when Catholics and Protestants decided to stop fighting and to live separately together. In the Dutch "pillar" system, which evolved over the centuries, Protestant, Catholic, and, eventually, secular/socialist communities formed separate but equal "pillars" of Dutch society, each with their own neighborhoods, schools, trade unions, hospitals, state-supported media, and political parties. "By the early twentieth century," Jane Kramer, describing "The Dutch Model," writes, "pillar society was for all practical purposes institutionalized. Holland had a Catholic pillar, a Protestant pillar, and a 'humanist' pillar . . . you could grow up Catholic, like [former Christian Democratic Prime Minister] Lubbers, in a big Dutch city and inhabit an entirely Catholic world; you could grow up secular and liberal, like [Theo] van Gogh, and never look at a paper or watch a channel that wasn't yours."

> Pillar society was permissive. It let you alone. You didn't have to love your neighbor, or even accommodate your neighbor, only to "tolerate" him and occasionally come together with him in places where the rules were clear, like parliament. It had nothing to do with

the hybrid adventures of contemporary urban life, and, inevitably, it was crumbling before the Rifians and Turks arrived. The Catholic pillar all but collapsed after Vatican II. But the ethos, and the legal structures, of separateness persisted, and it was the first and often the most enduring lesson about living in Holland that immigrants learned. In the nineteen seventies, when [immigrant labor] recruitment stopped and the Muslims who stayed were allowed to import their families, the world those families entered could, with very little effort, be made to resemble home. . . .

[The] Dutch model for efficiently integrating immigrant labor . . . assured the immigrants' right to "socioeconomic equality," to "inclusion and participation in the political domain," and, finally, to "equity in the domains of culture and religion"—which is to say, the right to be "authentically" themselves.[1]

Pillarization was an updated, egalitarian version of the Ottoman millet system and the very model of modern multiculturalism. As Kramer observes, "authenticity was a nice folkloric fiction—'integration, not assimilation.' . . . Paul Scheffer, a well-known Amsterdam intellectual . . . told me that the country had 'let its immigrants rot in their own privacy.'"

We said, "Leave the children their language of origin. Leave them their own history, because they're going back." It became a mantra. Twenty years went by and they didn't go back, and it was still a mantra. But, once you accept that multicultural argument against teaching them our history, you are excluding them from collective memory, from an enormous chance for renewal. So generation one tried to re-create the fantasy world of home, and generation two had no cultural context, no identification, either with its parents or with the culture here. September 11th gave many of them their narrative. To the extent that radicalization—radical, international Islam—is linked to preventing integration, that may be very difficult to control.[2]

The Dutch, even after recognizing that immigrants, their children, and grandchildren would not go "home," still imagined that Muslims could be incorporated into their own "pillar" even though traditional Catholic, Protestant, and secular/socialist pillars were collapsing under the weight of affluence, secularization, and cosmopolitanism. It produced a Muslim second generation who were deracinated and susceptible to radical Islamicist propaganda.

Since the 2004 murder of Theo van Gogh by an Islamicist fanatic, the Dutch have been agonizing, soul-searching, and trying to understand out how to deal with their Muslim religious minority, which represents over 5 percent of the population, approximately five times the percentage of Episcopalians in the United States. The Dutch still haven't figured it out and remain unhappy in their own way.

The French in Denial: The Will Stockdale Doctrine

In *No Time for Sergeants*, military officials worry about Private Will Stockdale's eyesight, sexual orientation, and sanity when Stockdale, cautioned by his sergeant to ignore female officers' gender, claims not to recognize that a buxom second lieutenant is a woman. The gender-blind policy Stockdale's sergeant urged him to adopt was the model for the French government's policy regarding race. According to the official French ideology, race did not, or at least, should not exist. All French citizens were French and anyone who spoke French, regardless of their race or ethnic origin—at least anyone who spoke decent French—was a citizen of Le Monde Francophone.

Our older son went through elementary school in a French immersion magnet program where he not only became fluent in French but also learned about Canadian coinage and, we discovered, was indoctrinated with cultural ideology. John remembers the world maps hanging in every classroom with countries and regions that belonged to "Le Monde Francophone" colored purple. These included not only France, Quebec, the French West Indies, and francophone Africa, but Vietnam, Lebanon, and Louisiana. According to the official French view, culture tracked language: if you spoke French, you were part of the grand culture; if you didn't, you weren't.

The program at John's school was excellent, the teachers were committed, and the principal was a dynamic woman who brought in speakers from all over Le Monde Francophone to address school assemblies. On one occasion she managed to get a high diplomat from somewhere in francophone Africa—a coup, since most students were black. The diplomat, John reported, began his talk by saying: "I am honored to be here at Knox Elementary School where *even* in America I can speak the civilized language of France."

This official French view was a revival of the ancient Greek scheme according to which the main cultural cut was between Greek-speaking people and Barbarians, where the latter were people "of unintelligible speech" that sounded like "ba-ba" to Greek ears. If you spoke Greek, whether you were male or female, slave or free, and regardless of race or ethnic origin, you were eligible for initiation into the Eleusinian Mysteries, the oldest, most prestigious, and most quintessentially Greek mystery cult in the ancient world, which guaranteed initiates a pleasant afterlife. If you didn't speak Greek, you were not eligible and could go to hell.

The Greeks were tribal, to the extent that citizenship in Greek citystates was strictly hereditary, but they were not racists in the modern sense and, unlike the French, admired other cultures. "Herodotus," Robert Irwin writes, "seems to have been singularly free of racial prejudice and because of his open-minded interest in other cultures he was known as the 'barbarophile.'"

> He wrote an admiring account of the achievements of the Egyptian pharaohs and he harped on the grandeur of Egypt and Lydia before those lands fell to the Persians . . . one thing that struck him about the Persians was their racism: "After their own nation they hold their nearest neighbours most in honour, then the nearest but one—and so on, their respect decreasing as the distance grows, and the most remote being the most despised."[3]

Irwin notes that "[t]he Persians certainly thought of themselves as a distinctive race and they referred to all foreigners as *anarya*, non-Aryans."[4]

The Greeks noticed race. Ancient freethinkers pointed out that

Nubians represented their gods as black, that Thracians depicted theirs as redheaded, and that if horses and oxen had had gods, their gods would look like horses and oxen. The Greeks just did not think that race was of much importance.

By the twentieth century, however, in the wake of the African slave trade, colonial expansion by European powers, and the popularization of Social Darwinism, the pseudo-science of race, and eugenics, race had become fetishized and was impossible to ignore, much as the official French view dictated that it should be invisible. French policy regarding immigrants and minorities assumed the official view that it was language and culture that mattered rather than race. On the ground, however, the French were unabashed racists. Nadir Dendoune, a native-born French citizen, complained that he was called a "Frenchman of Algerian origin." Outside of his hearing, when they were not being careful, his fellow citizens would have called him simply an *Arabian*.

In spite of the official view, it was race and not language or culture that mattered in France, where the fully acculturated, native-born, French-speaking children and grandchildren of immigrants from Northern and Sub-Saharan Africa continued to face discrimination in employment and a variety of social disadvantages. As commonly interpreted, however, the official view of race made it impossible to address ongoing racism. With impeccable logic, French policymakers inferred that since race could not be officially recognized, then neither could racism. Since racism could not be recognized, it could not be addressed. Impeccable logic, however, has its limitations, as I was reminded by a comment on one of my course evaluations for the logic class I regularly teach: "What's the point of being logical if no one else is?" French officialdom was color-blind—even though no one was.

In the aftermath of the 2005 riots in French immigrant suburbs, French policymakers have begun rethinking their policies and have considered adopting color-conscious policies in the interests of counteracting racism and, ultimately, producing a color-blind society—a goal that is currently remote. Until then, after decades of denial, the French remain unhappy in their own way.

Anglo-Saxon Empiricism: The Usual Muddle

Turning to the United States and United Kingdom, with side glances at Canada and Australia, where multiculturalism in its classic form has flourished for the past four decades, the goal of policies intended to address diversity has been unclear. Few Americans or Britons are seriously interested in pillarization or in the establishment of a millet system, yet few, apart from myself, would hold that the aim should be to establish a society in which members of racial minorities and immigrants shed their ethnic identities and become "unhyphenated" citizens. As far as I can tell, the goal of policies in Le Monde Anglophone has been, in the spirit of Rodney King, "getting along together" and accommodating cultural preferences to the extent that they are not socially disruptive.

English-speaking peoples have been remarkably consistent in the character of their own culturally specific unhappiness, and multiculturalist programs in the United States and the United Kingdom have been remarkably similar in spite of the fact that the "diverse" whom multiculturalism is supposed to accommodate have been very different.

In the United Kingdom, the diverse group that gets the most attention are Muslims, chiefly of South Asian origin. In the United States, the first group to receive the questionable benefits of multiculturalism were black Americans—native-born, English-speaking, US citizens with roots in America going back centuries, who were not by any stretch culturally alien and, indeed, were quintessentially American. Currently the focus of multiculturalism in the United States has shifted to Hispanics, a genuine immigrant group but one that, compared to immigrant populations in Britain and European countries, are about as unalien as any immigrant group can be: Catholics from next door who speak an easy Romance language.

In light of this, it may seem that whereas multicultural policies in Britain and continental Europe were intended to accommodate profound cultural differences, multiculturalism in America sought to perpetuate and enhance cultural identity or even to create it ex nihilo.

This, however, is not quite right, because in fact multiculturalism was instrumental in shaping, if not creating, Muslim identity in the United Kingdom. The 2007 report of the British Policy Exchange, *Living Apart Together*, notes:

> Although Muslims have lived in Britain since the nineteenth century, it is only in the last two decades that we have seen the development of a strong Muslim identity in the public sphere. Until the 1970s, it was ethnicity, not religion, which dominated the way Muslims perceived themselves. Older migrants are much more likely to identify with their ethnic or national identity, whilst identification with Islam is much more prevalent amongst the younger generation. ... The "Muslim identity" is therefore not an unchanging, monolithic entity, but something that has developed through a sequence of historical events and processes.[5]

Moreover, as the report notes, it is the younger generation of Muslims, native-born and acculturated, who exhibit the strongest Muslim identity. The report argues, compellingly, that multicultural policies figured significantly in the sequence of historical events that shaped and enhanced Muslim identity. Whether or not we agree with the results of the report, which issues from a center right think tank, a number of the trends, events, and policies are strikingly similar to phenomena that have figured on the American scene. It is worthwhile to consider some of these.

CULTURAL SELF-HATRED AND NATIONAL HUMILIATION

Leaving aside the authors' analyses, the data they report comparing young Muslims to members of their parents' and grandparents' generations is striking. The young are not only more likely to form a strong Muslim identity than their elders, they are more religious, more conservative, and more likely to express a greater sense of kinship with fellow Muslims around the world than with fellow British. Ironically, it seems, native-born, English-speaking young Muslims feel less British than less acculturated members of earlier generations. Intriguingly, the report suggests, this is not peculiar to Muslims but is rather a consequence of "confusion in the wider society about what belonging to Britain actually means."

> One of the principle factors in undermining British identity has been the rise of the politics of multiculturalism. Intellectual fashion has dictated that right-minded people should feel shame and guilt about Britain's imperial past and embarrassment about overt manifestations of national pride.[6]

Muslims were not alone in being confused about their national identity and embarrassed about being British, the report suggests, because confusion and embarrassment were cultivated and rewarded.

The same phenomenon was even more striking in the United States. Like most Americans of my generation, as a child I was infused with a sense of identity as an American, and even with a subidentity as a Patersonian and a super-identity as an inhabitant of Le Monde Anglophone. I had a jigsaw puzzle of the United States and paper dolls of the British royal family. I learned by heart the Preamble to the Constitution, the Gettysburg Address, all the presidents from Washington to John F. Kennedy, and the principle products and capitals of every state in the union. In eighth grade I learned the history of Paterson and the state of New Jersey—whose counties I can still recite in alphabetical order. I celebrated the American liturgical year including Memorial Day, Flag Day, Fourth of July, Labor Day, Columbus Day, Veterans' Day, and Thanksgiving. Some of what I learned was "patriotic," though none of it was partisan. However, much of it was not patriotic or even remotely political: I learned about crops and where they grew, industries and the land, and I learned stories about cultural worthies, from King Alfred and the Cakes to George Washington and the Cherry Tree to countless stories illustrating Lincoln's honesty and humor.

Like Stephen Dedalus, I knew *exactly* where I fit into the grand scheme of things: I was from Paterson, founded by Alexander

Hamilton in the Piedmont region of New Jersey on the Fall Line, in the United States of America, the history of which went back to the Civil War, the American Revolution, and the Pilgrim Fathers, part of the community of English-speaking peoples that went back to England, to Europe, to the Roman Empire, and finally to Greece, where I was born twenty-five hundred years ago. Beyond that, there was the World and the Universe. Now *that* was identity!

That thick sense of identity as an American collapsed when the Right appropriated it for political purposes, to promote support for the disastrous war in Vietnam and for the matchlessly abominable Richard Nixon. By the time I was in college, anything perceptibly American was for that reason alone the immediate object of scorn and derision or heavy irony. In the spirit of some feminists of the flaky fringe who called themselves "womyn" to get the "men" out, radicals spelled "America" with a "k" in place of the "c" to suggest that the United States was a Kafkaesque nightmare.

American identity had become politicized. America had ceased to be a piece of land with a history where people lived—it had become an ideology. America *was* racism, grasping materialism, international aggression, neocolonialism, and above all the war in Vietnam. No one I knew wanted to be American. It should hardly be surprising that there was an interest in alternative identities and affinity groups, and that Americans who hated the conservative political agenda preferred to identify as female, black, Hispanic, deaf or disabled, or, for that matter, as Capricorns, vegetarians, or Hare Krishnas. Anything but Amerikan!

MAKING OFFENSE

America had become so identified with an ideology that all symbols of American identity became politically loaded. The American flag in particular, which for most Americans had been a sacramental object— as I learned from my Girl Scout training, it couldn't touch the ground, had to be taken down before nightfall, and must be folded in a special, triangular pattern—became a symbol of the conservative political agenda at home and abroad. Within this system of meaning, the American flag necessarily made a statement, and a very different one from the statement any other flag made. Canadians could fly their maple leaf or sew it to their backpacks to show where they came from or which team they supported, but, from the Vietnam era to 9/11, flying the American flag was affirming support for conservative politics, militarism, and aggression, and making an in-your-face statement of American supremacy.

Regardless of your personal views on these matters, you could not display the American flag just to show where you came from or what team you supported, and you could not fly the flag on the Fourth of July simply because it was a holiday symbol, like the Christmas tree, Thanksgiving turkey, or Easter egg. Meaning is human-made but public: if, for whatever reason, a system of meanings becomes current within a community, no individual can opt out. You cannot change the meaning of a word or other symbol unilaterally by forming intentions that are different from other people's intentions or conjuring up different ideas in your head. Try saying "table" and meaning "chair." Once the American flag had been established as an ideological symbol, you could not display it without affirming a commitment to the ideology, regardless of what you may have had in mind, even if you only wanted to fly it because you liked doing holiday decorations.

Meanings are not in the head. They are socially created and public. As I discovered to my dismay as an undergraduate I could not go out in public wearing jeans and a T-shirt without making a political statement comparable to the ideological spellings "womyn" and "Amerika." Nowadays I dress exactly as I did when I was in college with exactly the same ideological intentions—namely none—but, because I'm older and because the symbolic conventions have changed, no one thinks that I'm making a political statement. They know I'm just a slob. Sometimes a cigar is just a cigar, but, unfortunately, because meaning is public when people think it's more than a cigar—so it is.

Because meaning is public, the widespread assumption that a

symbol or practice is offensive *makes* it offensive; common assumptions about meaning *confer* meaning. Multiculturalists, in the interests of cultural sensitivity, obsessed about the meanings of cultural symbols and the offense they might cause to minorities. Intent on avoiding offense, they publicized the offensive meanings they imagined they had discovered, in order to persuade the public to avoid using such symbols. In most cases it is debatable whether such symbols initially had the offensive meanings multiculturalists claimed to discover. However, once multiculturalists succeeded in persuading the public that these symbols had offensive meanings, they ipso facto *acquired* the meanings in question and became offensive. Multiculturalists engaged systematically in the project of making offense. They scrutinized linguistic usage, cultural symbols, and practices, "discovered" that they were covertly offensive, exclusionary, or demeaning, publicized their results and, to the extent that people believed them, *made* these usages offensive, exclusionary, and demeaning.

To see this, consider a stock case: multiculturalist objections to naming sports teams as "Indians," "Aztecs," or "Braves." I never understood what the problem was, since no one objected to calling teams "Vikings," "Celtics," or "Fighting Irish." Then I finally got it: a Native American group on campus had tacked up yet another sign objecting to the practice that screamed: "I'M A PERSON—NOT A MASCOT!" Fair enough, I thought. If that is what naming teams after Indian tribes *means*, they have a legitimate grievance. If it reduces Indians to two-dimensional figures, cartoon characters, pets, or toys, they have a reasonable complaint. But this meaning is not something that is inherent in the nature of things and, like all meanings, it is human-made. It seems likely, indeed, that it was made by the multiculturalists who imagined that they had discovered it.

Before the multiculturalist program was up and running, these Indian names did not offend Indians or anyone else. To name a team the "Aztecs" or the "Vikings" was to associate it with a group of people who were supposed to be brave, powerful, and capable of doing serious damage on the football field. It was not demeaning to their descendents and did not reduce them to mascots. No one imagined that naming the Minnesota team the "Vikings" reflected adversely on either the Vikings' direct descendents in Iceland or their peripheral descendents in Minnesota, and no one thought that naming the San Diego State team the "Aztecs" was any different. Multiculturalists, however, *guessed* that Indians were offended and believed that, even if they weren't, they *should* be—because multiculturalists thought that, through some program of speculative hermeneutics, they had teased out the true meaning of the practice of naming football teams after Indian tribes. In fact, this is not a meaning they discovered but one that they *made* by publicizing and promoting their supposed discovery.

Even worse, in some cases the multiculturalists' project of making offense began with offensive stereotypes. The Policy Exchange report describes how "[a]t Aberdeen University, army cadets were asked by the Officer Training Corps (OTC) to remove their uniforms when marching past a mosque." I cannot resist observing that Muslims had every right to be offended by naked cadets marching past their house of worship; however, as it turned out, Muslims had no objections to uniformed cadets on parade. The report notes: "A leading community figure and worshipper at the mosque, Habib Malik" said, with characteristic British understatement, "I am very surprised the OTC has done this . . . the Moslem community respects soldiers and thinks the Army is doing a wonderful job."[7]

The first thing that strikes one about this story is that the OTC never bothered to *ask* members of the mosque or their representatives whether they were offended by uniformed cadets marching past the premises. Multiculturalists rarely ask. They get the notion that women or blacks, Hispanics, Indians, or Muslims, will be offended by a practice and go from there, as the OTC did. At best, they may conjure up a member of the "community" who can be persuaded, or bribed, into taking offense. Even more disturbing is the question of why the officer assumed that Muslims would, or perhaps even should, be offended by cadets in uniform marching past their mosque. He might have had cause for concern if the cadets' route went past a Quaker meetinghouse. Muslims, however, are not known as pacifists, and it is hard to see what he imagined they would have found objectionable other than the exposure to the British military as such. His assumption seems to have been that Muslims were unpatriotic, did not support the British military, and were likely to make trouble if cadets in uniform marched past their mosque.

Multiculturalists quite often second-guess how members of "diverse" groups feel about things on the basis of assumptions that are not only false but offensive and patronizing. During the '90s, the Anglican Church's "Decade of Evangelism," when local churches went all out to attract minorities, a priest complained to me that, at a diocesan workshop on evangelism, clergy were warned to avoid the then fashionable turquoise and mauve shades in signage and "materials" because such colors were "exclusionary" and, in particular, sent the message to Hispanics that they were not welcome. Priests were advised to use "bright primary colors" in the interests of being "inclusive." I do not know whether his story was true, but it was close enough to be interesting. I sat on the diocesan Commission on Evangelism and heard innumerable proposals for attracting minorities by dumbing down, crapping up, sentimentalizing, simplifying, and vulgarizing what the church had to offer: the church, in an agony of multiculturalism, assumed that the minorities it was keen to win over were ignorant, stupid, illiterate, and tasteless, and that they were attracted by shiny objects and "bright primary colors."

Even when concern about the supposed sensitivities of disadvantaged groups did not reflect the bigoted or patronizing assumptions of bien-pensants, offense-making almost always backfired on members of the disadvantage groups whose interests they aimed to protect. Once linguistic usages, symbols, or practices had become objectionable to women, minorities, or members of other disadvantaged groups, those who took offense were castigated by the Right as hypersensitive.

When, for example, some feminists made a fuss about practices that in their symbol system "sexualized" or "objectified" women, the antifeminist Right was able to persuade the majority of the American public, who regarded these practices as innocuous, that feminists were silly, hypersensitive—and dangerous. A man hangs a girlie calendar in his workspace. What's the big deal? Men like to look at naked women; women like to look at Currier and Ives prints or cats. For the man, this calendar does not symbolize anything: sometimes a cigar is just a cigar. To a feminist-trained woman, however, this calendar has vast symbolic import. It "objectifies" women, represents them as little more than meat. This is offensive. Moreover, within this frame of reference, by displaying the calendar the man is marking his territory as a *guy space*, a He-Man Woman-Haters Club where women aren't welcome—except as sex objects. Feminists operating within this symbol system object. Their objections are legitimate to the extent that *if* the calendar had this symbolic value it would, and should, be offensive to women. It is not at all clear that the calendar had this symbolic import before it was "discovered" and the public was duly informed. Once the program of offense-making has progressed to this point, however, there is no turning back. Once a significant number of people have come to regard the calendar as a symbol of male dominance and female "objectification," that is what it becomes.

Now the antifeminist Right can make its case to men for whom the calendar is just a calendar, without symbolic import. First, this shows (as we've known all along) that women are overly emotional and hypersensitive. Second, if feminists make a fuss about a crappy calendar, it just shows that women don't have anything real to complain about. Discrimination in employment? Baloney—they're just huffy about dumb calendars and other trivia. Third—watch out! She can take you to court for "hostile environment." Women can sue you for girlie calendars, chance remarks they regard as sexist (because, as we know, they're hypersensitive), politically incorrect screen savers, and any number of other things that you can't even imagine. You have to be ultra-careful. It's probably safest just not to hire women—they're difficult to deal with and dangerous. Of course, if you have the guts and there's a woman around that you want to squeeze out, now you know how to create a hostile environment to make her life miserable.

Once again, offense-making backfires, and cultural sensitivity harms the very people it is supposed to benefit.

After this excursion into the dynamics of offense-making, let us return to the United Kingdom. Suppose the British government had made it a matter of explicitly stated public policy to "protect" Muslims from all contact with uniformed military personnel. Adopting and publicizing this policy would send the message to the public, including Muslims, that Muslim identity was inconsistent with support for the British armed forces and, presumably, with serving one's country in the military. The negative stereotype of Muslims would then become all the more firmly entrenched, and the prediction that Muslims would be hostile to the military would likely become a self-fulfilling prophecy.

This phenomenon is also familiar. It has become a tradition at my university to administer the Academic Integrity Pledge to entering students during the freshman convocation at the start of the academic year. Freshman, facing the solemn assembly of faculty in regalia, are required to stand and repeat a solemn oath not to cheat, administered by a high official in student government. In addition, student government provides stickers imprinted with the pledge to faculty, who are urged to paste them on tests. I do not believe that there is a single student who does not know that he is not supposed to cheat or who would be dissuaded from cheating by the Academic Integrity Pledge or the stickers. Indeed, the pledge and stickers send the message that cheating is a normal part of college life and predicts that students will cheat, or at least be strongly tempted to do so—a self-fulfilling prophecy.

I never cheated when I was a student because it never occurred to me. I thought of my academic work as my achievement, a test of my ability and performance, and would no more turn in a plagiarized paper than I would cheat in a race or other competition, lip-synch a vocal solo, or pretend that a store-bought sweater was my own knitting. Maybe even more importantly—possibly as a consequence of my Girl Scout training—I assumed that cheating was so bad and so likely to get you into big trouble that it wasn't even within the realm of normal badness: it was up there with shooting heroin or pouring sugar into someone's gas tank. The message that University of San Diego students were getting, by contrast, was that cheating was just normal undergraduate badness, like binge drinking or smoking dope. Much worse, the Academic Integrity Pledge, stickers, and other paraphernalia aimed at discouraging cheating contributed to defining the student role: students were not in the business of competing and achieving for their own satisfaction, with grades as an acknowledgment and reward. They were playing an adversarial game with faculty and promising to play fair.

In the same way, multicultural policies do not simply accommodate preexisting cultural identities: they help to create them and define their character. British multicultural policies helped to create Muslim identity in the United Kingdom by second-guessing what Muslims as a "community"—not Bengalis, Kashmiris, or Pakistanis—would and, presumably should, want and what would offend them.

Perhaps even more importantly, the government and other funding agencies bankrolled "community leaders," often self-appointed, and organizations that claimed to represent their ethnic "community." In the United Kingdom, until recently the government's primary "dialogue partner" for contact with the "Muslim community" was the Muslim Council of Britain, an umbrella organization representing only 20 percent of British Muslim organizations and that, according to the Policy Exchange report, only 6 percent of the Muslim population regarded as representative of their views. In the United States things are pretty much the same: government agencies, foundations, and private contributors fund individuals who set up as "community leaders" and agencies they imagine will represent the interests of ethnic "communities," who keep their members occupied and prevent them from causing trouble. Multiculturalism thus creates a class of stakeholders who define their respective "communities" and "eat off of" multiculturalism.

MULTICULTURAL PORK

The Policy Exchange report cites a remarkable statement in the suicide video of Mohammad Sidique Khan, the ringleader of the London bombings. Said Khan: "I have forsaken everything for what I believe in. Your democratically elected governments continue to perpetuate atrocities against my people all over the world."[8]

Other Muslims, the report notes, begged to differ.

> Nobody elected Khan. As far as we know, he did not have relations with anyone in Palestine, Bosnia or Chechnya. Indeed, he did not even bother to ask his family, friends or neighbours what they thought. At the local mosque near where three of the bombers grew up, one of the committee members, Muhboob Hussein, reacted with anger to 7/7: "This is not Islam, this is not *jihad*, these people are not Muslim. This man [Khan] never came to our mosque. . . ." As one Muslim respondant told us: "I thought they were just selfish and just scum."[9]

Reflecting, the writers of the report note: "With impeccable logic, Khan deduced that anyone who shouts loud enough and claims to speak on behalf of a community can win the ear of government. Instead of challenging Khan's pomposity, many commentators have instead urged the Government to see Khan as a voice of the angry Muslim world, or at least recognize the legitimacy of his demands."[10] Everything changes, yet everything remains the same. In 1970 Tom Wolfe published "Mau-Mauing the Flak-Catchers" as a companion piece to "Radical Chic," in which he described the strategies self-appointed representatives of ethnic communities used to extract funding from flak-catching government welfare bureaucrats and the white liberal establishment. Khan was the ultimate Mau-Mau, threatening violence to secure benefits for "his" people all over the world and blowing himself up to make good on his threat. Most Mau-Maus, however, were just looking for jobs and grants—which were readily available.

In the United Kingdom, the perception of Muslim victimhood and sensitivity created exaggerated anxiety about giving offense. Authorities operated on the assumption that Muslims where hypersensitive and needed to be accommodated and the fear that they were "so unruly and angry" that they needed to be appeased" and were so oppressed that they needed to be given "voice" through community organizations that purported to represent them.[11] The lengths to which they went were picked up by the media and, as the report suggests "helped to foster a belief that Muslims are unduly sensitive":

> In 2003 the local council in High Wycombe, Buckinghamshire banned an advertisement for a Christmas carol service arguing that religious issues could inflame tensions in the multi-ethnic community. In 2005 Dudley Council banned all images of pigs in its offices (including on calendars, cuddly toys, etc.) because one Muslim complained about a consignment of pig-shaped stress toys. The Tate Modern controversially withdrew an art work by John Latham which featured a copy of the Qu'ran, although no Muslim had actually complained. The London Underground banned a poster for an American television series, which pointed out that the central hero fighting terrorism was a Muslim. . . . In 2003, a prison officer in Suffolk was dismissed from his post after making a joke about Osama Bin Laden in the presence of Asian visitors, even though the tribunal could not establish whether they had even overheard the remark.[12]

Local authorities also established and funded social clubs and other facilities devoted to serving Muslims and other identity groups and organizations to represent their supposed interests. So, in 1997 the government established the Muslim Council of Britain to "give voice" to Muslim citizens. "Since the late 1980s the Government has consulted with Muslim groups in order to gauge Muslim opinion on a range of issues. This has been encouraged by the broader political framework of multiculturalism, which categorizes citizens into religious, ethnic and cultural groups. The Muslim Council of Britain (MCB) was set up in 1997 at the request of the then Conservative Home Secretary, Michael Howard, to act as the coherent and unified voice of Muslims to the Government."[13]

On the face of it, this program seems puzzling. Muslims, like other British citizens, had the vote and access to the political process. It is hard to see why the home secretary should have imagined that there was some special need to create a special organization to represent them. Moreover, as the report noted, only 6 percent of the Muslim population of the United Kingdom believed that the MCB *did* in fact represent their views and concerns.[14]

Most Americans, however, will immediately recognize what was going on: the government was dispensing "pork"—to Muslims. And once Muslims got their bacon and chops, other identity groups demanded their piece of the pork pie. "The politics of multiculturalism," the report notes, "has created a curious dynamic: some groups demand special protections for their particular identity, which in turn encourages other groups to make their own demands."[15] The story is familiar to all of us who come from tribal territories dominated by corrupt machine politics. In cities with large ethnically identified populations who bloc voted, politicians regularly negotiated with what the British called "community leaders" who represented their ethnic communities and were able to deliver votes (one way or another). During the latter half of the twentieth century, as white ethnicity waned and bloc voting became a thing of the past, classic machine politics disintegrated and most of us thought that was good.

The remarkable thing about the British program was that it not only represented an attempt to reproduce a corrupt system that most Americans found loathsome but that it was done openly, officially, and even piously. The British, it seemed, aimed to re-create Tammany Hall—and congratulated themselves on it. In much the same way, even though in the United States classic white-ethnic machine politics as we knew it had largely disappeared by the end of the twentieth century, the new ethnic politics was a vital force. Throughout the country there was a sense that locally significant ethnic minorities had to be accommodated, mollified, "given voice," and funded.

When we took our kids to the zoo in Balboa Park years ago, we used to pass by a squat cylindrical building decorated with murals in bright primary colors, which announced itself as the Centro Cultural de la Raza. I was never sure what this place was, until, while writing this book, I checked its Web site and discovered that the Centro Cultural de la Raza was a "non-profit cultural arts organization, established in 1970 (but housed in its current building since 1971) whose mission is to create, promote, preserve and educate about Mexicana/o, Chicana/o, Latina/o and Indigenous art and culture."[16] A "partial list of funders" at the site acknowledged that in addition to corporate sponsors, including AOL Time Warner, Bank of America, Merrill Lynch, and Washington Mutual, the project was financed by City of San Diego OSP, City of San Diego CDBG, City of San Diego ADA, City Council District 3, County of San Diego, and the San Diego mayor's office.[17]

Just down the road, I discovered that another building of the same size and shape housed the WorldBeat Cultural Center, "dedicated to promoting, presenting, and preserving the Indigenous cultures of the world through music, art, education, culture, and technology."[18] The WorldBeat Center, its Web site announced, was established in 1985 and "dedicated to the African and Indigenous Diaspora" presumably to achieve parity for blacks. Most multicultural projects in the San Diego area, however, were devoted to Mexicana/o, Chicana/o, and Latina/o concerns, including the nationally famous Chicano Park murals. The outdoor art project was initiated in 1970, during a protest movement, after the City of San Diego reneged on its promise to create a park for residents of the Barrio Logan neighborhood to compensate for homes and businesses that were demolished for freeway construction. The murals designed by local Mexicana/o, Chicana/o, and Latina/o artists adorning freeway support pillars are technically proficient and hideous. Dedicated to the Nation of Aztlán, they include a mural representing the Rage of La Raza, described by the Chicano Park Web page as an expression of "the rage of the people, of Mexican-American people."

The lower section of pylon number four contains the logo for Chicano Park. . . . A hand reaches up to place a blue dot on San Diego, illustrating the location of Chicano Park with the greater homeland of Aztlan, which is painted red within the map of the United States. . . . A male face peers outward with a look of intense distrust, while a nude woman confronts the viewer, with a gun in her left hand. She holds the hand of a child of the future who appears to be gliding upon an undulating green ribbon. "These images symbolized the inter-national and cosmic character of the [Chicano] movement. Above the Rage of La Raza, a cosmic landscape contains Saturn, the sun, and a swastika within a central radiating disc.[19]

The Wikipedia entry for Chicano Park history is especially entertaining:

On his way to school, a community member, San Diego City College student, and Brown Beret named Mario Solis noticed bulldozers next to the area designated for the park. When he inquired about the nature of the work being undertaken, he was shocked to discover that, rather than a park, the crew was preparing to build a parking lot next to a building that would be converted into a California Highway Patrol station. Since the community had many grievances against the local police and law enforcement in general already, this was considered a slap in the face. . . . Solis went door-to-door to spread the news of the construction. At school, he alerted the students of Professor Gil Robledo's Chicano studies class, who printed fliers to bring more attention to the affair. . . . Solis is reported to have commandeered a bulldozer to flatten the land for planting. Also, notably, the flag of Aztlán was raised on an old telephone pole, marking a symbolic "reclamation" of land that was once Mexico by people of Mexican descent.[20]

A large portrait of Solis, in his brown beret with the inscription "Varrio si, Yonkes no" dominates the Chicano Park display. The inscription alludes to the junkyards—"yonkes"—which blighted the neighborhood before Solis and his followers persuaded the city of San Diego to zone them out. Before researching the matter, I assumed that the subject of the portrait was Che Guevara and that the punning inscription meant "Barrio, yes; Yankees (that's *me*), no."

Unlike conservative opponents of multiculturalism, I am not in the least worried that Hispanics intend to reclaim the Southwest, either by violence or outbreeding, in order to establish a state of Aztlán. Residents of Barrio Logan were quite reasonably angry because the city of San Diego went back on its promise to build them a park. A college student from the neighborhood, with the cooperation of his professor, initiated a protest as a class project; local artists came up with the idea of painting murals in the revolutionary style of the period on pylons and managed to get funding for the project. It was harmless fun, and local residents got the park to which they were entitled.

Nevertheless, between Chicano Park, the Centro Cultural de la Raza, the Worldbeat Center, and innumerable other ethnic social, cultural, educational, and political projects funded by corporate sponsors and local government, there are legions of artists, "community organizers," folk dance instructors, political activists, and bureaucrats eating multicultural pork. They have an interest in preserving and promoting ethnic identity. Businesses, government agencies, and individuals, out of guilt and fear, or simply in the interest of public relations, financed cultural identity projects, and so it became possible to make a career of multiculturalism. Ethnicity, which individuals latched onto in their quest for identity and formed by the program of offense-making, was perpetuated by careerist stakeholders.

Once established, it is easy to see how the multicultural system perpetuated itself. The intriguing question is why corporate sponsors, government agencies, and middle-class white liberals began funding this system in the first place and why, in particular, they favored precisely those programs that, at least for rhetorical purposes, adopted oppositional identities and often represented themselves as foes of corporations, the government, and middle-class white liberals. The reason, I shall suggest, is that the "radicalism" of these groups was harmless and, indeed, that their funders and fellow-travelers believed that by supporting their projects they could mollify their members and supposed constituents.

NOTES

1. Jane Kramer, "The Dutch Model: Multiculturalism and Muslim Immigrants," *New Yorker* 82 (April 3, 2006): 60–67.

2. Ibid.

3. Robert Irwin, *Dangerous Knowledge: Orientalism and Its Discontents* (Woodstock, NY: Overlook Press, 2006), p. 13.

4. Ibid., pp. 11–12.

5. Munira Mirza, Abi Senthikumaran, and Zein Ja'far, *Living Apart Together: British Muslims and the Paradox of Multiculturalism* (London: Policy Exchange, 2007).

6. Ibid., p. 33.

7. Ibid., p. 34.

8. Ibid.

9. Ibid.

10. Ibid., p. 82.

11. Ibid., p. 78.

12. Ibid., pp. 75–76.

13. Ibid., p. 78.

14. Ibid., p. 80.

15. Ibid., p. 77.

16. Centro Cultural de la Raza Web site, http://www.centroraza .com/history.htm.

17. Ibid.

18. WorldBeat Cultural Center Web site, http://www.worldbeatcenter .org/.

19. Chicano Park Web site, http://www.chicanoparksandiego.com/ murals/logo.html.

20. "Chicano Park," Wikipedia entry, http://en.wikipedia.org/wiki/ Chicano_Park.

Chapter 10

IDENTITY POLITICS

The Making of a Mystique

And, behold, men brought in a bed a man which was taken with a palsy: and they sought [means] to bring him in, and to lay [him] before him. And when they could not find by what [way] they might bring him in because of the multitude, they went upon the housetop, and let him down through the tiling with [his] couch into the midst before Jesus. And when he saw their faith, he said unto him, Man, thy sins are forgiven thee. And the scribes and the Pharisees began to reason, saying, Who is this which speaketh blasphemies? Who can forgive sins, but God alone? But when Jesus perceived their thoughts, he answering said unto them, What reason ye in your hearts? Whether is easier, to say, Thy sins be forgiven thee; or to say, Rise up and walk?

—Luke 5:18–23

Within a decade of the passage of the Civil Rights Act of 1964, the culmination of a hard-fought century-long battle for racial integration, Martin Luther King Jr.'s dictum that individuals should be judged on the content of their character and not on the color of their skin was viewed as, at best, naive, and even the very word *integration* had become suspect. Identity politics, including the Story of Race, and more broadly, multiculturalism, became the new orthodoxy for political liberals. It is worth asking why.

The short answer is that, first, as a consequence of domestic legal history and international politics, the ideal of color-blindness mandated by the civil rights movement was appropriated by the political Right to push its agendas. Second, and perhaps more importantly, identity politics, for all its radical rhetoric, was essentially conservative. It did not challenge the widely held view that blacks, or at least most of them, could not cut it by "white" standards and it did not promote integration.

Multiculturalism valorized racial and ethnic stereotypes in order to promote respect for members of disadvantaged minorities. Respect, self-esteem, pride, dignity, and other intangibles were cheap, and American multiculturalists became convinced that they could fix social problems on the cheap by dispensing these intangibles: it is easier to say "your sins are forgiven" than to say "rise up and walk." They hoped in particular that they could curb the antisocial behavior of young underclass males by promoting self-esteem.

DECONSTRUCTING MALCOLM X:
THE HARMLESSNESS OF RADICALISM

Everyone I knew back in college liked Malcolm X—and everyone I knew back in college was white and rich. Why on earth did they like someone who hated rich white people? Even more mysteriously, within a decade after I graduated, Alex Haley's *Autobiography of Malcolm X* had become a staple of coming-of-age literature in high school English classes. Why, I wondered, would teachers set up Malcolm, a school dropout given to drinking, drugs, gambling, and criminal activity as a "role model" for high school students? And why, I wondered, did the Story of Race developed in the *Autobiography*, which was canonized in the Black Power movement and identity politics, become orthodoxy for privileged white liberals?

By reflecting on these mysteries, I believe we will be in a better position to make sense of the rise of multiculturalism in American culture as well as the making of the multicultural mystique.

One reason that Malcolm's *Autobiography* became a classic coming-of-age book was that by the mid-twentieth century adolescence had become deeply problematic, and so it was de rigueur for the heroes of such works to be countercultural—and Malcolm filled the bill. Because the standard educational program for Americans was extended into late adolescence or longer, there was a large population of individuals aged roughly fourteen to thirty, sexually mature and able to fend for themselves, who were socially defined as children— classified as "students," financially dependent on parents, unmarried, and officially expected to be celibate. Relegated to this limbo, we were angry with our parents and angry at the culture generally.

We looked for countercultural heroes. At their least offensive, countercultural heroes were sensitive preppies like Holden Caulfield, stewing about adult "phoniness," and the self-congratulatory junior members of Salinger's Glass family, dabbling in Eastern religions. At midrange they were greasers, like *Happy Days'* Fonzie, or his prototype, the young Elvis. At their worst they were bad black dudes like Malcolm. Holden, Fonzie, and Malcolm were attractive to adolescents because they challenged mainstream practices and values, but they were acceptable to adults because, in the end, they were tame.

Adults recognized that Malcolm was sufficiently countercultural to connect with disaffected youth and to address legitimate social concerns, but that in the end, he was tame enough to model the journey from confused adolescent rebellion to principled adult participation in a loyal opposition. School authorities adopted Malcolm X's *Autobiography* for much the same reason that the British government adopted conservative, politicized Muslims from the Muslim Council of Britain as representatives of "the Muslim community." The thinking was that Muslims who had the potential to cause trouble wouldn't pay attention to liberal Muslims, who were *too* tame. To keep a lid on the disaffected, the government had to negotiate with Muslims who would not be dismissed as Uncle Toms but who were just tame enough to promote its agenda to potential troublemakers. Disaffected young Muslims had to be inoculated with a live but weakened strain of the virus—dead viruses would not do.

This was the appeal of Malcolm X. He was bad enough and angry enough to get a hearing from the bad, angry young men school authorities wanted to control, but in the end, he was tame. And he was tamed in the standard way, by getting religion. It hardly mattered to most Americans at the time that the religion in question was Islam, or that it provided support for the ideology of black militancy and black separatism. It was strong religion, it was puritanical, and it promoted "family values," including the subordination of women—just the ticket, Americans thought, to get an angry young black man to give up drugs, drink, and petty crime and put his life in order. There was even some hint that after his pilgrimage to Mecca, Malcolm was in the process of repudiating some of his more radical antiwhite sentiments and that, had he not been assassinated, he might have become intolerably mellow as an elder statesman of American Islam and paterfamilias, lighting Kwanzaa candles with his wife and six daughters.

For all that, Malcolm X's *Autobiography* was an improvement over much of the Horatio Alger literature I read in school. Our ninth-grade reader included excerpts from Booker T. Washington's cringing autobiography *Up from Slavery*, as well as biographical sketches of other poor Americans who had achieved success, immigrants and even a woman—aviatrix Jacqueline Cochrane. The message was that individuals could overcome poverty, hardship, and the social handicaps of race and sex through persistence and hard work. I didn't believe a word of it or remember anyone in my class who did. The people in these stories were special cases, famous people—they were, after all, famous enough to have stories written about them—and the stories were just more of the usual baloney, the official story that had nothing to do with the way things really were. At my school I couldn't even take shop or mechanical drawing; I didn't see any way that I would get the chance to fly. Everyone knew that if girls went to college, they'd be teachers and if they didn't, they'd be secretaries. And black women cleaned houses. That was just the way things were.

The stories we read said nothing about the injustice of the disadvantages their heroes had to fight. If prejudice or discrimination got any mention at all, it was little more than as hardships inherent in the nature of things, which heroes could overcome with perseverance and hard work in the way that Helen Keller, the subject of another story, had overcome her handicaps. In the Booker T. Washington story, as in *Pinky*, there was some notion that if black people were diligent, humble, and sacrificed to "help their people," things might be improved. This seemed even less fair: why should anyone, because of their race, have to be more virtuous, work harder, and end up worse off anyway? I thought Pinky should have married the doctor: if it was OK for white girls who were nurses, like Donna Stone on the old *Donna Reed Show*, to marry doctors and live happy, suburban lives, why wasn't it OK for Pinky?

The Autobiography of Malcolm X was an improvement. The Story of Race it popularized was also an improvement because it recognized racism as an injustice and repudiated any obligation to be extra good or to work self-sacrificially without making waves to uplift one's people in order to please whites and get the benefits of second-class citizenship. So far so good—but there it stopped. The political agenda, if any, petered out in innocuous projects like Renee Rogers's unsuccessful campaign against American Airlines' anticornrow policy and funding for a bewildering array of programs intended to promote cultural affirmation and self-esteem.

Radicalism, as Americans were relieved to discover, was harmless. The civil rights movement made segregation illegal but almost as soon as integration was a reality, identity politics and black separatism became fashionable, a step backward that could only please conservatives who resisted integration. ("Sure—wear your big Afros, celebrate Kwanzaa, shake your fists, talk revolution, and read Malcolm X. Just don't move into our neighborhoods, send your kids to our schools or marry our sisters.") It refurbished racial stereotypes, which civil rights leaders had worked to dismantle and valorized them in order to promote self-esteem, which on the received view would curb antisocial behavior.

Radicalism was tame, so Americans learned to stop worrying and to love the Revolution. Revolution just turned things back around to where they'd started, and equality, at least the sort of equality multi-culturalists wanted, did not undermine separateness.

EQUALITY OF WHAT?

Most people think that equality, whatever it is, is a good thing. As Amartya Sen famously argued, all plausible political theories are egal-itarian: they just differ in their answers to the equality-of-what ques-tion. Welfarists want equality of welfare; free marketers want equal access to markets. Opponents of affirmative action claim to want equality of opportunity rather than equality of result. Libertarians want equality of rights.

Sen's point is a logical one: "equal" and other members of its family—including "similar," "identical," and "like," are syncategore-matic. The terms cry out for an answer to the question: "in what way?" My dog is a lot like yours. How so? In size, color, breed, or tempera-ment, or in some other respect? We're a lot alike, you know. Oh, really? How so?

We can understand the fundamental difference between assimila-tionists and multiculturalists as a disagreement about what sort of equality matters: equality of circumstance or equality of respect? Equality of fact, if you will, or equality of value? What is it that mat-ters most for people, in particular for members of disadvantaged groups: equity or sameness, having the same status, reward, or respect as the next guy or getting to live the same kind of life?

I mulled over this question while phasing out over my knitting during a conference titled "What Kind of Equality Should Women

Want?" As I drifted off, I remembered a TV fantasy—it might have been an old *Twilight Zone* episode—about a secretary who likes her job but is thoroughly fed up with the lack of respect she gets both from her boss and from local feminists intent on raising her consciousness because she doesn't mind being "just a secretary." And then . . . reminiscent of Alice through the looking glass, she falls into the Xerox machine and enters an alternative reality where secretaries are king. In the alternative boardroom, when she tells the assembled company at the boat-shaped table that she's a secretary, all conversation stops until, after a pregnant pause, one awestruck executive breathes: "You're a *secretary*—I guess I thought you'd be *taller*."

Height notwithstanding, she is treated to three-martini lunches, solicited by corporate headhunters, and generally shown a very good time while she tries to figure out how to get back through the Xerox machine—until, quite rationally, she decides not to bother. Alternative reality has worked out just fine.

The paper that was being presented as I drifted into alternative reality was by a legal scholar arguing that equal opportunity regulations should benefit both what she called "Tomboys" and "Femmes." Tomboys just wanted to be guys, have a fair chance to get "men's jobs," and be treated like guys. This was still very much not the way things were, and, she argued, there should be regulations to fix that. Femmes, like the *Twilight Zone* secretary, were OK with traditional women's jobs but should be getting respect, and pay, commensurate with their education and responsibilities. This was also not the way things were. At a major teaching hospital in the Pacific Northwest, the largely female nursing staff complained that hospital parking lot attendants, all of them male, were paid more than they were. The nurses demanded "comparable worth."

I agreed—and made a mental note to avoid this hospital, since, though I was fond of my car, I was much fonder of my body. However, I was and am a confirmed Tomboy. The trouble, as I reflected, was that some policies geared to accommodate Femmes set back the interests of Tomboys and vice versa. There was no free ride. Pure Femmes wanted separate but equal; pure Tomboys, like me, just wanted to do the kinds of jobs guys did, but we didn't really care that much about equality in pay, respect, or anything else when it came down to brass tacks. There probably weren't that many pure Tomboys or pure Femmes in the population, but there were certainly Tomboy interests and Femme interests represented, and the practical problem was getting the greatest good for the greatest number.

That is also the practical problem when it comes to adjudicating between assimilationists and cultural preservationists. Cultural preservationists want to behave in ways and live lives that deviate from the white, middle-class Anglo norm without being penalized for it. They want to live Amish lives or what Ken Livingstone called "Jamaican lifestyles"—whatever those might be—to wear hijabs, jilbabs, or cornrows and otherwise affirm their right to cultural difference. Like Femmes, they want to be separate but equal. The equality they want is equality of respect. Assimilationists, like Tomboys, just want to be regular guys, to do the jobs that white, middle-class Anglos do, get mortgages and car loans on the same terms, and be treated in the same way that white, middle-class Anglos are treated, without any special role obligations—even trivial ones restricted to Black History Month—and without pressure to identify with ancestral cultures or exhibit "authenticity." Assimilationists want equality of circumstance—the opportunity to live the same lives as white, middle-class Anglos.

In order to promote equality of respect multiculturalists supported the interests of cultural preservationists. They assumed that minorities could not, would not, and should not assimilate and that it was important to affirm their alternative lifestyles to boost their self-esteem. I worried that, in addition to making ethnicity more salient and chaining people to their roots, this assumption was a self-fulfilling prophecy.

When my oldest kid was in high school, he brought home a handout on "Seven Types of Intelligence" that had been distributed at a school assembly, which pitched the idea to students that everyone was beautiful in their own way. The aim of this talk was to promote equality of respect and instill self-esteem. Everyone, students were told, was intelligent: there were just different types of intelligence other than just academic intelligence, including, I recall, empathetic intelligence, which dealt with understanding people, and athletic intelligence, which facilitated achievements on the basketball court. From the way my son described the pep talk, I was not happy. The gist seemed to be: Girls—you may be bad at math, but you're really sensitive to people and that's great; don't worry about being scientists or engineers, you can be social workers. Black guys—you're not doing that well in school, but don't worry—you can still slam dunk and are good, valuable people with your own special brand of intelligence. Everyone, according to the talk, was beautiful in their own way, intelligent in their own way, and equally worthy of respect.

The goals this talk suggested for women and minorities were consolation prizes, if they were prizes at all. The whole promotion seemed to me both patronizing and counterproductive. Why was it so all-fired important to boost everyone's self-esteem and prove to them that they were beautiful, or intelligent, in their own way? Why weren't students being told: these are the standards for achievement—you've got to learn how to read and write well, learn math, science, and at least one foreign language. If you're too dumb or too lazy, tough on you. Some people are going to find these subjects easier than others and some will do better than others in school and in their subsequent careers. Work as hard as you can and do your personal best.

MULTICULTURALISM AND THE SELF-ESTEEM MOVEMENT

Why were educators offering consolation prizes and promoting alternative standards for achievement so that everyone could count as a success even at the risk of undermining their motivation to do well according to traditional academic and professional standards? The reason, I suspect, was a deep-seated pessimism about the capabilities of most students, minorities in particular, and perhaps even more importantly an interest in curbing antisocial behavior. When I asked teachers or faculty from our school of education why countries like Finland and Japan were able to run mass education systems where everyone went to school and everyone did reasonably well, they gulped, blushed, and stammered that the populations of these countries were "more homogeneous." The assumption was that in the United States by contrast there were lots of students (and we knew who they were) who couldn't cut it academically and who would run amok if they were discouraged or frustrated: they had to be mollified, flattered, and kept busy.

This soft racism was the only alternative they could see to the older hard racism of segregation and containment. It was an old story, going back to the 1960s, when, in the wake of the civil rights movement, Americans became painfully aware that formal equality under the law would not fix America's race problem. De facto segregation was still the norm. Black Americans were still as a group much poorer than white Americans, more likely to be unemployed, and more likely to belong to the criminal underclass that terrorized urban ghettos. After the first of a series of Long Hot Summers, the Kerner Commission, charged by President Johnson to investigate the causes of the riots, concluded: "Our nation is moving toward two societies—one black and one white, separate and unequal."

Many white Americans, still in the grip of the older hard racism, blamed the civil rights movement. Blacks were the barbarians at the gates, by their nature brutal and violent. In the old days they were kept under control or at least confined to ghettos where they could only beat up on one another. Now the Goths had crossed the Danube and were sacking Rome.

Liberal politicians and social reformers looked for an alternative explanation and a fix. And they wanted a simple explanation and a quick, relatively cheap fix that the public would accept. The received view during the period was that low self-esteem was the root cause of antisocial behavior and that the Story of Race explained why young, underclass, minority males were especially prone to crime and violence. This is how, in the United States, multiculturalism became inextricably linked to the self-esteem movement. The fundamental thesis of the movement was the doctrine that members of disadvantaged minorities behaved badly because, as a consequence of racism, they suffered from low self-esteem. Rejection of one's ethnic roots was a manifestation of self-hatred, according to the Story of Race, so to boost the self-esteem of minorities, it was crucial to instill ethnic pride.

The appeal of this doctrine during the 1960s when it was popularized was not difficult to understand. The 1954 Supreme Court ruling *Brown v. the Topeka Board of Education* prohibited racial segregation in the public schools, Jim Crow laws had been struck down, bogus "literacy tests," which disenfranchised blacks in the South had been declared illegal, and the Civil Rights Acts of the 1960s prohibited racial discrimination. At least nominally, the goals of the civil rights movement had been achieved. However, white Americans were flabbergasted to discover that after ten years of the civil rights movement—following over two hundred years of slavery, segregation, oppression, and disenfranchisement—black Americans were still poorer, less educated, and more likely to engage in antisocial behavior than white Americans. White Americans of good will were terrified that the persistence of social, economic, and educational inequality showed that blacks were genetically inferior; even in Mississippi public toilets were integrated, so why weren't all those black people working as doctors and corporate executives? The doctrines of the self-esteem movement purported to provide a psychological explanation that did not reflect adversely on the character of black Americans.

Psychology was in vogue and for almost two decades had provided explanations and, advocates hoped, cures for socially unacceptable behavior. So, during the heyday of the feminine mystique, women dissatisfied with suburban domesticity were diagnosed with penis envy and a variety of other psychological pathologies, juvenile delinquents were tagged as "emotionally disturbed" and sent into therapy, and gay men and women were classified as mentally ill. Psychology was, in the popular view, "scientific" and provided kinder, gentler solutions to social problems than religious moralism. Under the psychological regime, deviants would receive therapy and, if necessary, medication rather than blame or punishment.

Perhaps more importantly, psychological accounts were more acceptable to the American public than economic explanations, which suggested remedial measures that most white Americans found unpalatable, like the strict enforcement of equal opportunity regulations, affirmative action, school busing, and other efforts to dismantle the system of white privilege that persisted in spite of formal equality under the law. Pride, respect, and other intangibles, like the forgiveness of sins, were cheap. It was easier to promote self-esteem than it would have been to improve lives of individuals who were socially crippled materially, so that they could rise up and walk.

Self-esteem, as promoters understood it, was not only a matter of feeling good about one's choices or achievements but a matter of taking pride in ascribed characteristics and affiliations, in particular, racial identity. Here they drew on the work of revolutionary writer and activist Frantz Fanon, filtered through the growing literature of identity politics and the rhetoric of the Black Power movement. Fanon, trained as a psychiatrist, argued that colonized people, internalizing the racist categories inherent in the language and culture of their oppressors, suffered from inferiority complexes. Racism depleted self-esteem. However, whereas Fanon had argued for violent revolution as a means by which colonized people could recover self-esteem, the movement his work inspired sought to promote self-esteem in order to avoid violence and other forms of socially disruptive behavior.

Among politicians, pundits, social critics, and K–12 educators, it became a commonplace that low self-esteem was the source of academic failure and antisocial behavior. The Moynihan Report of 1965 had made the case that "black matriarchy," by undermining the self-esteem of black men, was at the root of a variety of social ills.[1] Unmanned by castrating black females, the story went, young black males asserted their masculinity by cultivating machismo and sticking up convenience stores. The solution, welcomed by liberals and conservatives alike, was to pull funding from black women and children in order to force them into dependence on black men, whose self-esteem—so the story went—would be boosted by female subservience.

The Moynihan Report in addition suggested paying black males ten thousand dollars a year, a very decent wage in 1965, to work as kindergarten teachers in ghetto schools in order to provide "positive role models" for black boys. The role model doctrine was a central feature of the self-esteem movement. The view was that it was good for children to have heroes to show them what was possible and encourage them to aim high—but that heroes were effective in this regard only if they were of the same sex and race as their admirers. Otherwise, according to the role model doctrine, children could not "identify" with them. Since "identity" on the multiculturalist account was essentially gendered, racial, and ethnic, black boys needed black men as role models.

No one, of course, worried about black girls. They were not likely to engage in violence—at least not outside the home—and most were not, in any case, big enough or strong enough to do real damage. It was the young males who had to be mollified and domesticated, and the Moynihan program, like the Promise Keepers' agenda that was briefly fashionable twenty years later, proposed sacrificing women to men in exchange for civilized behavior in the public square. In return for behaving themselves in public, men got to dominate their women at home.

In addition to their program for reconstructing the patriarchal family to protect fragile male egos, self-esteem advocates promoted cultural self-affirmation. Linguists were recruited to make the case that Black English was an authentic language with its own grammar and vocabulary.[2] History teachers contrived fantasies representing Africa as the cradle of civilization. No one shied away from admitting that before being colonized and incorporated into the Roman world, inhabitants of the British Isles were brutal, illiterate barbarians. Likewise, no one worried about British self-hatred because no one suspected that their descendents were genetically defective or worried that without special pleading they would take to sticking up 7-Elevens. Blacks, however, were thought to require more careful treatment.

And so the multiculturalist program emerged, pushed through by the self-esteem movement. Race and ethnic origin—ascribed and immutable characteristics—were essential features of individuals' identities that individuals who manifested healthy self-esteem affirmed. Repudiating one's race or ethnicity was a source of self-destructive, antisocial behavior. In a properly multicultural society, all cultural traditions would be honored and all individuals would take pride in their racial and ethnic identities. The self-esteem of members of disadvantaged groups in particular was to be promoted by the promulgation of good myths elaborating on the virtues of their ancestral cultures and providing "role models" for them from among people of the same color.

THE FAILURE OF THE SELF-ESTEEM MOVEMENT

The fundamental doctrines of the self-esteem movement concerning the importance of self-esteem, role models, and ethnic pride are so deeply embedded in popular culture that to most of us they seem commonsensical and innocuous. However, there are two reasons why we should reject them.

First of all, they are false. These were the doctrines that leaders of the self-esteem movement, commissioned by the State of California in 1986 as a Task Force to Promote Self-Esteem and Personal Social Responsibility, attempted to prove. Members of the task force set out to establish that low self-esteem was responsible for all manner of social pathologies, including academic failure, teenage pregnancy, and street crime. Remarkably, in spite of the task force's preconceived notions and agenda, their report, *The Social Importance of Self-Esteem*, failed to find any significant connection between low self-esteem and any of the pathologies they studied. As Neil Smelser noted in his introduction, "One of the disappointing aspects of every chapter in this volume . . . is how low the association between self-esteem and its consequences are in research to date."[3]

Second, practices built on the self-esteem movement's doctrines do not promote achievement or curb antisocial behavior. Indeed data suggested that promoting "global self-esteem," the general sense of pride in oneself not grounded in any skill or achievement, was counterproductive. In a report for the Center for Equal Opportunity summarizing this data, Nina H. Shokraii notes:

> When psychologists Harold W. Stevenson and James W. Stigler tested the academic skills of elementary school students in Japan, Taiwan, China, and the United States, the Asian students easily outperformed their American counterparts. That came as no surprise. But when the same students were asked how they felt about their subject skills, the Americans exhibited a significantly higher self-evaluation of their academic prowess. In other words, they combined a lousy performance with a high sense of self-esteem. As Stevenson and Stigler point out, Asian schools teach their students to indulge in self-congratulation only after they have paid their dues, through years of learning and hard work. While educators in most countries frown upon pride—one manifestation of a high self-esteem—American teachers actually encourage it as a positive personality trait.[4]

In addition to impeding academic performance by diminishing incentives for achievement, Shokraii suggested that boosting self-esteem did not promote good citizenship either:

> Those who think low self-esteem is the cause of high crime rates among blacks are also wrong. According to a recent study by psychologists Roy Baumeister, Joseph Boden, and Laura Smart, "first, [this notion] does not fit the transient shifts in the crime rate among African Americans, which is now reaching its highest levels as slavery recedes farther and farther into the background. Second, self-esteem levels among African Americans are now equal to, or higher than, the self-esteem levels of whites. Third, it is far from certain that slaves had a low self-esteem." A study by Jennifer Crocker and Brenda Major of the State University of New York at Buffalo,

similarly refuted the psychological theories that claim members of stigmatized groups (blacks, for example) should possess low global self-esteem. They argued that stigmatized individuals are not simply "passive victims but are frequently able to actively protect their self-esteem from prejudice and discrimination."

Ironically, adolescent African-American males living in impoverished neighborhoods are more likely to turn violent if schools bombard them with unearned praise. Baumeister, Boden, and Smart found that when high self-esteem is challenged by others' negative views, egotism is threatened. People will react in one of two ways. They either lower their self-appraisal and withdraw, or they maintain their self-appraisal and manifest negative emotions toward the source of the ego threat. This response can easily become violent in individuals who place high emphasis on their self-appraisal.[5]

Undeterred by the results of such studies, educators, members of the "helping professions," and community leaders continued to promote multiculturalism and ethnic pride without any results to show. Cultural affirmation and self-esteem did not boost math scores or discourage antisocial behavior. Bilingual education did not improve Hispanic children's academic achievement or encourage them to stay in school. The traditional patriarchal family and female subservience did not tame young lower-class males. Indeed, as subsequent developments showed, it seemed to have the opposite effect: youths in Arab immigrant ghettos, whose women were as subservient as Moynihan or any other neo-Freudian social reformer could wish, were as violent, directionless, and antisocial as young black men in American slums. Yob culture and thuggery among the lower classes, it turned out, were universal, had nothing to do with ethnic identity, and could not be fixed by playing identity politics or sacrificing virgins.

Nevertheless, even though the self-esteem movement did no good, dumping money into cultural affirmation projects let people off the hook: such projects were the socially acceptable alternative to politically unpopular programs that were proven to be effective in benefiting minorities—affirmative action, integrated housing, and school busing.[6]

Perhaps that is why, twenty years after the California Task Force's report, in the absence of any evidence of redeeming social value for purposes other than entertainment, it remains popular. It was easier, and cheaper, to say, "Thy sins are forgiven" than to say "Rise up and walk"—or to implement programs that would have made that possible.

THE MAKING OF A MYSTIQUE

In spite of the falsity of self-esteem doctrines, the failure of the self-esteem movement in the United States to achieve any worthwhile results, and the growing skepticism about the multicultural agenda in European countries, multiculturalism has not yet been discredited because it is a deeply embedded cultural "mystique" in the sense that the "feminine mystique" imposed on women during the 1950s was. A cultural mystique, understood along the lines that Betty Friedan suggested, is an ideology that obscures the unjust treatment of a disadvantaged group by invoking psychological, theological, or other obscurantist doctrines to establish that members of the group are not worse off than privileged individuals but just differently off—and to keep them in their place.

That is what the feminine mystique did for women. In retrospect, it is clear that during the 1950s women as a group were less well-off than men: they had few career options and fewer choices overall as to the kinds of lives they could live. They were poorly paid and so were for the most part economically dependent on men. Friedan's readers in particular—educated middle-class housewives—were most worse off than their male counterparts. Homemaking was dead-end, semiskilled drudgery—"For this I went to college?" According to the feminine mystique, however, women were not *worse* off than men but rather *differently* off. Promoters of the mystique regularly sang paeans to domesticity: "You're not *just a housewife* . . . you're a psychologist, a chef, an interior decorator . . . a corporate CEO."

When the feminine mystique was in force, female identity was highly salient and tightly scripted—and the script for women strictly forbade dissatisfaction with any features of the prescribed female role. Psychologists, educators, and others who were regarded as experts in these matters interpreted dissatisfaction as a manifestation of neurosis, maladjustment, or self-hatred. If you didn't like doing the sorts of things women were supposed to do, you didn't like yourself; if you were frustrated by the restricted range of jobs or life options available to women, you didn't accept yourself. During the period, the jargon of psychology was code for moral assessment, and obscurantist psychological doctrines were invoked to enforce social rules and role obligations.

Now compare the enforcement of multicultural role obligation. Blacks, Hispanics, Asians, and Indians who did not do ethnic according to the multicultural rules were characterized as inauthentic, self-hating "Oreos," "Coconuts," "Bananas," and "Apples." Deconstructing the fruit basket metaphor, Richard Thompson Ford notes that the suggestion was not that they were white "inside," essentially white and only superficially black, brown, yellow, or red, but rather that in failing to follow the rules for their ethnic classification they were hiding or rejecting what they "really" were or ought to be—like "neurotic" or maladjusted women during the days of the feminine mystique who rejected their feminine role.

As a thought experiment, Ford asks us to imagine a case in which a Catholic priest loses his faith and leaves the priesthood. No one suggests that he is still "really" a Catholic or condemns him for quitting his job. On the contrary, if he had continued to function as a priest, we should condemn him as a self-serving hypocrite and a fake. If the psychological reality, the beliefs, values, and commitments that make a person Catholic are gone, we believe, he shouldn't behave as if he were a religious believer, because that is not what he really is. By contrast, multiculturalists, Ford notes, hold that "Oreos," "Coconuts," "Bananas," and "Apples" ought to play their prescribed ethnic roles regardless of their beliefs, values, preferences, aspirations, or interests. Indeed, the suggestion is that having ethnically inappropriate beliefs, values, preferences, aspirations, or interests is in some sense a denial of one's true self, recalling social workers' concerns about the supposed dangers of interracial adoption earlier cited by Ford: "Black children belong . . . in black families in order that they receive the total sense of themselves . . . black children in white homes are cut of from the healthy development of themselves."[7]

Like the feminine mystique, the multicultural mystique was enforced by the invocation of obscurantist psychological doctrines about "healthy development" and individuals' "sense of self." In both cases, these psychological doctrines were peculiar, and they were peculiar in the very same way because they suggested that a psychology, a system of beliefs, values, character traits, aspirations, and the like, which would have been OK in a body of one sort, was "unhealthy" in a body of another sort. A white child, enculturated in a white home to acquire certain beliefs, values, aspirations, preferences, interests, and habits would be psychologically healthy; his black psychological duplicate enculturated in the same white home would be unhealthy and would lack a "total sense of himself." By the same token, under the feminine mystique, a female psychological duplicate of a "healthy" male would be ipso facto neurotic and self-hating.

Spelled out in this way, it should be clear that in suggesting that there is something wrong with such "Oreo" children or "neurotic" women, these psychological "experts" weren't really talking about individuals' psychological problems at all: they were talking about individuals' failure to conform to social expectations and rules imposed in virtue of gender, race, and social circumstance. Critics of the feminine mystique, most notably Betty Friedan, noticed this. Under the feminine mystique, she noted, mental health was defined as "life-adjustment" with the implication that where there was a lack of fit between women and the roles they were supposed to play, the fault was in women rather than in the sex role system and the restrictive social rules it imposed on them.

Following Friedan, feminists urged that it was the rules, not women, that ought to be changed. Unlike feminists, however, multiculturalists insisted that the rules were nonnegotiable and imposed role obligations on members of minorities in virtue of race and ethnicity. Reminiscent of psychological "experts" during the heyday of the feminine mystique, they declared "Oreos," "Coconuts," "Bananas," and "Apples" inauthentic. A "taint" clung to Nella Larsen for literary "passing." Keith Richburg was slammed for "forgetting his African roots" and for refusing to express a sense of kinship with his "African brothers." George "Macaca" Allen was accused of anti-Semitism for failing to exhibit "pride in his family heritage," and the blogosphere lit up with descriptions of him as a "self-hating Jew"— even white guys were not safe from the Identity Police!

Again, like the feminine mystique, multiculturalism preached *la différence*. Cultures weren't better or worse—just different. The privileging of the white male role was an illusion, so there was no point in trying to appropriate it. Men and women were "complimentary"; equal—but separate. By the same token, there were seven different types of intelligence, and everybody had at least one. Feminists ridiculed the doctrine that housewives were corporate CEOs, psychologists, chefs, interior decorators, and all the other items in the great litany of the feminine mystique, but multiculturalists proclaimed that all cultures were equally worthy of respect and some may have even believed that shooting baskets was as good as doing calculus.

Why did the feminine mystique collapse during the late twentieth century while the multicultural mystique flourished? Maybe it was because during this time there were compelling economic reasons for recruiting women into the labor force that the feminine mystique impeded. By contrast, there was no compelling reason to dispel the multicultural mystique and, moreover, taking it down would have been very expensive: it would require policies to which the American voting public had a deep aversion. Americans wanted women in the labor force to fill traditional pink-collar jobs in the rapidly expanding service sector, so the feminine mystique had to go. Americans, however, did not want school busing, reformed immigration policies that would regularize the status of undocumented workers, or the strict enforcement of regulations forbidding discrimination in employment or access to credit, so the multicultural mystique had to stay.

After forgiving the paralytic's sins, Jesus healed him just to show the Pharisees that he could do it. Politicians were not so ready to tell minorities, "Rise up and walk."

NOTES

1. D. P. Moynihan, "The Negro Family: The Case for National Action," Office of Policy Planning and Research, United States Department of Labor, March 1965.

2. In fairness, Black English is an authentic dialect with characteristic grammatical structures and is, in fact, continuing to diverge from Standard American English, though most linguists do not believe that its characteristic grammatical forms have their roots in the languages of West Africa. See, e.g., John McWhorter, *The Power of Babel: A Natural History of Language* (New York: HarperPerennial, 2003).

3. Ibid., p. 15.

4. N. Shokraii, "The Self-Esteem Fraud: Why Feel-Good Education Does Not Lead to Academic Success," Report of the Center for Equal Opportunity, http://www.ceousa.org/READ/self.html.

5. Ibid.

6. See, e.g., Alan Finder, "As Test Scores Jump, Raleigh Credits Integration by Income," *New York Times*, September 25, 2005, http://www.udel .edu/anthro/ackerman/raleigh.pdf, for information about the strikingly beneficial effects of school busing for racial and ethnic minorities. For information about the benefits of integrated housing, see the Fund for an Open Society at http://www.opensoc.org/.

7. Richard T. Ford, *Racial Culture: A Critique*, chap. 3 (Princeton, NJ: Princeton University Press, 2005), p. 8.

Chapter 11

POLICY

Sadek recently quit his job delivering groceries near Saint-Denis. . . . Sadek, 31, has a secondary school education and aspires to something better. But he knows his options are limited: "With a name like mine, I can't have a sales job." Telemarketing could be a possibility—his Arab roots safely hidden from view. Of course, he would have to work under an assumed name.

Sadek's story sums up the job prospects of the children and grandchildren of Muslim immigrants. They may be French on paper—but they know that Ali and Rachid are much less likely to get ahead than Alain or Richard. Racial discrimination is banned in France. But a quick look at the people working in any shop or office suggests the practice is widespread. The impression is confirmed by official statistics. Unemployment among people of French origin is 9.2%. Among those of foreign origin, the figure is 14%—even after adjusting for educational qualifications. . . .

"Doors are closed when you are an Arab," says Yazid Sabeg, a businessman and writer. For many young people, the first time they notice the closed door is when they try to go clubbing. "The first time the guy at the entrance says: 'You're not coming in,' you accept it," says Nadir Dendoune, a journalist from Saint-Denis. "But after two or three times, you go home carrying a bag of hatred on your shoulders."[1]

—BBC Report, November 2, 2005

Since 9/11, Americans and Europeans have been rethinking policies on immigration and multiculturalism. So in his December 2006 speech, carefully hedged with disclaimers about religious freedom and the right of minorities to maintain distinct "cultures and lifestyles," Tony Blair announced that members of minority groups had a "duty to integrate."

Duty is precisely what we do not *want* to do. Blair's remarks, though nuanced, echoed the old canard that members of disadvantaged minorities prefer to "keep to themselves," reject mainstream values, and are, as a consequence, disadvantaged. If I am right, this story gets things exactly backward. Immigrants and minorities want to assimilate but face discrimination and exclusion, are marked as Other, and are never fully accepted. It is members of the majority who have the "duty to integrate."

TOO DIVERSE?

Multiculturalism is a response to a legitimate concern: the worry that the only viable alternative to plural monoculturalism is exclusion. Immigrants do not become enculturated immediately, and some members of the first generation never do. If the choice were between accommodating culturally distinct ethnic communities and closing the borders, we should certainly prefer accommodating culturally distinct ethnic communities. Members of dominant ethnic groups discriminate against ethnic minorities, and if, as Appiah suggests, the choice were between Black Power and Uncle Tom, we should certainly prefer Black Power.

Even though these are choices that, Appiah argues, we do not have to make, ethnic diversity is, nevertheless, problematic. In his 2004 article in the *Prospect*, David Goodhart speculated that there was a trade-off between ethnic diversity and social solidarity. Scandinavian countries with the strongest welfare states, he noted, were among the least ethnically diverse nations in the developed world. At the same time America, with a minority population he reckoned at 30 percent, was the least committed to social programs identified with the welfare state. Progressives, Goodhard suggested, faced a dilemma: liberal immigration policies, by increasing cultural diversity and "thinning out" the national culture, would inevitably undermine the social solidarity. "And therein," he writes, "lies one of the central dilemmas of political life":

> [S]haring and solidarity can conflict with diversity. This is an especially acute dilemma for progressives who want plenty of both solidarity (high social cohesion and generous welfare paid out of a progressive tax system) and diversity (equal respect for a wide range of peoples, values and ways of life). The tension between the two values is a reminder that serious politics is about trade-offs. . . . It was the Conservative politician David Willetts who drew my attention to the "progressive dilemma." Speaking at a roundtable on welfare reform, he said: "The basis on which you can extract large sums of money in tax and pay it out in benefits is that most people think the recipients are people like themselves, facing difficulties that they themselves could face. If values become more diverse, if lifestyles become more differentiated, then it becomes more difficult to sustain the legitimacy of a universal risk-pooling welfare state. People ask: 'Why should I pay for them when they are doing things that I wouldn't do?' This is America versus Sweden. You can have a Swedish welfare state provided that you are a homogeneous society with intensely shared values. In the United States you have a very diverse, individualistic society where people feel fewer obligations to fellow citizens."

While Goodhart's essay was nuanced, the sociobiological thesis that some assumed it was intended to convey is false. Genetic kinship is neither necessary nor sufficient for social solidarity. As Goodhart himself notes, "The first clips of mourning Swedes after the murder of the foreign minister Anna Lindh were of crying immigrants expressing their sorrow in perfect Swedish." Biology is not destiny. One suspects that many white Englishmen feel a much greater kinship with black Englishmen of West Indian extraction than they do with white Frenchmen.

In addition, Goodhart's suggestion that American resistance to income transfers and the social programs associated with the welfare state is a consequence of ethnic diversity is questionable. The ideologies of self-reliance, the Protestant work ethic, and rugged individualism predate mass immigration and are bred in the bone. Moreover, American identity is thick and goes beyond an abstract sense of shared political commitments. Every American is obsessed with a shared history and identifies with it. Every American can identify the *Niña*, *Pinta*, and *Santa Maria* and the *Mayflower*; every American imbibes a rich mythos involving Pilgrims and pioneers, cowboys and Indians, Africans enduring the Middle Passage, the Irish fleeing the Potato Famine, and immigrants sighting the Statue of Liberty on their way to Ellis Island. The history of successive waves of immigrants is a part of the Great Trek story that every American schoolchild learns.

Nevertheless, sociobiological conjecture aside, people do hesitate to enter into risk-pooling schemes that they believe are likely to benefit individuals who are culturally alien and either unwilling or unable to buy into shared values and a shared culture. A century ago, during mass immigration from European countries, Americans gave generously to support schools, settlement houses, and other programs that benefited immigrants under the rubric of "Americanization." Even if anti-immigrant sentiment bubbled under the surface, the melting pot was official ideology. Americans assumed that immigrants could, should, and would become Americans—indeed, as Teddy Roosevelt famously proclaimed, "unhyphenated Americans." Goodhart seems correct in suggesting that where the native population assumes that immigrants or minorities cannot be absorbed or actively reject the fundamental values of the dominant culture, social solidarity suffers.

Where they assume, however, that immigrants and minorities can and will assimilate, they work and give to promote integration.

Goodhart is also correct in suggesting that "absorbing outsiders into a community that is worthy of the name takes time"—and effort. Oddly, considering his worries about the difficulties of promoting support for a welfare state in America, he cites "the old US melting pot" as a model for integrating immigrants:

> Immigrants who plan to stay should be encouraged to become Britons as far as that is compatible with holding on to some core aspects of their own culture. In return for learning the language, getting a job and paying taxes, and abiding by the laws and norms of the host society, immigrants must be given a stake in the system and incentives to become good citizens. . . . Immigrants from the same place are bound to want to congregate together, but policy should try to prevent that consolidating into segregation across all the main areas of life: residence, school, workplace, church. In any case, the laissez faire approach of the postwar period in which ethnic minority citizens were not encouraged to join the common culture (although many did) should be buried. Citizenship ceremonies, language lessons and the mentoring of new citizens should help to create a British version of the old US melting pot.

The American melting pot did melt—and the most striking evidence for that is the fact that Goodhart puts the minority population of the United States at 30 percent as distinct from the 70 percent he characterizes as "non-Hispanic whites." A century ago, the grandparents and great-grandparents of many members of that 70 percent were themselves classified as minorities and native-born Americans (whose grandparents and great-grandparents had immigrated a century earlier) worried about the ability of the United States to absorb mass immigration.

Few Americans advocate completely open borders. Short of that, however, there is no reason to believe that reasonably generous immigration policies will undermine the shared culture of the United States or of other countries that receive immigrants—so long as such nations reject multiculturalism and commit to proactive policies encouraging and facilitating assimilation.

Such policies need not be and, arguably, should not be color-blind. Racial discrimination, against both immigrants and native-born members of visible minorities, is a fact of life and, as we have seen in the aftermath of the riots in French immigrant suburbs, denial will not make it go away. Without intentional efforts to disperse immigrant populations, immigrants will cluster and form ghettos because they lack the language skills, coping strategies, and personal contacts to operate effectively in the larger society. Without proactive policies to ameliorate ongoing discrimination in employment, housing, and access to credit—including affirmative action—discrimination will persist. The pervasiveness of discrimination, social exclusion, and a variety of policies and practices that lock out immigrants and members of visible minorities, as well as their sincere avowals, suggest that most members of these groups would prefer to assimilate to the larger culture.

Multiculturalists, however, assumed that among immigrants and members of minority groups, cultural preservationists were in the majority and so they sought to accommodate them. That assumption was initially self-serving and eventually self-destructive. Europe, Johann Hari writes "inhaled immigrants from our former colonies to skivvy and scrub for us, and the most hassle-free approach seemed to be multiculturalism."[2] America, sociologist Alejandro Portes suggests, did the same, with a similar result: a native-born second generation, with few prospects in the mainstream society, who merge into what Portes dubbed "the rainbow underclass":

> Immigrants provide an abundant, diligent, docile, vulnerable, and low-cost labor pool where native workers willing to toil at the same harsh jobs for minimum pay have all but disappeared. . . . Business may think of them as nothing but cheap labor—indeed, that's why many business groups support pure bracero programs of temporary "guestworkers." But the vast majority of these immigrants want what everyone else wants: families.

So the short-term benefits of migration must be balanced against what happens next. The human consequences of immigration come in the form of children born to today's immigrants. . . . The low wages that make foreign workers so attractive to employers translate into poverty and inferior schooling for their children. If these young-sters were growing up just to replace their parents as the next gener-ation of low-paid manual workers, the present situation could go on forever. But this is not how things happen.

Children of immigrants do not grow up to be low-paid foreign workers but U.S. citizens, with English as their primary language and American-style aspirations. . . . The trouble is that poor schools, tough neighborhoods, and the lack of role models to which their parents' poverty condemns them make these lofty aspirations an unreachable dream for many. . . . Add to this the effects of race discrimination—because the majority of today's second generation is nonwhite by pre-sent U.S. standards—and the stage is set for serious trouble.[3]

The worry that mass immigration will make receiving countries "too diverse" or that it will "thin out" their cultures is a sham. The fear is that immigrants will not remain sufficiently "diverse" to accept second-class status, do harsh jobs for low pay, and conveniently dis-appear when their labor is not needed.

In a recent *New York Times* article, "Do Immigrants Make Us Safer?" Eyal Press announced the surprising discovery that they did: poor neighborhoods populated by recent immigrants had surprisingly low crime rates, and immigrants were much less likely to engage in criminal activity than native-born citizens. The downside was that their children were much more likely to do so. As the British discov-ered, it was not immigrants but their children, British-born and accul-turated but not assimilated, members of the rainbow underclass, who dabbled in radical Islam, adopted oppositional identities, and, on 7/7, did damage. No one should have been surprised. These were native-born citizens whose connections to ancestral cultures were at best attenuated, with the same expectations and aspirations as other Amer-ican and British citizens, who were stigmatized, rejected, and excluded. Understandably, they decided that if they could not join the system, they would beat it.

Affluent countries with minority populations who do not want to deal with young people carrying bags of hatred on their shoulders face three stark alternatives. They can send minorities back to where they, their parents, or remote ancestors came from, seal the borders and leave a diminished, aging population hogging the good life to figure out how to get their dirty work done. They can establish a multicultural millet system in which minority groups, housed in an archipelago of conveniently located Bantustans, can maintain their own institutions, perpetuate their ancestral cultures, and serve as a hereditary class of dhimmi to do the dirty work. Or they can facilitate the acculturation of immigrants and assimilate minorities: they can repudiate the self-serving sentimentalities of the salad bowl and admit immigrants and minorities into the mainstream.

AFFIRMATIVE ACTION TO ELIMINATE DIVERSITY

This is a hard saying because, as Goodhart notes, people take care of their own—though not, as I have suggested, their biological tribe mates so much as their neighbors and cultural kin. They are not only reluctant to provide the benefits of a welfare state to individuals they regard as alien, they are reluctant to offer them jobs, accept them as neighbors, send their children to school with them, and admit them to clubs. If you are Other, you are excluded and being excluded you remain Other: social exclusion perpetuates itself.

That is hard to fix. As we have seen, official color-blind policies do not make individual citizens in their professional or social life color-blind. Moreover, even with the best of intentions, fair treatment and inclusion are difficult to achieve because we are wired for "implicit bias." We expect things to look a certain way, expect people to play roles appropriate to their kind, and don't notice what would otherwise strike us as evidence of gross discrimination or social inequities. Economist Barbara Bergmann in *In Defense of Affirmative Action* remarks by way of a striking example that no one, including people who should know better, seems to notice that almost all servers in fancy hotel restaurants are white males: "Most of the hotel dinners I go to," she observes, "are sponsored by feminist, civil rights, or scholarly organizations. The hotels must not be too concerned with pleasing since, despite the 1971 decision, almost all of the waiters who serve those dinners continue to be white males. The sponsoring organizations tend not to complain, and most of the diners do not even notice."[4]

She notes further that when people's attention is drawn to arrangements that suggest unequal treatment by sex or race, they readily concoct reasons to explain why no unfairness is involved:

> In deciding which candidate should be hired, or which of two employees should be paid more, even well-meaning decision-makers may believe they are focusing only on merit while actually using biased methods. The psychologist Faye Crosby and her associates have done important experimental work that shows how this happens.
>
> Crosby created fictitious information about a supposed group of male and female managers, all working for the same fictitious company. Each manager's record showed his or her education, experience, efficiency rating, and current salary. An individual manager, male or female, might have a high score on some factors and a low score on others. Crosby made the males' and females' scores about equal on average in each of the three factors, so the overall merit ratings for the two sexes were equal on average. Crosby assigned the male managers considerably higher salaries on average than the female managers. . . .
>
> Crosby randomly assigned the people reviewing the records to two groups; both groups saw the same sets of records. The members of group 1 were shown the records in pairs, each pair consisting of a male manager's record and a female manager's record. After seeing a pair, members of group 1 were asked to judge whether the salaries of the man and the woman in the pair were aligned fairly. . . . By the time the members of group 1 had seen all the pairs, contemplated each set of salaries, and arrived at an overall judgment of the

company, they had convinced themselves that in almost all of the pairs the male manager was more qualified than the female and deserved his higher salary. In each pair, the man was judged to deserve a higher salary than the woman if he was superior to her on any single one of the three factors used to measure about their relative merit. In other words, any factor that favored the man was given heavy weight, and any factor that favored the woman was ignored.[5]

People, she concludes, "want to believe, and are very ready to believe, that the better treatment of a member of a privileged group is justified by that person's merit." More broadly, people have notions about what is normal, what looks right, and when pressed will come up with reasons why things should be that way even where differences in privilege, status, or pay aren't involved. I recently stumbled on an ad in a local newspaper for a couple to manage an apartment complex. The ad read something like this: "*She* must be an aggressive renter, capable of handling all office work; *He* must be a skilled handyman, able to maintain the property and do minor repairs." In spite of a legal prohibition on advertising that violated antidiscrimination regulations, the ad was published, and I doubt that anyone but me noticed or was bothered by it. Men do manual labor and women do office work: this is the normal, ordinary way things are, so we don't notice.

We are biased in favor of the normal and ordinary way of things whether we like it or not and even where this bias works against us or thwarts our agendas.

One widely cited study showed that when applying for a research grant, women need to be 2.5 times more productive than men to be judged equally competent. The famous "McKay" study asked subjects to rank comparable academic papers by John T. McKay or Joan T. McKay; the "Joan" papers were ranked about one point lower on a five-point scale than the papers by "John." And since the arrival of "blind" orchestra auditions, in which candidates are evaluated from behind a screen, the percentage of women hired by the top five U.S. orchestras has risen from less than 5 percent to 34 percent.[6]

Funding agencies, which finance research grants, want the biggest bang for their buck, and the best way to ensure that is by awarding them to academics with the best track records. Unlike employers, they do not have to worry that employees who do not look the part will displease customers or that "nontraditional" workers will not be able to get on with coworkers. And yet, in all sincerity, with a compelling interest in awarding grants to researchers who were most likely produce the best work, individuals with professional expertise exhibited bias.

Transgendered Stanford neurobiologist Ben Barres, née Barbara, notes that even when it comes to trained scientists who should, presumably, be best equipped to make objective judgments, "it doesn't seem to matter so much what the facts are—many men have already decided that women are innately less good at this or that, and data saying otherwise won't always get them to change their minds." After he began living as a man in 1997, Professor Barres recalls overhearing another scientist say: "Ben Barres gave a great seminar today, but his work is much better than his sister's work."[7] Neither professional expertise nor goodwill nor self-interest effectively eliminate implicit bias or stop discrimination.

Even where employers have a compelling interest in avoiding discriminatory practices, bias is difficult to avoid. The last thing anyone in charge of hiring for positions in symphony orchestras wants to do is to discriminate. What matters for an orchestra is just the way it sounds—particularly these days when major symphony orchestras are primarily CD factories. Nevertheless, implicit bias played a role in auditions, and individuals in charge of hiring instituted blind auditions to eliminate that bias—not because of any abstract, moral interest in fairness but because they wanted to hire the most qualified candidates. And, when they did so, the number of women hired increased dramatically.

"Blind" procedures, however, are not feasible in hiring for most jobs and are never feasible when it comes to offering pay raises, training, or other opportunities for advancement to employees. Moreover, criteria for performance in most positions are not objective or quantifiable. For some jobs there are clear, objective, quantifiable criteria for competence: the qualifications for a typesetter are speed and accuracy—whoever wins the race with the fewest mistakes gets the job, and that is that. Most jobs are quite another matter. When we, as an academic department, do a search for a new colleague, we get between one hundred and fifty and three hundred and fifty applicants, most of whom are well qualified. We read their publications, look at their course evaluations (which may reflect student bias), observe them teaching sample classes, interview them formally, chat with them over dinner, and make our decision on the basis of a thousand considerations, including gut feelings and hunches, most of which are subjective and sensitive to implicit bias.

Most hiring, whether for tenure track assistant professors or convenience store counter personnel, is like this, and most hiring decisions are sensitive to implicit bias. Equal opportunity regulations, even when they are actually enforced, cannot effectively counteract implicit bias, which distorts our assessments of qualifications and merit. In addition, it is in employers' interest to cater for the bias of customers, clients, and coworkers. That is why, arguably, only stringently enforced affirmative action policies, including hard quotas for women and minorities, can effectively counteract the direct and indirect effects of bias and go some way toward achieving equality of opportunity.

After rioting in immigrant suburbs, French politicians began to rethink color-blind French policies, which were not effective in achieving integration and assimilation given the color-consciousness of French employers and club gatekeepers. Then interior minister Nicolas Sarkozy called for race-conscious affirmative action policies in the interests of achieving an authentically color-blind society in which visible minorities would be recognized as fully French by their countrymen.

Closer to home, Justice Stevens, defending an affirmative action plan that sought to retain minority teachers over white ones in *Wygant v. Jackson*, observed that the program did not promote differences among the races but rather sought to teach students that racial differences were irrelevant.

"The fact that persons of different races do, indeed, have differently colored skin," he maintained, "may give rise to a belief that there is some significant difference between such persons. The inclusion of minority teachers in the education process inevitably tends to dispel that illusion, whereas their exclusion could only tend to foster it. . . . Justice Stevens' insight that governmental consciousness of color can be the best path to social colorblindness flirts with irony but not with contradiction. And it answers, in a way other arguments do not, the adherents of colorblindness on their own terms."[8]

Denial will not make racism go away. Arguably, the most effective means for dismantling the tyranny of multiculturalism and for facilitating assimilation is by means of vigorously enforced race-conscious affirmative action policies.

Employers hate affirmative action because it restricts their autonomy and because they fear that firing "affirmative action hires" who don't work out will land them in legal difficulties. And, after extensive conservative crusading, affirmative action is anathema to the general public because they imagine that it constitutes "reverse discrimination," privileges women and minorities over white males, forces employers to hire unqualified applicants, and promotes color-consciousness. On every count they are wrong.

Affirmative action gets bad press in the United States for three reasons. First, Americans do not recognize the extent of ongoing discrimination. Second, they have been led to believe that the rationale for affirmative action is either compensation for past injustices or the promotion of "diversity." Finally, the cases in which affirmative action has been most publicly pursued, and challenged, are precisely those cases in which affirmative action policies are least motivated, specifically, those where decisions could easily be made on the basis of objective criteria or blind review.

In 2003 the US Supreme Court, in separate but parallel cases, considered the University of Michigan's affirmative action policies concerning undergraduate and law school admission. The Court, in a 5–4 decision, upheld the law school's affirmative action policy—which favored minorities—but struck down an affirmative action policy for undergraduate admissions that awarded twenty points for blacks, Hispanics, and Native Americans by a 6–3 vote. For the American public, the Michigan case, and prior to that the *Bakke* decision, defined the paradigm of affirmative action as a race-conscious program favoring minorities over whites who were better qualified for admission in terms of grades, test scores, and other quantifiable, objective criteria. In *Bakke*, the court had ruled that affirmative action policies could not be justified as remedies for "societal discrimination." In the Michigan cases, the Court narrowly ruled that it could take race into consideration in the interests of promoting "diversity"—a goal for which, Sandra Day O'Connor opined, affirmative action would soon be unnecessary—and that in any case the use of a points system violated equal protection provisions in the Constitution.

These cases were the paradigms in terms of which the American public understood affirmative action. The role of affirmative action in counteracting implicit bias and ongoing discrimination against women and minorities in circumstances where criteria were neither objective nor quantifiable and where blind review was not feasible was never considered. No fancy restaurant, as far as I know, has ever adopted an affirmative action program in the interests of getting more women or people of color to wait tables, much less found itself obliged to defend such a policy in court. Since the end of World War II there have been few if any serious efforts by businesses or unions to get more women into sex-segregated blue-collar jobs or to promote the employment of underclass minority youths in decent, steady unskilled or semiskilled positions. If such affirmative action programs exist, I am unaware of them, and so are most members of the American public.

It is in precisely these cases, where there are no objective qualifications or where the jobs can be done equally well by a wide range of applicants and where blind review is not feasible that affirmative action is clearly justified and most needed. In general, officially color-blind policies do not stop discriminatory color-conscious behavior. Only stringently enforced, intentional, proactive color-conscious policies, including affirmative action, can effectively counteract implicit bias, promote assimilation, and put an end to cultural diversity.

THE FUTURE OF A DANGEROUS IDEA

The assimilationist views, which I have defended here, suffer guilt by association with conservative politics and exclusionary policies. Until recently, most attacks on multiculturalism came from the Right. Literature rehearsing the arguments I have developed here, in favor of assimilation and individual choice, almost invariably carried conservative punch lines: "And that is why we should restrict immigration" or even more frequently, "And that is why we should reject 'reverse discrimination.'" Indeed, conservatives appealed to Americans' distaste for plural monoculturalism to promote their agendas: lampooning "political correctness," the self-esteem movement, and the silly excesses of multiculturalism, they persuaded the American public that liberal policies intended to benefit immigrants and other minorities would inevitably lead to balkanization.

Google "multiculturalism America," and conservative screeds rehearsing these themes pop out as fast as your Internet connection can pull up the screens. At this writing, the lead article turns out to be a rant from *Frontpage Magazine* explaining "How Multiculturalism Took Over America," and declares, "The first principle of multiculturalism is the equality of all cultures," then moves quickly to derive corollaries concerning the worthlessness of the Western tradition and the commitment of multiculturalists to dismantling it. In support of these claims, the author cites an innocuous remark by Henry Louis Gates recommending the study of non-Western cultures.[9] Following a harmless site for elementary school students promoting tolerance, a slick item by Roger Kimball, from the *New Criterion*, on "Institutionalizing Our Demise" occupies the number three slot. After a long description of "The Star-Spangled Banner" show at Fort McHenry, Kimball notes with dismay that "while 90 percent of Ivy League students could identify Rosa Parks, only 25 percent could identify the author of the words 'government of the people, by the people, for the people (Yes, it's the Gettysburg Address)'" and predictably, after a ritual swat at affirmative action, goes on to deplore at length the disintegration of Anglo-Protestant American identity.[10]

Following Kimball and rehearsing the perennial theme that "[t]his latest wave of immigration is different," Maria Hsia Chang, in a snit reminiscent of Henry James's horror at discovering a century earlier that "New York was full of Italians and Jews," suggests that hordes of unintegrated and unassimilable Hispanics, outbreeding their competition, are poised to establish an independent state of Aztlán comprising California, Arizona, Texas, New Mexico, and portions of Nevada, Utah, and Colorado.[11] One did not have the heart to open the next document, "Multiculturalism and the No-Think Nation," which began "Multiculturalism teaches that all cultures are equal with the exception of traditional American culture, which is racist, sexist, homophobic."

It should hardly be surprising that most political liberals, who favored social programs to benefit minorities and immigrants, supported generous immigration policies, and did not wish to associate themselves with the sentiments expressed in this literature, were reluctant to criticize multiculturalism of any variety. If the choice were between the Jingoist Bigot and the Plural Monoculturalist, I would, of course, choose the latter—but I would like not to have to choose.

Until recently, it was very difficult for political liberals to criticize multiculturalism without being accused of aiding and abetting the enemy or breaking the solidarity of the oppressed. It was only the publication of Susan Okin's essay "Is Multiculturalism Bad for Women?" and subsequent world events that made it feasible to join in a liberal critique of multiculturalism. Okin spilled the open secret that oppressed groups were more oppressive to women than privileged groups and that even if women had not achieved equality in liberal societies rooted in the Enlightenment, they were much worse off in illiberal ones. Okin's essay signaled the end of the liberal taboo on criticizing the practices of non-Western cultures, and subsequent world events made it impossible to ignore the glaring truth that people who were badly off themselves behaved badly.

These are, indeed, all dangerous ideas that conservatives have seized upon for generations to make the case for colonialism, to support racist theories, and to justify treating people who are badly off badly. However, it has become impossible to ignore the fact that denying these ideas is even more dangerous. As Janet Halley noted in her friendly amendment to Okin's essay, "Culture Constrains." It also oppresses and kills—and well-meaning attempts to accommodate cultural differences do no favors to individuals who are oppressed by their cultures.

This poses hard, and perhaps insoluble, questions about how liberal nations and international agencies ought to deal with sovereign states whose governments permit or perpetrate human rights violations.[12] I do not have even the beginning of an answer to these hard questions except to note that military operations, in the interest of spreading "freedom and democracy," appear to be counterproductive.

There are, however, easier questions concerning how liberal democratic nations ought to deal with diverse cultural groups within their territories, where national sovereignty is not an issue and the state is entitled to intervene in their affairs. Should European countries with large immigrant populations accommodate their cultural practices by exempting their members from laws and regulations intended to protect vulnerable individuals from coercion and harm? Should liberal states de jure or de facto grant illiberal societies within their borders virtual autonomy and allow them to run their own affairs so long as they do not bother members of the larger community? Should the French police have allowed gangs of thugs free rein within their housing projects so long as they confined their violence, rape, and drug dealing to their own turf? Should the US government and its agents have exempted the Amish from compulsory education beyond eighth grade and turned a blind eye to practices that imposed hardships and set back the interests of children because the Amish did not impose a burden on the taxpayer or cause trouble in the larger community, and because they were a desirable tourist attraction?

To these questions I have suggested answers based on the intuitive assumption that only individual sentient beings have interests and can, within a civil society, have rights. Individual humans—and nonhuman animals to the extent that they have desires and interests—have rights. Groups do not have interests or desires in any literal sense and so cannot have rights. Trees don't have rights, the environment doesn't have rights, and, most significantly, cultures don't have rights. They have no intrinsic worth and have value only to the extent that they serve the interests of sentient beings. Illiberal "traditional" cultures constrain the options of their members and thwart individual self-gratification. Arguably, their curio value to outsiders is outweighed by the burdens and constraints they impose on their members. Liberal states should not make special accommodations to preserve them but should facilitate members' exit and integration into the mainstream community.

Even where the distinctive practices of diverse cultural groups are not inherently objectionable, the question of whether cultural diversity as such should be encouraged, tolerated, or discouraged, which has been the primary focus of this book, is still on the table. Should multiethnic societies encourage and facilitate the assimilation of immigrants and other ethnic minorities or should they adopt a salad bowl model that, minimally, imposes scripts on members of ethnic minorities and in a significant range of cases ramps up the cost of exit from immigrant communities and ethnic enclaves?

Again, I have argued that multiethnic societies should encourage and facilitate assimilation for the simple reason that that is what most people want. They do not want to be locked into ethnic enclaves unto the nth generation or to "do black," even if only for the month of February, or to be pressed to identify with ancestral cultures to which they have no real connection.

It is worth rehearsing some truisms, which at least have the virtue of being true. Culture is not genetically coded. If you are born, raised, and educated in a country, speak the language, and follow the customs, you are part of that culture and of its history. There is no reason why you should identify, or be identified, with an ancestral culture of which you know nothing. Immigrants do not become fluent and enculturated as soon as they arrive in a country, but most do become fluent and enculturated eventually, and their children invariably do. We should not expect or demand that immigrants become indistinguishable from natives, but we should recognize that most want to be part of the countries where they have chosen to live and want their children to belong. We should be generous in welcoming immigrants and provide every resource that we can afford to help them assimilate. We should accommodate cultural differences as a temporary consequence of generous immigration policies so long as they do not violate the rights of members of immigrant groups, but we should not promote them and we certainly should not attempt to impose them on subsequent generations. And, of course, we should judge people by the content of their character and not the color of their skins.

I have argued that we should reject the salad bowl in favor of the melting pot and discourage practices that promote cultural diversity, because such practices render ascribed, immutable identities salient, impose scripts on members of minority groups, and restrict individual choice. This is the liberal case against "diversity."

NOTES

1. Henri Astier, "French Muslims Face Job Discrimination," BBC News online, November 2, 2005, http://news.bbc.co.uk/2/hi/europe/4399748.stm.

2. Johann Hari, "A 'Eurabian' Civil War—or the Slow Start to an Islamic Enlightenment?" JohannHari.com, http://www.johannhari.com/archive/article.php?id=1051.

3. http://www.prospect.org/print/V13/7/portes-a.html.

4. Barbara Bergmann, *In Defense of Affirmative Action* (New York: Basic Books, 1996), p. 68.

5. Ibid., pp. 72–74.

6. J. D. Nordell, "Positions of Power: How Female Ambition Is Shaped," Slate.com, November 21, 2006, http://www.slate.com/id/2154331/fr/rss/.

7. Roger Highfield, "Studies Showing Sex Bias Are Ignored, Says Transsexual Professor," Telegraph.co.uk, July 13, 2006, http://www .telegraph.co.uk/news/main.jhtml?xml=/news/2006/07/13/women13.xml &sSheet=/news/2006/07/13/ixnews.html.

8. Kenji Yoshino, "Blind Side: An Argument for Voluntary School Integration That Conservatives Should Like," Slate.com, December 7, 2006, http://www.slate.com/id/2155091/.

9. L. Auster, "How Multiculturalism Took Over America," *Frontpage*, July 9, 2004, http://www.frontpagemag.com/Articles/ReadArticle.asp?ID =14164.

10. R. Kimball, "Institutionalizing Our Demise: America vs. Multicul-turalism," *New Criterion*, 2004, http://www.newcriterion.com/archive/22/ june04/america.htm.

11. M. H. Chang, "Multiculturalism, Immigration and Aztlan," pre-sented at the Second Alliance for Stabilizing America's Population Action Conference, Breckenridge, CO, August 6, 1999, http://www.diversity alliance.org/docs/Chang-aztlan.html.

12. Carolyn Fluehr-Lobban, in "Anthropologists, Cultural Relativism and Universal Rights," *Chronicle of Higher Education* (June 9, 1995), notes: "Anthropologists generally have not spoken out, for example, against the practice in many cultures of female circumcision, which critics call a mutila-tion of women. They have been unwilling to pass judgment on such forms of culturally based homicide as the killing of infants or the aged. Some have withheld judgment on acts of communal violence, such as clashes between Hindus and Muslims in India or Tutsis and Hutus in Rwanda, perhaps because the animosities between those groups are of long standing."

INDEX